Simpler Times; Better Times
Growing up in the 1940s and 1950s

By

Jack D. Atchison

Jack D. Atchison

Copyright © 2012 by Atchison Publishing LLC

Cover design by Michael D Atchison

Interior design by Michael D Atchison

All rights reserved. No part of this publication can be reproduced or transmitted in any form or by any means, electronic or mechanical, without permission in writing from Atchison Publishing LLC, excepting brief quotes used in reviews.

Simpler Times; Better Times

Table of Contents

Preface 4
CHAPTER ONE 7
CHAPTER TWO 19
CHAPTER FOUR 36
CHAPTER FIVE 50
CHAPTER SIX..78
CHAPTER SEVEN 89
CHAPTER EIGHT 134
CHAPTER NINE...175
CHAPTER TEN 184
CHAPTER ELEVEN...201
CHAPTER TWELVE..229
CHAPTER THIRTEEN...247
CHAPTER FOURTEEN 265

Jack D. Atchison

Preface

Many of us who are sixty-years-of-age or older believe that we grew up in an era (the 1940s and 1950s) when life for a child was simpler and better than it is today. Younger people might find this hard to believe because we were certainly less affluent then, as the middle-class really didn't take hold until in the early 1950s; we suffered illnesses that children do not suffer today; and we lacked many of the devices and products that are commonplace now.

Most of our homes did not have air-conditioning, or even gas or electric furnaces for that matter. We did not have refrigerators, freezers, microwaves, dishwashers, washers or dryers, televisions, CD or DVD players, touch-tone or cell phones, electronic games, vacuum cleaners, coffee makers, portable radios or computers.

There were no frozen foods. Coke and Pepsi came in glass bottles. There were no shopping centers, malls, or big-box stores. No lotteries or casinos, except in Las Vegas.

There were no McDonalds, Wendy's, Burger Kings, Taco Bells, Subways, Pizza Huts, Domino's, Papa John's, Applebee's, TGI Fridays, IHOPs, Outback Steakhouses, Red Lobsters, KFCs, Chinese restaurants, or Sushi bars. No Home Depot, Lowe's, Office Max, Wal-Mart, Costco, Best Buy, Gap, Toys 'R' Us, PetSmart, Walgreens, or CVS.

Our roofs were covered with asbestos shingles. Our walls were painted with lead paint. No seat belts in cars. Weeds were sprayed with DDT.

No antibiotics. No CAT Scans or MRIs. We suffered the measles, mumps, chicken pox, and, too many children in those days, polio.

More than one car in a family was a rarity. There were no school buses; we walked to and from school. We walked to the store and lugged grocery bags home. We walked to the movies or wherever else we wanted to go. At around the age of ten, we

Simpler Times; Better Times

started to stand on the curb, stuck our thumb out, and hitch-hiked longer distances or, if we owned one, we rode a bike.

Most yards didn't have fences. Most people did not lock their car doors or the doors to their homes.

At school, home, or even at a neighbor's house, if you misbehaved you likely got spanked on the seat of your pants. If you acted up in school, you got spanked. If you continued to act up, you were suspended from school. And if that didn't get your attention, you were expelled.

There were no multiple-choice tests in school; all tests required a written answer. If you didn't answer questions correctly, you failed the test. Fail too many tests and you failed that grade and had to repeat it; in some cases, more than once.

When you got home from school, your mom usually was there waiting for you. Every evening, we sat around the dinner table as a family and ate a meal that was prepared at home. During dinner, each family member reported on her or his day, sharing the pleasant and unpleasant things that had happened with the rest of the family, and accepting the comments and advice offered by the rest of the family with respect to the reported events. In that fashion, the ties that bound the family together were reinforced and expanded.

When younger people hear about life in the 1940s and 1950s, they tend to focus on what we did not have and the seemingly harsh discipline to which we, as kids, were subjected. But what they don't focus on, as we older folks do, is how very rich and uncomplicated our lives were in those days.

Our playgrounds were vast and varied: fields, swamps, woods, backyards, parking lots and streets; all safe to play in, day or night. Our games were simple, challenging, and fun, and the only equipment required was a tin can; two sticks and two rags; a flashlight; a ball, any kind of a ball; our feet; or a little snow—no money required; just imagination.

We didn't have television, but we did have drive-in theaters. We didn't have fast-food places; but we did have soda fountains, candy stores, ice cream parlors, and ice chests full of cold soda pop at every gas station. We didn't have big-box stores, but we had five-and-dimes and dairy stores that sold gallon jugs of fruit punch and lemonade.

Jack D. Atchison

We didn't get allowances from our parents, but when we needed money we could always mow or trim lawns; rake leaves; babysit; shovel snow from driveways and sidewalks; deliver newspapers; carry grocery bags to cars; collect and return bottles for deposits; paint a fence; wash cars, or do other jobs that people were more than willing to hire us to do—and, as such, most of us always had all the cash we needed.

When we played, we, not adults, determined the game to be played; picked the playing venue; established the rules; chose the teams; refereed the game; and, if we decided to, kept the score. We played not to win or lose; but to have fun. And we played almost every day—snow, rain or shine; sweltering hot or freezing cold—from the time school let out until it was time for bed, breaking only when we had to do homework or eat dinner.

We had incredible freedom to choose how we would spend our days. We had the latitude to try new things, to take chances, to make mistakes and, sometimes, bad choices, and to learn from these experiences, good and bad.

We understood that the flip-side of freedom is responsibility: there were rules to follow and obey and, if you breached those rules, there were expected consequences. When it was time to pay the piper, you did not make excuses; you accepted your punishment because you knew you deserved it.

The brief stories on the following pages describe how two boys lived and matured during those wonderful days and tell about the people who accompanied them during their journey through childhood. The stories were written to show my children and grandchildren how their father's and grandfather's childhood differed from theirs. Hopefully, the stories will entertain and bring back fond memories to those of my age who elect to read them—and, if they do evoke old memories, maybe you will write down your own stories for your children and grandchildren, so that they can better understand you and where you came from before *progress* completely overcomes and erases the beauty of those simpler and better times that we oldsters so miss and long for today.

CHAPTER ONE

For nine months life was a sweet deal. I had a comfortable home and all the eats I could handle, free of charge. Suddenly, this tranquil existence came to an abrupt end. A pair of big hands grasped me by the ankles, yanked me from the warmth of the womb, held me upside down, and swatted me on the butt until I cried. A precursor of things to come.

A few days after my cruel, callous entry into the world, I found myself in the loving arms of two kids—eighteen-year-old Marjorie and nineteen-year-old James Robert; forevermore Mom and Dad to me. They carried me from the cold environment of Sparrow Hospital, my port-of-entry, to an apartment and, awhile later, to a rather remarkable structure located on Gunson Street in East Lansing, Michigan. The year was 1942.

The structure on Gunson Street was the house in which Dad had been raised. His parents, James Henry and Ina May—known as "Gramp" and "Gram" after my arrival—had just moved into a new home on Elm Place, making this one available to their son and his young family. It wasn't a gift; Mom and Dad paid a fair rental for the house, as gifts of houses to one's children were not commonplace in those days.

The house was typical of those built during the period of 1910 to 1930—a wooden shingle-sided affair with two stories above ground and a basement. In order to save money, always-frugal Gramp did most of the construction work on the house himself; so it had some unique characteristics.

A coal-fired furnace located in the basement heated the house. When Gramp built the chimney leading from the furnace, he used a plumb line—a piece of string with a lead bob attached to one end—to determine the vertical line against which he would lay the bricks for the chimney. Theoretically, if the plumb line remained steady, and the bricks were laid on the line that the plumb established, the chimney would be perfectly straight. So much for theory.

Jack D. Atchison

While he laid the first few tiers of bricks, Gramp strayed from his intended course, causing the plumb line to move when bricks pushed against it. As the chimney rose in height, he eventually discovered that the plumb line had been pushed outward by tiers of bricks and saw that the chimney tilted somewhat to the left. Being a resourceful guy, and not wanting to start over, he simply adjusted for his error by edging the next few tiers of bricks to the right. He expected this would offset the original error and the chimney would return to a straight, vertical line.

Unfortunately, he overcompensated. Now, the chimney leaned first to the left and then to the right. He made another correction, overdoing it once again. And so it went—a tilt to the left, then to the right, and back to the left. The chimney zigzagged upward for more than three stories with no more than a few feet actually conforming to a vertically-straight line.

Gramp used to say—in a joking fashion—that when the furnace was operational, smoke rose through the chimney in a corkscrew design. He said: "On winter days, smoke rises from the chimneys of the other houses in the neighborhood in nice, straight lines, so it is easy to spot our house from a distance. We just fix our eyes on the column of smoke that looks like a snake slithering through the sky."

His construction skills didn't start nor end with the chimney. No room in the entire house was square. As such, doors and windows hung at odd angles and wind and cold air whistled in around them. None of the floors were level. One could place a marble on one side of a room, give it a slight nudge, and watch it roll to the other side, picking up speed as it went. The floors also creaked and groaned at all hours of the day and night.

The barren, unadorned concrete walls and concrete floor in the unfinished basement were latticed with cracks that leaked water whenever it rained or snow melted, creating a damp, dank, dark tomblike atmosphere that represented ideal housing for spiders, bugs, and mice. Two suspended lights, the bulbs in which were prone to blow out whenever the switch was turned on, provided the only lighting, meaning that one better carry a flashlight anytime they ventured down the basement stairs.

Gramp also built the raised, covered porch that extended across the front of the house, as well as the steps that led from the

Simpler Times; Better Times

porch landing to a ground-level walkway. In order to construct the steps, he used two-by-fours and other lumber to build a form into which wet cement was to be poured. With the wooden apparatus in place, he started pouring the cement. Immediately, another major flaw in his construction techniques reared its ugly head: The weight of the wet concrete was too much for the wooden form. As the amount of cement entering the form increased, the form spread, threatening to break apart altogether. But luck was on Gramp's side that day and, though somewhat askance, the wooden form held and the concrete dried. When he removed the frame, a series of uneven steps emerged, all sloping toward the street, as if melting.

The steps presented interesting climbing challenges for young kids, especially in wintertime when the steps were ice covered. More than a few tushies suffered bruises when kids failed to negotiate the slopes.

The only positive thing the house had going for it was size. With a living room, dining room, kitchen, two bedrooms and a bath on the first floor and three bedrooms and a bath on the second, it had more than enough space for a small family. This space would prove invaluable in the years to come.

And, with all its apparent defects, the house on Gunson Street had been "home" to Gramp and Gram and their sons for some twenty years prior to when Mom, Dad, and I moved into it.

Mom was the middle child in a family of seven children—three boys, four girls. Her father, along with his brothers and sisters, operated a large farm that had been passed down by my great-grandfather. The farm extended eastward from the borderline separating Lansing and East Lansing and, for much of its existence prior to the 1930s, was planted in wheat and corn. And, at one time, the farm also featured dairy cattle and chicken coops. By 1942, however, Mom's Dad had started to move away from farming and toward homebuilding, and much of what had been farm acreage was being converted to housing subdivisions; although, some acres of corn and wheat still existed at that time.

Mom's extended family was very influential in the Lansing area. Members owned banks, hardware stores, brickyards, drug stores, dry cleaners and other kinds of businesses in the area.

Jack D. Atchison

As the middle child, Mom was more rebellious than her older siblings. Extremely attractive, popular with her classmates, intelligent and an outstanding student, she was constantly in her parent's doghouse. By the time she reached her teenage years, her relationship with her mother was strained, to say the least, due to her mother's unrelenting attempts to impose her will upon a headstrong daughter, ultimately producing an almost loveless relationship between the two of them that never healed.

Dad's family was smaller and much less affluent than Mom's. His mother—Gram—was a former schoolteacher and his father—Gramp—was career military. Dad had an older brother, Jack, and a younger sibling, Bill. Jack, a bright kid and promising athlete, endured a painful illness that shook the family to the core, dying of Leukemia at the age of eleven.

Dad, while very bright, was not a particularly good student. Rather than hitting the books, he spent his time on the football field, basketball court, baseball diamond, and in the boxing ring, where he garnered accolades and awards. He was also somewhat of a street kid, participating in and relishing more-than-occasional fisticuffs and brawls. Most significantly, he was not my Mom's parent's idea of a suitable husband for one of their daughters.

In the fall of 1941, when Mom and Dad were entering their senior year in high school, the country was on the verge of entering the most devastating war in history. Hitler's Nazi forces were plundering Europe, attacking and destroying one nation after another. In the Pacific, the Japanese were rattling their swords. It was clear to any seventeen- or eighteen-year-old male that he would soon be entering some form of military service, as it was simply a matter of time before the United States would be at war.

The overhang of impending military service intensified many school-age romances, as young people clung to each other for emotional support and a way to deal with the uncertainties facing them. Mom and Dad were no exceptions. Puppy love matured—if that is the proper word—into a bond of commitment that forged two individuals into a single unit.

The bitter relationship between Mom and her mother reached its lowest point when I was conceived. This event occurred while Mom and Dad were still seniors in high school and before they had secured a marriage license or exchanged wedding vows. And, while Gramp and Gram viewed my birth as a welcome and happy event, my maternal grandparents viewed the event much as one views a car wreck.

The attack on Pearl Harbor by the Japanese on December 7, 1941, assured that American forces would soon be entering battle. The entire nation supported the war effort and everyone was committed to fulfilling their patriotic duty. Dad wanted to do his part. Not long after he graduated from high school, along with most of the males in his high-school class, he voluntarily, and without reservation, enlisted in the armed services. He signed up for the Army, expecting to fight Axis forces in Europe.

At five-feet, six-and one-half-inches tall and weighing less than one hundred and forty pounds, he wasn't big, but was tougher than nails. So, passing the Army's induction physical shouldn't have been a concern.

When he showed up at the induction center, he passed the Army's written tests with flying colors. Then, he easily passed the physical examination. Only the vision test remained.

He approached the vision-testing room with trepidation. Without his glasses, which looked like the bottoms of two inverted coke bottles, he was as blind as a bat. And he had to meet the Army's minimum vision standards, without wearing glasses, before he would be accepted.

An Army physician instructed Dad to stand before an eye chart, which was posted on a wall about ten feet away. Dad was instructed to remove his glasses. Immediately, he knew he was in trouble. The chart on the wall was one big blur—he couldn't make out a single letter, not even the big, bold "E" that he knew was at the top of the chart.

"Okay," the army physician said, "read the third line from the top."

"I can't see it."

"Okay, can you see the second line?"

"Nope."

"How about the top line?"

"Nope."

Jack D. Atchison

The physician paused for a moment. "Okay, what do you see in front of you?"

"Just the wall," Dad said; disappointment etched in his voice.

"Well, at least you know it's a wall. You pass. Next!"

Even though Dad knew he would be sent to a foreign land to face a hostile and well-armed enemy, he was happy that the Army had accepted him. He was determined to serve his country and was anxious to get started. His attitudes toward military service were no different from those held by most of the men of his generation. They firmly believed in duty, honor, and country and were prepared to sacrifice their lives in defending those beliefs.

When we moved into the Gunson-Street house, Mom and Dad converted the upstairs into a dormer that could be rented to students attending nearby Michigan State College (later Michigan State University). The rents paid by the students, combined with Dad's military pay, would provide Mom with meager, but sufficient, funds to pay household bills while Dad was in training and overseas.

Work on the upstairs conversion happened quickly, because Dad had to leave for basic training. When he left, Mom was on her own—an eighteen-year-old with a newborn and a gaggle of college-student renters.

Life was no piece of cake for housewives in the 1940s.

Instead of a gas furnace or electric heat pump, the Gunson Street house had a coal furnace. Coal was delivered into the basement via a chute and was stored in a large bin. Several times a day during colder months, Mom had to walk down rickety stairs to a dark, dank basement and shovel coal into the furnace. Every few days, she had to remove cinders from the furnace and haul them outside to a trash bin.

Her washing machine was also in the basement. The washer was nothing more than a metal tub with an agitator in the center. Clothes were washed in the agitator tub and then were transferred to a separate rinse tub with a wringer attached to it. The wringer was an apparatus consisting of several hard-rubber rollers and a crank-like handle. She dunked clothing in the rinse water and

Simpler Times; Better Times

then placed the clothes between the rollers. She then cranked the wringer handle, drawing the clothes between the rollers in order to squeeze the rinse water from them. This process had to be repeated several times before all the soap residue was squeezed out of the wet clothing.

The wringing process had its dangers. If a person wasn't mindful of what they were doing, their hand could accompany the clothing into the wringer, becoming painfully trapped between the rollers. And it wasn't just hands that could fall victim to the wringer; other parts of the anatomy were also vulnerable. Hence, long after the wringer became obsolete, this phrase "don't get your tit caught in the wringer" is still a part of our language.

Once the clothes were wrung out, Mom carried them to the backyard and, using wooden clothespins, hung them on the drying line. After they flapped in the breeze for a few hours, she removed and ironed the dry clothes.

Thus, washing clothes was an all-day event; each load requiring an hour's hard labor. The process became even more imposing when a household had children in diapers, as ours did. Disposable diapers didn't exist in those days; instead, diapers were made of cloth and needed to be washed, as only the most well-to-do of families could afford laundry service. And, for obvious reasons, mostly olfactory in nature, washing diapers was a task done each day.

Food preparation and storage also were real chores. We didn't have a refrigerator. Instead, the kitchen featured an icebox—an appliance consisting of two insulated and interconnected cabinets. In one cabinet—the larger one, located on the bottom—perishable foods were stored. The smaller, top cabinet held a block of ice. The ice reduced the temperature of both cabinets, allowing foods, which would otherwise spoil, to be kept for several days. The temperature wasn't low enough, however, to freeze items or to keep previously-frozen items in their frozen state.

The block of ice melted over time, producing more tasks. Mom had to periodically empty a drip pan that caught the water produced by the melting ice. Some households, however, were more fortunate than ours; they owned a technologically advanced icebox with a hose extending from the drip pan to a drain, thus eliminating the need to empty the pan manually.

Jack D. Atchison

Once the block of ice melted, it had to be replaced. Twice a week, a horse-drawn wagon from the icehouse came through the neighborhood selling ice. The arrival of the iceman was one of the highlights of the week, especially in the summer. While the iceman used his steel tongs to lug a twenty- to thirty-pound block of ice into the house, kids in the neighborhood fed his draft horse carrots and cubes of sugar. Each time the horse snapped a carrot from your hand, you counted your fingers to assure yourself that the horse hadn't eaten them as well.

As a reward for feeding the horse, the iceman treated the kids. Using an ice pick, he chipped off fist-sized chunks of ice and gave them to the kids who were standing by the wagon. Kids then sat on the curb, sucking on ice, and watched the horse clomp down the street. Even to this day, I don't know of anything better than a cold piece of ice on a hot summer's day.

Because the icebox was only cold enough to keep perishables for a day or two, it affected how a family shopped for groceries. There were no frozen vegetables or prepared meals. Even if there had been, without a freezer, we couldn't have stocked up for a week or more, as we do today. So, Mom visited the meat market and produce stand almost every other day, buying just enough for two days' worth of meals on each trip.

This was a hassle. She didn't drive (she wouldn't have her driver's license until the 1960s). It probably didn't matter that she didn't have a license, because we didn't have a car—cars were a luxury, especially for a young family. So, she either got a ride with a friend or relative or she walked to and from the stores—usually she walked, arms loaded with groceries, kids in tow.

Now, Mom didn't have to go to the store for every grocery item; many were delivered to the door. A few times a week, a milkman traveled through the neighborhood selling milk, butter, cheese, ice cream, juice, and eggs. With about the same frequency, a bread truck also sold door-to-door, offering bread and other baked goods. And, at times, a butcher, fishmonger, or produce vendor made deliveries to the home.

Milk deliveries were the ones I remember best. An insulated box, into which the order, money, and empty bottles were placed, sat next to our back door. The milkman put the ordered

Simpler Times; Better Times

goods into this box. His delivery times were usually early in the morning, well before sunrise.

The milk was pasteurized, but not homogenized, so cream rested at the top of each bottle. Before drinking the milk, the bottle had to be shaken in order to blend the cream with the lighter milk.

In the winter, temperatures, especially in the predawn hours, often were well below zero. If the bottles were not removed from the milk box in time, the milk froze in the frigid morning air and expanded. When this happened, a frozen column of cream rose at the top of the bottle and popped the cardboard cap sealing the bottle. And many bottles couldn't withstand the force of the expanding milk and shattered.

In the summer, there were other problems. If the milk box was not emptied in time, the milk soured, producing a truly incredible odor that lingered in the box for days, even weeks. So, winter or summer, someone in the family was assigned the task of getting up early in the morning to empty the milk box.

There were ways to get around the absence of refrigerators, freezers, and readily available frozen foods. Some people—those who had a car and sufficient economic resources—rented food lockers in the local icehouse or butcher's shop. With a locker, they could freeze items, such as cuts of meat and certain produce.

Gram and Gramp had such a locker. They'd buy a quarter section of beef or pork, have the butcher cut it as they desired—steaks, roasts, and ground meat—and store it in their locker. This allowed them to buy larger quantities at better prices. But it also meant that whenever they wanted a cut of meat, they had to drive to the icehouse and retrieve it from the locker.

The most common way of storing food for later use was canning. The canning process involved converting fruits into jam or jelly; pickling fruits or vegetables; or preserving them in their whole state.

With each item, the process was time-consuming and laborious. Cherries needed to be pitted. Corn removed from the cob and peas from their pods. String beans cleaned and snapped into pieces. Apples cored. Next, whole fruit was cooked in sugar and water, converting it into to jam or jelly, or fruits and vegetables were cooked or soaked in vinegar or salt brine and spices to create tart, sour, pickled products.

Jack D. Atchison

After an item was processed, the actual canning started. Glass jars were sterilized by boiling, and then the fruit or vegetable was placed into them. Once the fruit or vegetable was in the jar, paraffin was melted and poured into the top of the jar to seal it. After the paraffin cooled a little, lids were screwed onto the jar.

All told, it took the better part of a day to can a given variety of fruit or vegetable. Mom canned cherries, strawberries, raspberries, blueberries, green beans, and other fruits and vegetables. When toddlers were around, her task was more difficult because, as she pitted cherries or cleaned strawberries, little hands grabbed handfuls of the fruit. By the end of a canning day, my hands and mouth were stained from the fruit I managed to pilfer whenever she turned her back.

Mom's labor didn't end with food preparation. For example, there was sewing—not as a hobby, but as a normal part of her duties. Except for underwear and socks, Mom made most of our clothes—shirts, blouses, dresses, shorts, pants, and pajamas. She bought bolts of cloth and, using patterns that she either purchased or made herself, cut out the various pieces needed for a garment. Then she sewed the pieces together, either by hand or by using a sewing machine.

Her sewing machine was a pedal-like affair that she pumped with her feet in order to drive the needle and turn the spindle. There weren't attachments to do fancy stitching and detail work, such as button holes; that was all done by hand. With these relatively crude tools, it took days to make a simple shirt or dress.

Even cleaning the house was complicated and time-consuming. Wall-to-wall carpeting was a luxury that few families could afford, certainly not our young family. The floors of the rooms in the Gunson Street house were wooden, except for the kitchen and bath, which were covered with linoleum. While rugs covered some of the floor area, most of the wooden floor was exposed, meaning it had to be scrubbed and waxed on a regular basis, as did the linoleum.

With no self-cleaning, self-shinning, wax products or electric scrubbers and buffers, Mom got down on hands and knees; washed the floor with soap and water, scrubbing hard enough with steel wool or a hard-bristled brush to remove the old wax; applied a new coat of paste wax; let the wax dry; and then, by hand, using

Simpler Times; Better Times

only a cloth, buffed the wax to a shine. It was hard labor, leaving her with sore knees, throbbing arms, and a stiff back.

We didn't have a vacuum cleaner to clean the rugs. Instead, Mom took the rugs to the backyard, hung them over the clothesline, and, using a metal rug beater, pounded the dust from the rugs. Again, this was tough, hard, dirty work, especially on a hot, humid, summer's day or on a frigid winter afternoon.

There were no cleaning products, such as Windex, toilet-bowl cleaners, soap-scum removers, aerosol dust removers, furniture polish, and stain removers. In their place, Mom used homemade concoctions of ammonia, abrasives, soap, and water, combined with large measures of elbow grease.

There were no dishwashing machines or garbage disposals. After every meal, plates, pots, and pans were scraped, washed, rinsed, and dried. Nor were there any of the other small, labor-saving appliances—microwaves, electric can openers, coffee makers, blenders, or self-cleaning ovens.

So, in the 1940s, the role of a housewife, even without the presence of children in the home, was a demanding one. It became Herculean when children were added to the mix.

Raising a child under any circumstances is hard work. Feeding, changing diapers, and bathing the child—repeatedly every day—drains one's energy. Listening to the child's inevitable crying and being constantly vigilant of the child's welfare takes a toll on one's nerves. Mix this in with demanding household chores and it is a wonder that women like Mom made it through their twenties with any semblance of sanity and health.

Yet, with all the demands placed upon her, she always found the time for daily walks, to read stories to her son, and for frequent, warm hugs and loving kisses.

As Dad was completing basic training, and shortly before he shipped out for Europe, Mom and I visited him at the Fort where he was in-training. One of Mom's brothers-in-law was training at the same Fort, and Mom's sister and her infant son were visiting at the same time. We spent several weeks there, although I remember none of the experience, as I was only several months old at the time.

It did prove to be an eventful trip, however, because about nine months later—December 1, 1943—Gary James was born.

Gary's arrival increased Mom's burdens. She was a few months away from her twentieth birthday, had two kids, neither of whom had reached his second birthday yet, and a dormer full of college students. She could not drive, had no car, lived in a hard-to-maintain house, had almost no money, and was, for all intents and purposes, a single parent.

Nor did things become easier when, in 1945, Dad returned from his duties in the Army. He had his education to complete, so he enrolled as a student at Michigan State, majoring in metallurgical engineering. During the day, he attended classes. At night, in order to provide for his family, he worked a full-time shift in a local manufacturing company that built tractors and other farm implements. He was gone all the time. We didn't see much more of him during his college years than we did when he was in the Army. His busy schedule still left Mom with the tasks of maintaining the home and dealing with the antics of two mischievous sons.

CHAPTER TWO

While Dad was overseas and, later, attending college, Mom did not have to cope entirely on her own; her extended family helped her with some of the burdens of raising two kids and running a home.

Though Mom's relationship with her parents was strained, they did live nearby and we did occasionally go to their farm. More importantly, Mom knew, if she was caught in a bind, one of her sisters or brothers, particularly her youngest sister, would make themselves available to watch Gary and me.

Mom's real help came from Dad's family—Gram and Gramp and Dad's younger brother, Bill—all of whom lived in East Lansing. They baby-sat. Gramp drove Mom to the store and the doctor's office and helped with maintenance and repairs around the house. And, always, they were there when Mom needed them— ready and willing to help however they could.

Gram and Gramp were born in the late 1800s and grew up in rural, southern Indiana.

Gram's family was more or less middle-class and she had a somewhat traditional upbringing—graduating from high school at the normal time; earning a teacher's certificate; and teaching grammar school.

Gramp was a different story. He grew up on small, hardscrabble farm. Had there been such a measurement at the time, his family would have lived well below the poverty level.

Gramp's father was a crusty, mean-spirited character who abhorred anything that resembled honest labor. He spent most of his days poaching game from neighbors' farms or dangling a fishing line in local ponds and streams. His philosophy was one of living off the land, rather than working it. He charged his kids with milking the cows, feeding the chickens, and plowing the fields. So, in the mornings, before going to school, Gramp performed a fair number of chores around the farm.

Then, if time still permitted, he walked a considerable number of miles to a one-room school house. On the way, he set traps to catch rabbits and muskrats, selling their pelts to earn a little extra income for the family.

One day, as he came upon his traps, he discovered that he'd trapped a skunk. The animal was alive and kicking in the trap, trying to free itself. Gramp didn't know what to do. He couldn't abandon his trap; it cost too much. But he didn't know how to free the skunk.

After some deliberation, he picked up a large stick and decided to club the skunk, hoping to kill it, so he could remove its body from the trap. With club raised, he slowly approached the struggling skunk. At a distance of only a few feet, and before he could strike with his club, the skunk raised its tail and sprayed him. Immediately, Gramp's nose filled with an awful odor and his eyes started to tear. Fearing that the skunk would spray him again, he retreated, deciding that, if not freed, the skunk would die in a day or two anyway.

With his clothes reeking of skunk odor, Gramp continued on to school. When he arrived and entered the classroom, the teacher chased him out, demanding that he remove his offending clothing before reentering. Outside, he took off his coveralls and shirt, but it didn't help much; the odor remained. Seeing no other option, he put his clothes back on and started the long walk home.

When he got there, his dad made him strip, bury his clothes—one of only three changes that Gramp owned—and wash himself with lye soap before he could come into the house.

So went his childhood; one small crisis and one hardship after another.

In his early teens, Gramp dropped out of school and went to work for a railroad company, serving as a conductor's assistant. It was hard work and low pay, but better than life on the farm.

A few years after he started the railroad job, during a stopover in a small Indiana town, a young lady entered the diner where he was eating lunch. He was immediately smitten by her good looks, warm smile, and cheerful laughter. His train was not scheduled to leave until the next day, so he worked up the courage

Simpler Times; Better Times

to introduce himself to the young lady, hoping to ask her to join him for dinner that evening.

A few minutes into the conversation she asked him when he had graduated from high school. He reluctantly admitted that he had not even completed one year of high school. That ended any chance of taking her out to dinner, as she firmly stated that she had no intention of striking up a relationship with an uneducated person.

Her rejection was the last straw; he'd had enough. When he returned home, he quit the railroad job and, at age nineteen, re-enrolled for his first year of high school. While it was somewhat embarrassing to be the oldest in his class, a man among little boys, he stuck with it and graduated in 1915 at the age of twenty-three.

Immediately upon getting his diploma, he returned to that little Indiana town, and sat in the diner from morning until closing time for several days. On the third day, the beautiful young lady who had rejected him four years earlier entered the diner and took a seat at table by the front window. Gramp walked up to her, laid his diploma on the table, and said, "Now, will you join me for dinner?"

During the ensuing courtship, Gramp entered the Army with the intention of making it his career. His choice of a stable career with growth opportunities appealed to his now equally-smitten lady friend. The romance bloomed and they were married, forming a partnership that would endure for more than sixty years.

After serving several years in the regular Army, Gram and Gramp moved to East Lansing, where he assumed a position in the Army's ROTC program at Michigan State. There his reputation as a "character" flourished.

Michigan State's ROTC unit consisted of two disciplines: the cavalry and artillery. The purpose of the ROTC program was to train officers for the Army. During his early years at Michigan State, Gramp was a sergeant in artillery, tasked with instructing the cadets in drill techniques. As he barked out commands, the sound of his voice carried all across the small campus, making "Sarge," as Gramp came to be known, one of the more recognized people on Michigan State's campus.

Jack D. Atchison

Cavalry and artillery instructors occasionally ventured onto each other's turf. One day, a cavalry instructor wanted to show his students how a mortar—the province of the artillery—worked. He came to Gramp and asked if he could borrow a mortar tube and projectile—a mortar shell—so he could demonstrate their operation to his class.

Gramp got a tube and projectile from the armory and gave them to the cavalry officer, saying: "If you use these in class, don't use the tube and projectile at the same time. Show them how the tube functions and then put the tube aside before explaining how the projectile works. Again," Gramp cautioned, "don't use them together at the same time."

"Got it," the cavalry officer said, as he headed to his classroom on the first floor of Demonstration Hall, the primary ROTC facility on campus, mortar tube and projectile in hand.

The cavalry officer placed the mortar tube's base plate on the concrete floor in the front of the classroom and began to explain how the device worked. He showed his class that by changing the angle of the tube's elevation, the flight of the projectile was altered, increasing or decreasing the height and distance of flight, thereby allowing the user to determine where the projectile would hit the ground.

Then, holding the projectile in his hands, he explained how the person firing the mortar simply dropped the projectile down the tube. When the projectile struck the bottom of the tube, a mechanism in the base plate sent the projectile skyward.

One of the cadets raised his hand. "I don't get it. You mean all you have to do is just drop the thing," pointing to the projectile, "and that's it?"

"Right," the cavalry officer said, "you just hold it over the tube, like this," positioning the projectile into the open end of the tube—and completely forgetting Gramp's admonition—"and drop it." As the words were leaving his mouth, the projectile slipped from his grasp. With a loud "Whomp!" the projectile blasted into the air, rocketing through the ceiling of the classroom—one that also served as the floor of a classroom on the second floor in which Gramp was lecturing a class of cadets. The force of the blast kicked the base plate and mortar tube through the thin classroom wall and into the hall outside.

Simpler Times; Better Times

Upstairs, the projectile tore through the floor between two rows of seated cadets, slammed into the ceiling and, its power spent, crashed down onto the floor. The occupants of the classroom hit the deck, heads covered and hearts pounding, certain that death was upon them. The projectile, mercifully a dud, bounced several times and came to rest amidst the frightened cadets.

While the cadets were diving to the floor, Gramp, who was standing behind a lectern in the front of the room, barely looked up from his notes, all but ignoring the missile tearing through his classroom. When the projectile hit the floor, he cleared his throat, looked down on the cadets, who were still scrambling around under their desks, and calmly said, "The damn cavalry is playing with the mortar again," before returning to his lecture without further comment.

That was but one incident involving armaments on the campus; there were others.

In order to train artillery officers, a gunnery range, of sorts, was constructed on the south side of the campus. There, several cannons were used to fire shells with dummy warheads into a large mound of sandbags. One day, a young cadet, under Gramp's tutelage and new to the artillery range, sighted one of the cannons too high. When the round discharged, it sailed over the sandbags and arched toward the campus, where it penetrated the third-floor wall of a women's dormitory, traveled through a community bathroom, careened down a hallway that ran the width of the building, crashed through another wall, and fell to rest in the front lawn. Miraculously, no one was injured, although a few young coeds were damn near frightened to death by the incident.

Then, there was the time when a general visited the campus. A military post, which the ROTC unit at Michigan State was considered to be, was expected to greet an officer of general's rank and status with an appropriate salute.

A series of old, iron, Civil-War-vintage cannons sat in front of Demonstration Hall. None had been fired since they had been installed on the campus—they were there for decorative purposes only, at least until the general's visit. One of the senior officers decided it would be a nice touch to salute the general with those iron cannons.

Gramp was tasked with figuring out how to fire them. He spent hours in the library, reading about how to build fuses and how to load the cannons with black powder and wadding. While the books he consulted described the process in general terms, none of them provided specifics, such as exactly how much powder to use.

Believing he had enough of an understanding to get the job done, he turned to the next stage in his planning—getting the black powder. He heard that a construction crew was blasting a highway right-of-way a few miles away from Lansing. He met with the crew's foreman and negotiated the purchase of several kegs of black powder.

On the summer morning of the general's scheduled arrival, Gramp and a couple cadets placed homemade fuses into the cannons; tamped in black powder, guessing about the amount required; and filled the rest of the cannons' barrels with wadding composed of old rags and newsprint. When they were done, they had two kegs of powder left over. Gramp ordered the cadets to store the extra powder in the loft of an Army maintenance building located near the center of the campus.

With cannons at the ready, Gramp and a group of cadets awaited the arrival of the general's staff car; a convertible-type affair. A cadet stood by each cannon, each holding a torch to light the fuse on his respective cannon. The plan was to light each cannon in succession, starting when the general's car neared the front lawn of Demonstration Hall, where the Cadet Corps and regular Army personnel were standing in parade formation, waiting for the general to inspect the troops.

When Gramp saw the general's staff car turn the corner of the road leading to Demonstration Hall, he raised his arm, signally the cadets to light their torches. Then, when the car turned to pass before the assembled troops, Gramp signaled to the cadets to touch the fuses of the cannons. In a practiced interval, each fuse was lit.

Suddenly, the campus reverberated with the thunderous sound of cannons exploding. Windows all over the campus cracked and shattered. The eardrums of anyone within a half-mile of the roaring, iron cannons were battered and bruised. Simultaneously, as makeshift wadding was expelled from one cannon after another, the air was filled with a dense cloud of rags and shredded paper. The general's car and the ranks of cadets were covered by debris that fell from the sky. Through it all, Gramp stood, mouth agape, awed by the sound and fury of his handiwork, wondering whether his military career had just reached an abrupt and unplanned end.

The general's car beat a hasty retreat from the campus, bypassing any attempt to inspect the troops, probably fearful that the enemy had landed in East Lansing.

In the weeks that followed, the incident with the cannons was investigated and discussed and was the subject of several tersely worded memos which passed through the Army's communication channels. Near the end, when Gramp was explaining for the umpteenth time how the whole thing had come about, an officer asked: "Where did the damn powder come from?"

"I got it from a civilian construction crew."

"Is there any left?"

"Yes, Sir. There are two kegs in the maintenance building."

"Is it safely stored?"

"I don't know, Sir."

"Well, find out," the officer ordered.

Following those orders, a couple cadets accompanied Gramp to the maintenance building, where the kegs were sitting in the loft. They pried open the lid on one of the kegs. The powder inside was warm to the touch, heated by the summer sun that beat down on the building's sheet-metal roof, a sign that the powder could ignite at any moment. If it had, there was enough in the kegs to put a good-sized dent in the middle of Michigan State's campus.

Without delay, Gramp and his cadets, acting ever so carefully, removed the kegs and cautiously carried them to the Red Cedar River which flowed through the center of the campus. There, the powder was poured into the water, closing the file on the cannon incident.

Gramp's reputation as a campus character was further enhanced by his quest for knowledge. Even though he never enrolled as a student at Michigan State, he was a frequent visitor to the college classroom, attending those courses that were of interest to him. In hit-or-miss fashion, he learned algebra, geometry, trigonometry, and calculus, as well as some physics, chemistry, history, and literature. He was always reading and, by middle age, was as well-read and knowledgeable as many college-educated men holding advanced degrees. More importantly, in acquiring his book-based knowledge, he never lost his innate common sense and wisdom.

He often told a story about sitting in on a class dealing with advanced mathematics. The professor's explanation of a complex equation was baffling. At one point in the lecture, Gramp turned his chair around and faced the rear of the room. The professor noticed his odd behavior and asked: "Sarge, is something wrong?"

"Nope," Gramp said over his shoulder. "But this stuff is going so far over my head that I'm just trying to catch it when it rebounds off the wall."

Gramp was, indeed, a colorful character—a crusty military man, dressed in sharply creased khaki and shoes that shone like mirrored glass. He had a deep, booming voice that was accustomed to shouting out commands on the drill field; a stoic, gruff exterior; an inquiring mind, making him a veritable fount of knowledge; and an inner core that was as soft as a well-roasted marshmallow.

Over the years he became our mentor, favorite playmate, protector, and source of inspiration.

Gram, with her roly-poly figure, rosy cheeks, and ever-present good humor, was everyone's prototypical grandmother.

She brought three sons into this world: Jack, Dad, and Bill. Jack's death from leukemia left Gram with an emotional scar that never healed. Fifty years after Jack's death, the mere mention of his name, or the recounting of a story about his brief life, brought tears to her eyes and choked her voice. This constant mother's grief was a demonstration of the depth of Gram's love for her children and grandchildren.

As I grew older, every person to whom I introduced this gentle woman called her "Gram," and immediately thought of her as their own surrogate grandmother.

CHAPTER THREE

For the first year or so of his existence, Gary was, from my perspective, not much better than our pet dog. He did nothing; except sleep, eat, burp, barf, fart and poop—pretty much in that order—day after day. He was, for the most part, a little, fat blob that smelled up our bedroom.

Hearsay has it that during my first year, I acted a lot like Gary did; but I never believed that—marked it down as a ugly rumor intended to quell my constant criticism of Gary's rather obvious inadequacies.

As he grew, Gary gradually changed from a smelly blob to a klutz. His hair was bright red—almost orange—his face dotted with freckles. And he always did the unexpected.

Just after he started eating regular food, we gradually noticed that a foul odor surrounded him. It took a while for this to register, as Gary smelled none too good on the best of days. With each passing day, the putrid, rotten, smell grew worse. The closer one got to Gary, the more repulsive the odor.

Mom was concerned that he was suffering from a serious malady. She consulted the family medical book, but couldn't find any illness that had a strange odor as one of its symptoms. Fearing the worst, she scheduled an appointment with the family doctor.

When we arrived at the doctor's office, it didn't take the doctor long to understand the nature and origin of Mom's concern. Gary stunk like a wet compost heap. The odor was overpowering, literally almost causing the doctor to retch as he approached his little, red-haired patient.

The doctor started his examination by looking into Gary's mouth, but found nothing out of the ordinary. An inspection of Gary's ears yielded nothing that accounted for the odor. Next, the doctor used an instrument resembling a small, pointed flashlight to peer into Gary's nostrils. He looked once, smiled, and looked again. "I think I've found the problem."

Jack D. Atchison

He got a tweezers-like instrument from a tray in a cabinet. Very carefully, the doctor inserted the instrument into one of Gary's nostrils and extracted a gray, foul-smelling object, placing it on a tray before reentering the nostril to retrieve similar and equally odorous objects. He then worked on the other nostril, retrieving several similar objects. Then, using the flashlight, he once again peered into Gary's nose. Removing the flashlight, the doctor turned to Mom. "That should cure the problem."

Mom looked at the offensive objects on the Doctor's tray. "What are those?" she asked; fearing they were the product of some terrible illness—tumors or malignant growths.

The doctor laughed. "Lima beans."

Mom was stunned. "Lima beans?"

"Yes. Somehow those beans," pointing to the tray, "got into your son's nose...he probably put them there while playing with his food. They've been in his nose for days, maybe weeks, and have rotted, producing the odor."

Mom, now relieved, joined the doctor in laughing at the absurdity of the situation. Gary, the little klutz, simply sat on the examining table, a customary grin of complete innocence spread on his freckled face.

Because of the limitations in our family budget, Mom made the decorations for the Christmas tree. In addition to stringing popcorn and cranberries, she made hanging decorations out of pine cones. She gathered the cones from a stand of pine trees located near Michigan State's campus. Then, using the same type of paint used by builders of model airplanes, she painted the cones silver and gold. When they dried, she attached hooks to the cones and hung them on the tree, using them as substitutes for store-bought glass decorations.

One Christmas season—1946 as I recall—Gary and I watched with interest as Mom made her pine-cone decorations. It was fascinating to see drab, brown cones turn into brilliant silver and gold ornaments. When they were hung next to the strings of white popcorn and red cranberries, our tree was as bright and festive as anyone could hope to see.

One night, in the wee hours of the morning, three-year-old Gary decided to help Mom with her decorating activities. He rose

Simpler Times; Better Times

from his bed and waddled to the living room, where the now fully-decorated Christmas tree stood, and added his own personal touches to the effort before returning to his bed an hour or so later.

In the morning, when Mom entered the living room, she was shocked to find portions of the living-room walls painted in gold and the wooden floor in silver. Finding the culprit wasn't difficult. Leading from the living room to the door of the room that Gary and I shared was a tell-tale track of tiny silver and gold footprints.

Mom walked to our room, opened the door, and followed the footprints directly to the bed in which Gary was sleeping. She pulled back his covers to find that his sheets were also marked with silver and gold paint. Mom shook Gary by his shoulders to awaken him. When his eyes opened, she asked, in an accusatory tone: "Young man, are you the one who painted the living room?"

Gary's freckled face split into a wide grin. "Yes. It's pretty, isn't it?"

Looking on from my bed, I fully expected to see Mom tan Gary's little fanny. I was surprised. Whatever anger she felt as a result of the mess in her living room instantly disappeared when she saw the look of undisguised pride on his face. Instead of paddling his behind, she simply hugged him and laughed.

When Mom needed a little relief, which was frequent, Gramp took me with him when he drove around town to take care of errands. Since we didn't have a car, I always looked forward to these trips in his "truck," as I called the car. More often than not, our trips featured a stop at one of the ROTC buildings on Michigan State's campus.

The cavalry unit maintained several stables of horses and, whenever we visited the campus, I always begged Gramp to stop, so we could visit the horses. He usually granted my request—it was either that or listen to me cry all the way home. We'd feed the horses carrots and sugar cubes—he always had a supply of both, knowing he'd need them when I was in the car.

My favorite horse was an old chestnut-colored draft horse named Norwegian. The cavalry officers would seat me atop this huge animal and then lead us on a walk around the stable area.

Jack D. Atchison

After a dozen or so of these rides, I came to view Norwegian as my personal pet and was completely unafraid of him.

One day while we were visiting the stable, Gramp and a group of officers stood next to Norwegian while they discussed ROTC business. I kept asking for a ride but, absorbed in their discussion, they ignored my requests. Growing impatient, I decided to take matters into my own hands.

Norwegian's back stood six feet or more off the ground. The top of my head stood about three-feet off the ground. Somehow, I had to negotiate the three-foot difference if I was to ride the horse. Studying the problem, I concluded that the only way to get on the horse, without assistance, was to climb up its tail. So, I went to the rear of the horse and grabbed the tail. As soon as I tugged on his tail, Norwegian let out a loud snort and lashed out with a hoof, catching me right in the solar plexus and sending me flying. I landed about ten feet away, the wind knocked out of me. I believed my days on earth had ended.

Hearing Norwegian's snort, Gramp and the others turned around—just in time to see me hit the dirt. When Gramp picked me up, he didn't have to ask what happened: the hoof print on my shirt said it all.

After that, I wouldn't get within twenty yards of Norwegian, or any other horse in the stable. I may not have been very smart when I grabbed the horse's tail, but I wasn't stupid—one swift kick in the belly was the only lesson I needed

One day, Gramp babysat us while Mom ran a few errands. I was in the front yard playing with a truck that belonged to Gary—one to which he had taken a strong proprietary interest, protesting strongly if anyone else touched it, let alone played with it as I was doing. Gary was leaning over the porch railing, bawling loudly, demanding that the truck be returned to him without delay. Gramp was sitting in a rocking chair on the porch, trying to read; his concentration disrupted by Gary's incessant wailing.

Having heard enough of Gary's screams, Gramp yelled down to me: "Jackie, give Gary his truck."

"But I'm playing with it," I protested.

"It's mine. I want it," Gary yelled, tears streaming down his cheeks, his face nearly as red as his carrot-colored hair.

Simpler Times; Better Times

"If it's Gary's, give it to him," Gramp said, his patience sorely tested by Gary's ever-louder crying.

"But—"

"No buts," Gramp said, his voice rising, "toss it to him."

"Oh, okay." I picked up the truck and gave it a mighty heave. It sailed over the porch railing, over Gary's head, past Gramp, and, with a loud crash, through the living room window.

Gramp lurched out of his chair, his face reddening with anger. "Why did you do that?"

"You told me to toss it. I tossed it."

That brought him up short. He had, indeed, ordered me to throw the truck. He looked over his shoulder at the broken glass, obviously wondering about Mom's reaction to this latest of many similar accidents; an inordinate number of which seemed to happen on Gramp's watch. He looked back to Gary and me. "We've got to get this mess cleaned up."

I breathed a sigh of relief. Fixing the window had taken on a higher priority than fixing my little red wagon—the expected spanking was now unlikely to occur. Gary must have come to the same realization, because the smile on his face—the one signifying that his older brother was in hot water—disappeared.

During the next hour, we went to the hardware store and got a new piece of glass. Gramp replaced the broken pane. The shards of glass were swept from the living room floor. And the three of us—all co-conspirators now—entered into a tacit agreement to withhold any talk of a broken window from Mom.

We all gained something from our pact to remain silent. I avoided a spanking for throwing the truck. Gary avoided a similar fate as punishment for his annoying crying. Gramp escaped the task of explaining that he'd been the one who had suggested that the truck be thrown.

During the years that followed, the three of us engaged in many more of these mutually beneficial conspiracies, covering up transgressions which we wished to keep from either Mom or Gram.

One of Gary's and my favorite places to be babysat was Gram and Gramp's house on Elm Place, which was located just one block north of Michigan State's campus. We spent at least one night a week there. It gave Mom and Dad a needed break and our grandparents liked us to stay with them. But, there were a few drawbacks to staying at their house.

The first occurred if one of us happened to display any sign of sickness—sniffles, runny nose, sneezing, or a cough. On those occasions, we were subjected to Gram's medical care. She had a deep, abiding faith in the healing powers of Vick's VapoRub—a strong-smelling, Vaseline-type substance. She thought the stuff could cure almost any ailment. As soon as she heard a sniffle, or watched one of us wipe our nose on the sleeve of our shirt—a kid's ideal substitute for a handkerchief—she ran for her jar of Vick's.

She started by rubbing a gob of the stuff into my chest and around my neck. Then, she put a dollop between my nose and upper lip. And, before bedtime, she put some in a vaporizer, and then put the vaporizer and my head under a blanket, forcing me to breathe Vick's-filled steam. When she was done, I smelled bad enough to gag a maggot.

Surprisingly, the stuff seemed to work, because the sniffles and runny nose disappeared. I suspect the germs couldn't stand the smell and left to find a less odorous victim.

Another problem was her breakfast treats. I really hated fried eggs with runny yolks, burned toast, and undercooked bacon—and Gram knew it. So, without fail, each morning, my plate contained two eggs that looked like they were right out of the shell, having bypassed the frying pan; a few rashers of near-raw bacon; and two pieces of toast that were so badly burned that they resembled charcoal briquettes. When Gram served this daily culinary disaster, her smile stretched from ear to ear, as she anticipated the fit that I invariably threw. As I ranted and raved about the mess on my plate, Gram, the picture of innocence, would say: "My, my, is something wrong with your breakfast?"

About then, Gramp, who would eat anything put in front of him, would say: "Looks okay to me; eat up, son." This, of course, would evoke an even wider grin from Gram.

To be fair, after she got her morning chuckle at my expense, another plate, filled with perfectly fried eggs, golden-brown toast lathered with melted butter, and several strips of crisp bacon, would be placed in front of me. As for the offending plate,

Simpler Times; Better Times

Gram simply slid it under Gramp's nose and in a flash the gooey eggs, burnt toast and raw bacon disappeared down his gullet.

Over the years, our arguments over Vick's and burned toast persisted. And Gram played it to the hilt. Every year, for as long as Gram was alive, two of my Christmas presents were a jar of Vick's and several pieces of burnt toast—all carefully wrapped in colorful paper and ribbons by her loving hands.

The upstairs windows in the Elm Place house had three round ventilation holes in the bottom of each frame. At night, when moonlight shined through the holes, they projected an eerie yellow glow. I imagined that they were the eyes of tigers, lions, and wolves that were about to attack me.

When I first noticed the holes, I was sharing a bed with Gary. As images of ferocious beasts filled my thoughts, fear set in. I turned to Gary's side of the bed and burrowed my way beneath his body, not stopping until he was completely on top of me. In the process, he woke up and started to yell: "Get off my side of the bed! Get away from me!"

Gary's yelling brought Gramp to the bedroom door. "What are you guys doing?" He asked as he turned on the light.

"Jack's on my side of the bed. He woke me up."

"What's your problem?" Gramp asked me.

I slid out from under Gary. "I...I thought that I saw something."

"What did you see?" Gramp's patience was wearing thin.

I pointed toward the window. "An animal's eyes. It was coming after me."

Gramp grunted. "What kind of animal?"

"I don't know...a lion...a tiger."

Gramp laughed. "There aren't any lions or tigers in East Lansing." He paused and scratched his head. "What were you doing underneath Gary?"

"Hiding."

"Under Gary?" Gramp said with a laugh.

"Yeah."

"Why?"

Jack D. Atchison

"Well, I figured if an animal came into the room, it would get him first...then it would go away." So much for being my brother's keeper.

Because we tended to keep each other awake, Gram and Gramp started having us sleep with them. One of us would go to one bedroom with Gram, and the other would sleep with Gramp. They sang songs and told us stories until we fell asleep. We got to hear hundreds of stories and jokes—many of them time after time, as both Gram and Gramp had a few favorites they liked to repeat. And it was great for all of us—they didn't have to listen to us fight and we were thoroughly entertained.

Gram and Gramp also babysat us at our own house on Gunson Street.

One summer's day, Gary and I were playing with the water hose in the backyard, squirting each other and running through the water to cool off. Gram came outside to check on us. When I saw her descend the steps of the back porch, I figured, if the water felt good to us, a shot from the hose would cool her off, too. So, I turned the hose on her, thoroughly drenching her from head to foot.

Her reaction was not what I expected—I had failed to take into account that she was fully dressed and might not appreciate getting her clothes soaked. Well, she was madder than a wet hen and she came after me with fire in her eyes. Fortunately, I'd had experiences like this one before. I knew that Gram traveled at a snail's pace, even when angry, and, if I continued to run, she'd never catch me, providing time for her anger to disappear.

Again, I miscalculated a little—I hadn't factored Gramp into the equation. He saw me squirt Gram and he thought it was hilarious. He stood on the back porch and laughed so hard that his face turned red and he started to wheeze. That really got to Gram. The more Gramp laughed, the madder she got, and the faster she chased after me. Luckily for me, her anger gave out before my legs did. As she stopped to catch her breath, she gradually saw a little humor in the whole situation.

A few days later, Gary and I were once again playing with the hose in the backyard when Gram and Gramp stopped to visit.

Simpler Times; Better Times

Gram was going to stay with us while Gramp went to the campus on ROTC business He was dressed in his military uniform—sharply creased khakis, tie, hat, and highly polished shoes.

Gary, who was a slow learner, had the hose in his hands. With a wide grin, he turned it on Gramp, squirting him worse than I had done to Gram just a few days earlier. Boy, did Gary make a mistake. Gramp let out a bellow, as only a drill instructor can, and his face reddened in anger—gone was the laughter of a few days before. He was on Gary like a mongoose after a snake, ready to tan his little bottom. But this time Gramp miscalculated—he hadn't factored Gram into the equation.

Before Gramp could bring his hand down on Gary's fanny, Gram called for him to stop, informing him that what's good for the goose is good for the gander. If it was funny when she got doused with the hose, it was equally humorous when he got soaked.

Gramp let Gary go without spanking him, in part, because of Gram's words and, in part, because he knew he'd have to answer to Mom if he spanked Gary.

Discipline was the one area over which Gramp and Mom clashed. Mom had made it clear that if either of her sons required a spanking, it would be either she or Dad who administered the punishment—no one else, including Gramp. This didn't necessarily sit too well with Gramp, who was used to disciplining his troops without interference from others, but he went along with Mom's wishes and only rarely administered a spanking to either of us (and, on the few occasions when he did, we fully deserved it).

Jack D. Atchison

CHAPTER FOUR

The only kid close to Gary's or my age living within two blocks of our Gunson Street house was a girl who lived across the street. She was a year older than I was and spent her playtime with dolls and dressing up in old clothes. She also viewed boys to be only one step up from stray alley cats, or maybe it was one step down. Either way, she had no intention of spending her playtime with Gary or me, and we shared the same view of spending time in her company. Thus, by default, Gary and I were expected to entertain each other. Neither of us found the situation to be satisfactory.

Without television to occupy our time—television did not appear in American homes on a widespread basis until the early 1950s—Gary and I passed away the hours by inventing games and getting into mischief of one kind or another.

In order to reduce the damage caused by playtime activities, Mom constantly laid down one rule after another. Do not run while holding a sharp object in your hands. Do not jump on the beds. Stay away from all electrical appliances. Do not play with matches. Do not stand up in the tub. Stay away from the stove. Do not hit each other. Do not throw things in the house. Keep the basement door closed. And on and on—the list grew exponentially with each passing day, usually prompted by very specific events.

For example, around the age of three, one of the upstairs borders gave me a tin horn—the kind used as a noisemaker at a New Year's or birthday party. I carried it around the house, blowing through it from morning to night, producing, to my ear, beautiful music.

It's amazing how sounds that are music to a child's ear are perceived so differently by adults. As I blew on my little horn, melodies filled the air. But to my surprise, Mom kept yelling: "Will you put that thing away! You're driving me crazy!"

The boarders upstairs, who were trying to study, threatened to shove the little horn into various parts of my anatomy.

Simpler Times; Better Times

Undeterred by the threats, I continued to march around the house acting out a passable imitation of the Pied Piper.

One afternoon, as I sat on the living-room floor, my eyes were drawn to an electrical outlet on the wall. Curious as to the function of the outlet, I approached it, tin horn still in hand. After studying the innocuous-looking outlet for a moment, and learning nothing new about its purpose, I thrust the pointed end of the tin horn into one of the openings.

"Bam!"

Flames shot from the wall. A tremendous burst of energy shocked my hand, traveled through my body, threw me into the air, and unceremoniously deposited me in a heap on the floor in the middle of the room. My head was filled with stars and flashing lights. My body tingled.

Mom was sitting in the dining room and was startled when the lights flickered and she heard a loud thump in the living room. She got up to see what was happening. When she turned the corner to enter the living room, she saw me stretched out on the floor, dazed, my eyes filled with tears.

"What happened?" she asked, as she knelt by my side.

Without saying anything, I pointed at the wall, some eight feet away.

Mom looked to where I was pointing and was shocked to see my little tin horn fused to and jutting out from the electrical outlet—an outlet now surrounded by a large, dark smudge.

She turned back to me. "Are you okay?"

I nodded that I was.

"Do you hurt anywhere?"

I nodded that I didn't.

I wasn't hurt, just frightened. I still didn't know what had happened. But the flight through the air, the tingling, and stars of white light that danced in front of my eyes had scared the living daylights out of me.

Mom picked me and deposited me on a sofa, where she gave me a stern, and well-deserved, lecture about what little boys should and should not do around electrical outlets. Another rule emerged and I assure you, she had my complete and undivided attention. One encounter with the power of electricity was all I needed to get the message—loud and clear.

Jack D. Atchison

Later, the power was turned off and the tin horn was pried from the damaged outlet. It's amazing that the whole house hadn't gone up in flames.

Gary and I shared a bedroom and between our twin beds was a large dresser.

And though we had been told numerous times not to, one of our favorite pastime activities was to jump up and down on one of the beds, seeing how far we could soar into the air. During one of these sessions, I jumped higher than expected and catapulted from the bed onto an open dresser drawer. When I landed head first on the corner of the drawer, a sharp edge tore at my ear, producing a nasty gash.

My first inclination was to say and do nothing about the cut. We knew we weren't supposed to jump on the beds, having been lectured countless numbers of times that it wasn't good for the box springs. If I drew attention to my injury, I'd have to confess that we'd violated one of Mom's rules, which would surely result in a whipping, merely adding more pain to what was already coming from my throbbing ear. This inclination was rapidly dismissed when I looked down at the blood that was pooling at my feet and staining my clothes. So, hand over torn ear, I sought out Mom.

When she saw the blood streaming through my fingers, she knew we were in for another of our all-too-frequent trips to the doctor's office. Once there, I received about a half-dozen stitches from the doctor's new assistant, a foreign student doing his final training here in the States. When he had the sutures in place, the assistant covered them with some kind of goop, saying it would prevent dirt from getting into the wound.

Five or six days later, we returned to the doctor's office to get the stitches removed. By now, having made the trip so many times, Mom could find her way from our house to the doctor's office in her sleep. When the doctor looked at the stitches, he just shook his head and went, "tsk, tsk." It seems that the goop his assistant had used had hardened, making it impossible to remove the stitches without reopening the wound.

Removing the stitches turned out to be much more painful than the original accident—a fact that I communicated to the doctor by screaming at the top of my lungs and kicking frequently,

Simpler Times; Better Times

but unsuccessfully, at his groin whenever he ventured close enough to grasp my ear in order to tear out another suture. We had a similar series of communications over his decision to re-stitch the now profusely bleeding ear.

The whole experience convinced me to assiduously avoid physician's offices whenever possible.

Despite the lesson learned from the ear accident, we found ourselves returning time and time again to the doctor's office. Many of the trips were for the routine illnesses that children contract—measles, croup, flu, and the like—but many were to get stitches to close small wounds. In fact, because we made so many trips to his office and knowing that Mom had severely limited economic resources, the doctor felt sorry for us and often treated us free of charge.

Mom knew one of the favorite activities of her young boys was chasing each other at full speed, both inside and outside the house. When the pursuer—in our case, usually me—caught the pursued—generally Gary—a wrestling match normally ensued and lasted until one of the combatants—most often Gary—screamed for help. Thus, Mom was frequently forced to divert her time and attention from household duties to serve as referee and peace arbiter. And two more rules were established: (1) no running in the house and (2) no fighting.

One afternoon, Gary and I were actively engaged in chasing each other throughout the house—he in panicked flight and me hot on his heels, determined to give him a good pummeling when I caught him. Gary sped from the kitchen into the living room, jumped over the couch, dodged around a chair, and sped out the front storm door, slamming it behind him. The door banged into the frame and, because the frame was a product of Gramp's skill with a plumb line and, thus, was canted at an angle, the door jammed when it closed, leaving it as snug as it would have been had it been locked.

As I neared the door, running as fast as my short little legs allowed, I extended my left hand to push the glass storm door open. I hit the door in the middle of one of the glass panes. Instead of the door opening, my hand and arm crashed through the glass, shattering it into a bunch of sharp shards. By then, Gary had made it safely down the porch steps and was in the front yard. When I crashed through the door, he knew the chase was over and turned to laugh at my predicament, knowing I was in deep trouble for breaking the glass out of the door.

Extracting my hand from the door, I heard Gary's cackling laugh and, like him, knew the razor strap was looming in the near future. When I pulled my hand back, I noticed a growing pool of blood on the floor. I looked at my hand, expecting to see that a finger was gone, but none were. I raised my right hand and checked my nose; it wasn't bleeding either. Then, I noticed my left wrist; blood was squirting out of it in big spurts and it was beginning to throb. I yelled for Mom.

Hearing the panic in my voice, she hurried from the kitchen to the living room, noticing the broken glass on the floor and assuming it was the cause of my concern. Then, she, too, saw blood spurting from my wrist. She clamped her hand over the cut and took me to the kitchen where she got a towel to use as a compress. With one hand pressing against the wound to stem the flow of blood, she called Gramp and told him that we needed to make another trip to the doctor's office.

The doctor, acutely aware of my dislike of stitches and, perhaps, desirous of protecting his privates from being assaulted by my kicking feet, closed the wound with a quick series of stitches. For my part, I saw a silver lining in the trip to the doctor's office—Mom would surely overlook the shattered storm door and the damage I had caused—no razor strap. I was wrong. Mom's sense of discipline was stronger than her maternal sympathy and I got my just desserts.

One day, Gary and I heard Mom screaming from the kitchen. Her cries were filled with fear and panic. We rushed to the kitchen to see what was wrong. There was Mom, sitting in the sink—a sink filled with water, soap suds, and dirty dishes. With fear in her eyes, she pointed her finger toward the floor.

Our eyes followed her finger and, when we saw the object of her panic, Gary and I started to giggle. Our giggling turned to laughter. Scurrying around on the kitchen floor was a tiny, gray mouse. The poor thing had probably ventured up from the basement, which was a fertile breeding ground for the creatures, to

Simpler Times; Better Times

get a morsel of food. Instead, he was greeted by the panicked screams of a frightened human. Now, the little guy was on the verge of a heart attack, scared out of his wits, desperately trying to find an escape route to the basement.

I stopped laughing long enough to get a broom and took a few feeble swipes at the poor mouse. The little guy easily avoided the broom and darted from the kitchen, presumably finding his way back downstairs.

When Mom climbed out of the sink, her clothes were soaked and the expression on her face was a combination of embarrassment and anger—anger that her two sons were so unsympathetic to her plight and were mocking her with their laughter. But then, she, too, saw the humor in the situation and joined in the laughter.

We had several similar situations. Other mice ventured into the kitchen, as did a bird or two. On warm days, we left the kitchen door ajar and opened the windows to create a cooling cross-draft and, occasionally, a disoriented sparrow flew into the kitchen. When that happened, Gary and I were called to shoo it away with a broom. It was great fun to chase the bird all over the kitchen and to watch Mom's reaction every time it swooped in her direction. So, naturally, we were never in a hurry to let the bird escape to the outdoors.

We also got used to disposing of mice. Because they kept coming up from the basement, traps were set in all the closets and in the darker corners of the house. The traps were baited with pieces of cheese. Every week or so, we'd find a dead mouse in one of the traps. Then, Gary, Gramp, or I would remove the mouse from the trap, pick it up by the tail, and take it outside to the garbage can. Mom wouldn't touch them.

One night, our dog, Panda, a black Spitz and Chow, ran down the basement stairs and started to snarl and bark. We assumed that Panda had spotted a mouse and was hunting it down. When the barking continued, and intensified, Dad, who was now home from the War, decided to check out the situation. When he descended the basement stairs, Panda was engaged in a fight with a sewer rat that appeared to be damn near the size of the dog. The rat had scruffy fur; a long, naked tail; little beady eyes, which at times appeared to be red; and fierce, pointed teeth from which froth flowed. Dad picked up the flat-nosed shovel we used to fill the coal-fired furnace, waded in between the dog and the rat, and swung the shovel at the rat.

Gary and I sat on the basement steps and watched the battle. It was a heck of a scene. The dog was barking and charging at the rat. The rat was snarling and trying to bite everything in sight. And Dad was swinging the shovel as fast as he could at the two snarling animals circling his feet. Suddenly, the shovel found its mark and with a loud "clang" the rat bit the dust. When Dad lifted it up by the tail to take it to the garbage can, it looked to be over two-feet long.

From that point forward, it was almost impossible to get Mom to go to the basement. It was bad enough when she knew it housed itty-bitty mice. But now that she knew huge rats could be hiding in the dark corners, there was no way she was going down those steps.

With no one else to play with, Gary was my shadow. Wherever I went, he followed. If I stopped to scratch my butt; he stopped and scratched his, too. If I picked my nose; he picked his. We became a two person parade. I dressed in baggy shorts, Buster Browns, droopy socks, and a tee-shirt; he dressed the same. The only thing distinguishing one of us from the other was that I was a little taller and had curly blonde hair and his was bright red; otherwise, we were clones, literally almost joined at the hip because he followed so closely behind me. With each passing day, his constant presence and whining voice became increasingly more annoying, even to a five-year old. Something had to give.

A big, green doghouse sat in the backyard—the home of our sizable black dog, Panda. The doghouse had a door, but it was never used to close the house. Instead, the door lay on the ground, serving as a ramp for Panda to use to enter his dwelling. One day, as I eyed this ugly green structure, a brilliant solution to the problem of my younger brother flashed into my mind.

I went to our combination garage and storage shed, Gary at my heels, and got a hammer and a few big nails.

"What are those for?" Gary asked.

"You'll see." I walked to the backyard. When we got to the doghouse, I pointed to it and said to Gary: "Get in there."

Simpler Times; Better Times

"Why?"

"Because, you'll like it and I have a surprise for you." He looked unconvinced. His eyes shifted from the doghouse to me, and then back to the doghouse. "Come on. You'll like it. Trust me." The magic words.

"Okay." Still somewhat dubious, he crawled into the doghouse.

As soon as he was completely inside, I pulled the door from its ramp-like position and shoved it up to block the opening that Gary had just crawled through. With the door in place, I started securing it by hammering in the handful of nails I had gotten from the garage. Every pound of the hammer produced a wail from Gary, each louder than the one that had preceded it. Undaunted by the noise coming from inside the doghouse, I finished the task of nailing the door shut, noticing that the last few wails emanating from Gary were, by far, the loudest and most intense.

Satisfied with my work, and ignoring the incredibly shrill screams Gary was now unleashing, I tossed the hammer aside and strolled from the backyard—a free man—the constant shadow no longer dogging my heels.

I'd barely cleared the backyard when Mom, alerted by the uncanny sonar system mothers seem to possess, came out the front door. "I hear your brother crying. Where is he?"

"In the backyard."

"What's wrong with him?" Mom asked as she came down the porch steps.

"I don't know," I said; hoping to end her line of inquiry.

She took my hand. "Let's go see."

We walked to the backyard. When we got there, Gary's wailing was louder, but he was nowhere to be seen. Mom looked perplexed as her eyes searched the yard. Then, she turned to me. "Where's Gary?"

Very quietly, I said, "In the doghouse."

"Where?"

"In the doghouse," I repeated in an even more hushed tone.

Mom rushed to the doghouse, noticing for the first time that the door was shut. She tugged at the door. Gary's screams were louder now. The door didn't budge. "What did you do to the door?"

Pointing to the hammer, I said, "I nailed it shut."

Jack D. Atchison

Mom didn't say anything. She didn't have to; her look was enough. I knew I was in for another session with the razor strap.

She picked up the hammer and, using the clawed end, started to pry at the door. As she worked on the door, Gary's crying became louder and louder. With the nails apparently free, Mom gave a firm tug on the door. When it pulled away from the doghouse, Gary came with it. Mom and I saw the problem at the same time—the reason for his incessant wailing: The door was nailed to his forehead.

He must have been leaning against the door when I pounded in the nails, and one of them hit him square in the middle of the forehead. Mom, shocked by what she saw, released the door—it just hung there, suspended from Gary's head. Mom grabbed the door again and gave it a swift tug. With a little "pop," the nail released and the door pulled free. A trickle of blood seeped from a small hole in Gary's forehead.

Gary's wound wasn't serious, although, always cautious, Mom made another of her many trips to the family doctor. As for me, I had the expected session with the razor strap, probably experienced almost as much pain as Gary had.

Behind the glass front of the druggist's counter was a sight that made my eyes sparkle and stomach growl in greedy anticipation. Red and black licorice whips; red, yellow, orange, and green gumdrops; lemon and cherry sour balls; jawbreakers; chocolate babies; malted milk balls; and every kind of candy a kid could ever want.

Even at the age of five, I knew a nickel bought a small bagful of these wonderful confections. A dime's worth gave you a king-sized stomachache. I wasn't sure how much the crumpled, green piece of paper that I clutched tightly in my right hand would buy, but I knew it was a lot—certainly more than I'd ever been able to buy before.

Deciding where to start was a tough decision. I really liked gumdrops; except the green ones, that is. But they stuck to my teeth. Since I'd recently lost my two front teeth, and a few more were kind of wobbly, I didn't think gumdrops were a good idea. Jawbreakers were my second favorite, but, again, they were tough

Simpler Times; Better Times

to handle given the current condition of my remaining teeth. This left the chocolate stuff.

Chocolate is okay. It tastes good; no problem there. But it melts in your hands, and is the one kind of candy that really made me sick—sick enough to throw up, especially if I ate as much as I thought this piece of paper would buy. I saw visions of myself lying on the bathroom floor, holding my cramped stomach, tasting bile in my throat, and listening to Mom say: "It's your own fault. You know better than to eat that much candy." It wasn't a pretty picture.

So, here I was, trying to decide whether to punish my teeth or my stomach—gumdrops, jawbreakers, or chocolate. Life's full of hard decisions, but this was really tough. Who knew if I'd ever have this much money again? A guy doesn't want to make the wrong choice when he knows an opportunity like this might not come his way again for a long, long time—if ever.

As I was lost in these deep thoughts, the druggist came out from behind the soda fountain where he'd been tending to other customers and approached me—a little towhead, dressed in baggy shorts and white tee-shirt, with my nose planted on the glass of his candy counter.

"Jackie," he said, pointing to my right hand, "what have you got there?"

"Money." I held up the green piece of paper. "How much candy can I buy?"

The druggist reached for the money I had clutched in my hand. "Let's see how much you've got."

There was no way that I was going to surrender the cash—not until I had the goods. I held up the crumpled bill for him to see—just a quick peek   then put it behind my back.

"That's five dollars, Jackie. It'll buy a lot of candy. More than you can carry home."

I knew it! I'd hit pay dirt!

"Okay. I'll start with a bag of gumdrops."

The teeth lost. They were coming out anyway. Gramp will tie a string around them, hook the other end of the string to a door knob, slam the door, and yank them out, or I lose them to the sticky gumdrops.

Jack D. Atchison

The druggist didn't move. He just stood there looking at me. Finally, he asked, "Does your mother know that you have this money?"

Oh, oh, decision time. A lie gets me the candy. The truth gets me in trouble. What to do? I lowered my eyes and shuffled my feet, deep in thought.

The druggist saw my dilemma. He squatted down, putting us at eye level. "Does your mother know you've come to the store to buy candy?"

What's with this guy? Here I am, I thought, cash in hand, ready to buy, and he's giving me the fifth degree. What kind of salesmanship is that? Worse, he's coming close to blowing the whole deal.

It should be noted that every merchant in the neighborhood knew every kid in the neighborhood. They knew where we lived; they knew our general economic circumstances; and, they knew our parents.

Before I could answer, he took my hand and led me to the soda fountain, where he lifted me up and deposited my fanny on one of the stools.

"I'll tell you what, before I put your candy in a bag, let me talk to your mother." He lifted the telephone and started to dial. As was the case with most of the neighborhood merchants, he knew the telephone numbers of his regular customers and, with the number of prescriptions and bandages we bought in this store, we were, indeed, regular customers.

Rats! There's no way that Mom is going to buy this deal. I glanced over my shoulder and looked pensively at the candy counter. So close and, yet, so far. My vision of bags full of gumdrops, jawbreakers, and chocolate gave way to the image of a razor strap being applied to my backside.

I heard the druggist say: "Marge, I've got your son, Jackie, here." He paused and listened. "He's by himself." Another pause. "No, Gary's not with him." Yet, another pause. This was painful. "He's got five dollars and wants to buy candy." There goes the deal. "Alright, I'll keep him here."

I couldn't hear Mom's side of the conversation. That's probably just as well, because I didn't figure that she was very happy about what the druggist told her. Sold out by a squealer!

Simpler Times; Better Times

It didn't take long for Mom to walk from our house to the drugstore—a distance of two blocks. At the time—the summer of 1947—Mom, who was twenty-three years old, was a seasoned veteran in dealing with the mischief that her sons generated.

She entered the drugstore and walked briskly to the soda-fountain counter where I was sitting. The expression on her face was a mixture of concern, anger, and bewilderment—a typical expression for a young mother. She pried the five-dollar bill from my fingers and, in a tone I was becoming all too familiar with, asked: "Where did you get this?" Followed rapidly by, "Where's your brother?"

Interesting questions. The answers were certainly linked, and ones which were difficult to give to her. I was more certain than ever that the truth would produce the spanking that was looming ever larger on the horizon. But truth it had to be. "I sold Gary."

"You did what?" Mom's voice now contained elements of concern, panic, bewilderment, and more than a hint of threatening anger.

"I sold Gary."

"When? To whom?"

I shrugged. "A little while ago. To a kid down the street." I pointed in the vague direction of home.

"Why?" she asked, still somewhat bewildered.

Why, indeed. It was a good deal—both for me and the other kid. Gary was a little, red-haired pest. He followed me everywhere. He always got me in trouble with Mom or Gramp. He served no useful purpose—at least not from my perspective. Heck, I couldn't even lock him up in the doghouse. But for the other kid, it was a different story. For five bucks he acquired his own personal slave—someone to clean his room, fetch things for him, and do whatever he wanted. In turn, I got five bucks—and all the candy it would buy—along with freedom from my little brother. It was, as far as I was concerned, a win-win situation.

Before I could explain the beauty and unquestionable logic underlying the transaction, I was lifted from the stool. Mom firmly grasped my hand and led me from the store with the following command: "Take me to your brother!"

Jack D. Atchison

As we exited the store, I glanced back at the candy counter. Any possibility of enjoying its contents was gone. The druggist stood by the door to the store, a smile on his face, apparently finding humor in a situation that held none for either Mom or me.

We covered the blocks between the store and to what I thought was Gary's new home in record time—Mom walking purposefully and me struggling to keep up with her. As she pulled me along by the hand, I had to run with a weird kind of hopping motion to keep from falling flat on my face. And run I did. I knew better than to make a deteriorating situation worse.

When we approached a white house located on a street one block away from our home, I pointed. "Gary's in there."

Mom hurried up the porch steps, with me firmly in tow, and knocked on the door. A woman in a work dress and apron opened the door. "I believe my son, Gary, is inside with your son. Would you please send him out?"

"Your son's not here."

"Yes, he is. Jackie," pointing to me, "said that he `sold' Gary to your son for five dollars."

The look on the woman's face made it clear that she thought Mom was demented. Undeterred, Mom extended the five-dollar bill to the woman, "This is yours. Now, please send Gary out here."

"I told you that your son isn't here," the woman said; her voice piqued. Nonetheless, she took the five bucks.

At this point, we heard faint sounds coming from inside the house. With the uncanny knack that mothers have to hear and identify the cries of their offspring, Mom honed in on the sounds coming from within the house. "I hear my son."

The woman looked over her shoulder toward the door behind her.

"I'd like to see if Gary's down there," Mom said, pointing to a door that led to the basement.

With some reluctance, the woman let us enter the house. Mom opened the door and we descended a flight of stairs into a dark, dank basement.

We found Gary tied to a post by a rope; much like a leash for a dog. He was sitting on the floor, crying, with big tears streaming down his freckled cheeks. Mom untied the rope, took him in her arms, and fixed me with a withering look.

The woman turned to her son—a kid of six or seven. "Where did you get this money?" She asked, holding up the well-crumpled, five-dollar bill, obviously accepting the idea that her son had, indeed, used it to purchase Gary from his slave-trading, older brother.

"From...from your...your purse," the kid stammered, knowing he now faced the same fate I did—a session with a razor strap or belt. We looked at each other—two defeated deal makers.

"I'm sorry," the woman said to Mom as we headed up the stairs. "I didn't know that your boy was down here."

"That's okay. I guess we both have some talking to do with our sons," indicating me and the other kid, who still appeared to be taking refuge in his basement.

Mom escorted us home. Gary was on one side of her, feeling better, his tears dried. I was on her other side, apprehension about what awaited me rising with each step.

Later, I received my expected fate—a few swats with the razor strap. They were administered by Dad, who I think saw some humor in the whole event but, because he was in charge of family discipline, was nonetheless compelled to carry out the fully deserved punishment.

Like most of these attitude adjusters, the swats stung, but the only thing that got bruised was my ego—and only for a few moments at that. Nonetheless, my days as a slave trader had come to an end.

CHAPTER FIVE

In 1948, Dad received his engineering degree from Michigan State and, upon graduation, accepted a job with Republic Steel in Canton, Ohio. For him, it was the end of an arduous grind of working nights, attending classes, slaving over homework, and trying to care for a wife and two boisterous boys. Both he and Mom were ready for a change.

Soon after Dad accepted Republic Steel's offer of employment, Mom and he visited Canton to look for a house. A new subdivision was being started in which "affordable housing" was being constructed for veterans of World War II. Through a program sponsored by the Veterans Administration that allowed for a minimal down payment and a low-interest-rate mortgage, they purchased a new home—one not yet completed—in the new subdivision. For them, it was a "dream house," and they were anxious to move in and begin pursuing a more normal and, hopefully, less hectic and demanding life.

Gary and I were not as enthusiastic about a move to Ohio. We would be leaving Gram and Gramp, who we saw and spent time with almost every day. They were our best friends, our surrogate parents, our teachers and playmates, and, aside from Mom and Dad, the most important people in our worlds. The thought of being away from them was both troubling and painful. And they felt the same.

In early December of 1948, we made the move to Canton. Dad hooked a trailer to his old Chevrolet and, after loading it mostly with clothing, we set off on the first of what would be many trips between East Lansing and Canton.

It was a long and fatiguing drive. The top speed for the old car, pulling a trailer, was about forty-five miles per hour, provided it was going downhill with a good tailwind behind it. Otherwise, we crawled along at under forty miles per hour. There were no interstate highways and the Ohio Turnpike had not yet been built, so we traveled along a series of two-lane roads, passing through

Simpler Times; Better Times

every little burg and hamlet between East Lansing and Canton, which meant stopping for each of their single traffic lights.

It was a cold winter's day and the car's heater cast out a meager draft of warm air, not enough to keep the occupants from the cold. So, we were all bundled in coats and sweaters, gloves on our hands. Our collective breathing caused frost to form on the windshield. Every few miles Mom or Dad wiped the glass with their gloved hands in order to keep it relatively frost-free.

Gary and I huddled in the back seat, wrapped in coats, scarves, and blankets. As the trip progressed, we contributed to the conversation and threatened Mom's and Dad's sanity, by saying things like: "I've got to go to the bathroom"; "I need a drink of water"; "He's on my side of the seat"; "He's hitting me"; and "I'm hungry." These comments, made every few minutes, especially each time we passed through a small town, were invariably followed by the question: "Are we there yet?" And, as the miles passed by, the whine in our voices and the punches we exchanged increased, causing Dad to frequently threaten: "Do I have to stop this car and spank you guys?"

About halfway through the trip, my skin started to itch. Starting around my neck, particularly under the collar of my jacket, the itch spread to my arms, stomach, and back. As the irritation intensified, so did my whining, resulting in a new threat from Dad: "I'll find space for you in the trailer behind the car if you don't keep quiet."

We arrived in Canton late in the day. Because our new home was not yet ready for occupancy, we were going to stay with friends of Gram and Gramp. When we arrived at their house and removed our coats and gloves, I discovered the source of the maddening itch. My neck, arms, and stomach were covered with large, red spots—the chicken pox. By the next morning, the spots had spread to virtually every inch of my body and fever had set in—it was all Mom and Dad needed to make their lives complete.

For the next week or so, Gary and I stayed with our grandparents' friends while Mom and Dad made repeated trips back and forth between Canton and East Lansing to move the remainder of our household goods. I spent most of my time trying to remove the mittens Mom put on my hands to prevent me from scratching the pustules of chicken pox, while Gary spent his time teasing me and taking great delight in my discomfort. By the time Mom and Dad had completed all their trips, their friends were tired of our constant fighting and were more than happy to get rid of us. For the same reasons, Mom and Dad didn't seem overly enthusiastic about the prospect of getting us back.

Nasty childhood illnesses were more common in the 1940 to 1956 era than they are today. The chicken pox was followed by measles, scarlet fever and then the mumps. Once one kid in the neighborhood was afflicted, it was just a matter of days or weeks before every other kid caught the malady de jour.

As this was before many common antibiotics had been developed, medical care was pretty much the same for every aliment—a couple dollops of Vicks, bed rest, and liberal doses of fruit juices and soup. No immunization shots—except for small pox and tuberculosis. No magic pill. Just Vicks and rest.

The mumps were almost as bad as the chicken pox. I got them first. Looked like a chipmunk that was storing acorns in my cheeks for several weeks. I couldn't swallow without intense discomfort. And I complained constantly. Gary caught the mumps two weeks later and Mom got to undergo the same experience twice within a month—one of the real joys of motherhood.

We also suffered through one or two bouts of tonsillitis every winter. Nasty stuff. Yet, to the best of my recollection, none of the kids in the area—Gary and I included—ever had our tonsils removed.

Polio was the truly scary disease of our childhood era. None of our friends ever contracted polio, but many kids in East Lansing and, later, Canton did. Many were confined to huge iron-lung machines to aid their breathing; others were crippled for life; and, unfortunately many kids died from the disease. It remained a horror until 1952 when Jonas Salk discovered a cure and preventative vaccine.

Many of our childhood diseases—chicken pox, measles and mumps—are now prevented by inoculations. And many, if not most, kids have their tonsils removed before they reach the age of eight. Some "progress" of a desirable nature has, indeed, been made.

Simpler Times; Better Times

Our new house was on Grandview Avenue, near the northwest edge of Canton's city limits, in what is known as the Harter District—named after the local elementary school which, in turn, was named after the founder of a local bank. The house was at the bottom of a hill, three houses removed from the end of the street. At the time of our arrival, only a few dozen houses had been completed in a subdivision that eventually would contain several hundred houses.

Grandview dead-ended at the edge of a swamp, which extended south for several hundred yards or so, ending at the bottom of a hill leading to Canton's main east-west road, Tuscarawas—one heck of a name to spell, so it was usually just referred to as "West Tusc." The road immediately west of Grandview, where the subdivision ended, was Whipple Road, a major thoroughfare that marked the boundary of the city's limit.

Grandview wasn't paved. Instead, it consisted of gravel and cinders that were covered with oil and compacted by a heavy roller. Because the street was lightly traveled, the gravel had not thoroughly bonded together. As we drove down the street to our new house, gravel pinged against the underside of the car and shot from the back tires, flying in all directions like bullets sprayed from a machine gun.

Our house was typical of the "starter homes" in the subdivision. It consisted of two above-ground stories and a basement. The first story contained the living room, dining area, kitchen, two bedrooms, and bathroom; all compactly arranged in about eight-hundred square-feet. The second story was unfinished—a cost-saving consideration. The basement contained a gas furnace—a far step up from the coal furnace in the Gunson Street house. And, as was the case with all the other houses on the block, there was no garage—another factor that kept the house affordable for a young family with a limited income.

The materials used to construct the house were also selected to keep costs down. The floors were pine, with some kind of caulking compound inserted between the flooring boards to seal the seams. The walls were wood frame covered by plasterboard. The exterior consisted of wooden, shake shingles. The roof was tarpaper covered by asbestos shingles.

The interior finish was minimal. The walls were painted white. There were no draperies or other window coverings. There were no built-in appliances. And, with the exception of linoleum in the kitchen and bath, there was no carpeting or other floor coverings. The expectation was that the new owner would do all the interior decorating.

The yards in the neighborhood were unadorned dirt, laced with a liberal supply of grapefruit-sized rocks. When we moved in, winter snow covered our front and back yards, which were frozen solid. When the days got warmer, the top layer of frost melted and the yards became a sea of mud dotted by gravel driveways that stood like small islands in the midst of the mud. All in all, the yards represented ideal playing conditions for a couple boys.

Even with all the economy measures, the house looked like a castle when we drove into the gravel drive for the first time. It was new and, compared to Gunson Street, open, light, and airy. It was, indeed, a dream home.

Within a few days of moving in, Gary and I learned that a boy our age, also named Jack, lived in one of the houses located behind us. A few weeks later, two more boys, one my age, Johnny, and one a year younger than Gary, Chuckie, moved into a house behind ours.

As we played in our own yards, we frequently glanced at each other, trying to work up the courage to introduce ourselves. For Gary and me, having playmates our own age so close by was a new experience. So, we had to overcome a sense of shyness and, perhaps, fear before we could garner the courage to meet our new, prospective playmates.

In large measure, they, too, had to summon up enough courage to meet us. They, also, had been uprooted from their former homes and now found themselves in a new environment, inflicted with the same fears and uncertainties that Gary and I were experiencing.

Gradually, with runny noses and rosy cheeks, the parties inched closer and closer to one another. In the end, we met at the boundaries of our respective yards. After a few awkward minutes of feeling each other out, we entered into fast friendships and literally overnight became constant companions. Each day, as soon

Simpler Times; Better Times

as we wolfed down breakfast or school ended, we donned our outdoor clothing, met our new friends, and played nonstop until darkness arrived.

We were a motley little band. Because it was wintertime, we dressed in snowsuits, rubber boots, and mittens, with scarves tightly wrapped around our heads to protect our faces from the cold winter air. Because our families were on tight budgets, our winter clothes were often hand-me-downs. Some of the snowsuits had been patched so many times they looked more like quilts than clothes.

Because Johnny and I were the oldest in our respective families, we occasionally got new clothes. But for Chuckie and Gary, it was different. All their clothes were handed down from Johnny or me after we outgrew them or they were castoffs from friends and relatives. Not that it really mattered, because none of us was fashion conscious. Our only concern was that the clothes were warm. Besides, within a few minutes after leaving the house, we usually were covered with mud, so no one could tell whether our clothes were new or not.

The neighborhood was a great place to play. At any given time, a half-dozen houses were under construction. Basements had been built with cement blocks and most were framed out. We rapidly learned how to scale the framed walls and rafters. The two-by-fours became our own private playground—informal sets of monkey bars built for us to climb and swing on. As we played, people passing by saw a band of four- to six-year-old boys swinging from the first-floor rafters, as we played tag or cops and robbers.

The most exciting structures were those where the framing was in place but the flooring boards had not yet been installed to build the first-story floor. In these cases, as we climbed the structure, we could see all the way to the basement floor—a drop of almost twenty feet when we were hanging on the rafters for the first-story ceiling. The possibility of falling and plunging onto the basement floor added an exciting element of danger to our play. It also made us careful and skilled climbers, as no one wanted to use his body to test the hardness of a concrete floor.

Of course, our mothers weren't too crazy about our playing in these partially-completed structures. They worried about us falling into the open basements, stepping on nails, or falling from the framing as we climbed toward the roofing rafters. In some respects, their fears were justified. We did step on nails and there were more than a few spectacular falls. Fortunately, our heavy winter clothing served as padding, cushioning falls and preventing any serious injuries. Moreover, we weren't stupid. All minor mishaps were concealed from our parents, serving to cement the bond that had grown between the members of our little gang as we became co-conspirators in cover-ups of various injuries.

    When the mud was too deep, or the temperatures plunged to near zero, we congregated in one of our basements. No one's basement was finished. That is, they were just big open spaces, devoid of partitions, making them great places to play.

    The only drawback came when we played in Johnny's and Chuckie's basement. The duct work leading from the furnace to the upper floors was exposed between the rafters that formed the basement's ceiling. The duct work consisted of thin sheet metal and it conducted noise like the skin of a drum. When we played, a ball or other object periodically struck the duct work. Their mother was petrified that we would hit the furnace and cause the house to explode in flames, so with each sound that resonated through the house, Johnny's mother screamed out: "Stop it! You're going to kill us all!" Then, she'd run down the basement stairs and deliver a heated lecture on the dangers of hitting furnaces—lectures that we quickly learned to ignore.

    There was another thing about Johnny's mom. She was paranoid that kids might get dirt on her furniture, which had been purchased just after they moved into their new house. In order to protect the furniture, she encased everything in clear plastic. It was the darnedest stuff. As a little kid, who wasn't very tall, once I'd managed to climb onto a chair or the couch, if I shifted position, I'd slide off the furniture and land on the floor. It was like she oiled the stuff every morning in order to make it as slippery as possible. The funny thing is, ten years later, when we were all in high school, the plastic was still there, covering every piece of furniture. It still may be there, because the family still lives in the same house.

Simpler Times; Better Times

Privacy and home security were not concerns in our childhood era like they are today. When completed, our subdivision ran north-south for five blocks and east-west for another five blocks. Each block contained around 20 homes, on average, meaning there were around 500 houses in total in the subdivision. Less than thirty homes had fenced backyards; none had fences in the front yards. The backyard fences were not constructed to keep people out, but rather to keep dogs in. The rarity of fences was attributable to the rarity of dogs in the neighborhood.

The houses were cookie-cutter replicas; except for the color they were painted, each looked like every other house in the neighborhood. Each had about a thirty-five-foot by twenty-five-foot footprint; each had two above-ground stories and a basement. The top floor and basement were in every case unfinished when the occupants moved in. The typical family consisted of husband and wife and usually two or more kids; although, there were a few childless households—probably not more than fifty out of five hundred households fell in that category. With little space, a large family, and low budget, few families wanted a dog—one that took up space and needed to be fed. Hence, little need for fences.

None of the doors on our friends' houses were ever locked. If I wanted to visit one of them, or they wanted to visit me, you knocked on the door, waited a minute, walked in, and yelled for the person you wanted to see. If, perchance, they were not home, you simply exited the house and closed the door—no harm; no foul. I do not recall a single incident of a home robbery ever occurring in the neighborhood.

Until a shopping center was built at the end of the street, we never saw a police car in the neighborhood; and then, we only saw them around the shopping center.

The first time I ever had a key to a place in which I lived was when I got a key to my dorm room in college. Until then, I never had a key to any house I lived in—never needed one—the door was never locked.

Many of today's safety concerns simply did not exist then; perhaps in some cases because of a lack of research and knowledge but, in most cases, because common sense prevailed over government regulations.

Jack D. Atchison

The shingles on our roof were made of asbestos—advertised to prevent fire damage. The paint on the walls contained lead, as did all gasoline at the time. We sprayed the flower beds with DDT and used DDT to kill mosquitoes in the spring and summer. Most of the farmers in the country used DDT to kill crop pests. Some sixty years later, most of us are still alive. Why? Maybe because we aren't experimental mice. Maybe because we didn't work where any of the stuff was made and, therefore, it was not possible to breathe or ingest enough of the stuff to ever really get sick from it.

We ate copious amounts of dairy products, potatoes, and red meat—and no kid in my group of friends and few adults in the neighborhood were fat because our play and work was strenuous. We did not sit around on our butts watching television or playing computer games; instead, we played hard and got plenty of exercise.

There were no seat belts or airbags in cars. No safety helmets for bicycle riders. No knee and arm pads for roller-skaters. Instead, you tended to be careful and avoided accidents; and when accidents occurred, you accepted the consequences.

No one sued their doctor when a treatment did not work out as intended. When a fender-bender occurred, the parties, without the aid of lawyers, settled with each other. You did not sue your neighbors over every argument and disagreement; you worked it out.

Kids knew the rules—the rules at home and in school. If you broke the rules, and every kid did every so often, there were consequences. If you acted up in class, fought on the playground, or talked back to a teacher, you knew you were going to the principal's office where you would receive several whacks with a nasty wooden paddle—most of us got a taste of the paddle at least once during our school years. If you still misbehaved—and the paddle did not get your attention—you were suspended. If the suspension did not work—you were expelled. There was no gnashing of teeth about depriving a poor youngster of the education to which he or she was "entitled"—rules were rules. Students, parents and teachers all agreed—the education of thirty people was not going to be disrupted by the misbehavior of one student.

Simpler Times; Better Times

If there was any question about the principal's authority to whack your little butt, it was rapidly dispelled when you got home. Because there, your fanny received a few more whacks. If I said to Dad: "It wasn't my fault." Or "I didn't mean to do it." Or "The other guy started it." He would listen, nod his head in understanding, and then whack, whack, whack. Excuses didn't cut it. You were responsible for your own actions and responsible for the consequences of those actions—period—end of story.

If you damaged another party's property or person, you paid for it. You paid for it even it took all your allowances for weeks or months to do so or if you had to mow a hundred lawns or shovel a hundred sidewalks. Right was right; wrong was wrong; fair was fair.

If a whipping was not a sufficient penalty by itself, added measures were taken. Allowances were surrendered. You spent every Saturday and Sunday for weeks painting the house, digging flower gardens, washing windows—sometimes the same windows over-and-over again. In the end, you learned to follow the rules or suffer the consequences. The "devil made me do it" excuse just made things worse.

Then Doctor Spock came along and screwed everything up.

When Christmas break ended in early January 1949, and I was completely over the chicken pox, Jack, Johnny and I had to go to school. Gary and Chuckie were too young, so they got to stay home and play.

Jack was going to attend a parochial school, while Johnny and I headed for public school. I was surprised by Jack's announcement that he was attending a different school. I hadn't heard of parochial schools before and when he told me that all his teachers would be nuns or priests, my surprise grew. I didn't know anything about the Catholic Church and it seemed strange to me that Jack was going to school in his church—actually the school was next door to the church, but the way he described it made it seem like the classes were in the church itself.

From my perspective, it sounded like Jack was being punished by having to attend this strange school, separate and apart from the rest of us. But Jack made it sound like a good deal, stating that he'd get a better education than Johnny and I would because Catholic schools were better than public schools.

Jack's declaration started a debate: Which was, indeed, better, Catholic or public schools? The debate grew more intense as time passed, as most arguments among kids tend to do. And because we didn't attend school together, we didn't see much of Jack, except on the weekends. The debate and our lack of daily contact gradually created a distance between us and, as a consequence, Jack didn't become part of the gang of kids that Johnny and I later associated with in the neighborhood. The kids who attended public school tended to hang out together and the parochial school kids did the same. For the first time, I experienced the divisive effects that religious differences can produce, even among six-year-old kids.

Mom walked me to Harter Elementary School for my first day of classes. The school was located about eight blocks from our house, a distance of close to a mile, making it a long walk for a kid with short legs, especially when one was bundled in a snowsuit and boots in the wintertime. As we trudged along, I was filled with apprehension—the fear of meeting new people and encountering a new experience. Mom, seeing the fear in my eyes, tried to quell my concerns by offering words of encouragement. Despite her efforts, I entered the classroom on shaky legs, wishing, for the first time in my life, that I was at home with Gary.

It was the start of the second semester of the first grade. Johnny and I were the only new students joining the class at the semester break. So, we were the subjects of curious stares from the other students as we made our way to desks in the back of the room—stares that fueled my feelings of discomfort and apprehension.

The actual schoolwork did not worry me. Mom, Gram, and Gramp had already taught me basic arithmetic and I could add, subtract, multiply and divide by the time I had started the first grade in East Lansing. I could also read books written for children and good portions of popular magazines, like *The Saturday Evening Post, Look,* and *Life*. And when I came across a word I did not understand or could not pronounce, one of the adults in the house was always eager to answer my questions. So, the first

Simpler Times; Better Times

semester in East Lansing had been very easy. That was about to change.

Miss Julian, our teacher, was a tall, skinny, blonde-haired, unmarried woman whom I rapidly learned had the disposition and temper of a PCP-crazed rattlesnake, prone to strike out in venomous attacks of rage against any of her wards who had the temerity to upset her by failing to adhere explicitly to her instructions.

The class was engaged in learning the alphabet; something I had learned before my fourth birthday. As a teaching aide, Miss Julian gave each student a piece of colored construction paper. The students were instructed to fold the piece of paper and draw a letter of the alphabet on it. They were then to use scissors to cut out the letter they had drawn. If done correctly, when the paper was unfolded, the student had two identical versions of the letter, joined at the center by the fold in the paper.

When I joined the class, they were about halfway through the alphabet. Miss Julian decided that Johnny and I should start with the letter "A" and catch up to the rest of the class. This didn't sound too bad, at least not until it dawned on me that it had taken the rest of the class a few weeks to get to the point where they were. It took an hour or so to draw and cut out each letter, primarily because Miss Julian insisted that each letter had to conform to her very stringent quality standards, requiring several attempts by most students before she declared their effort satisfactory. To catch up, Johnny and I had to do two letters in the same time that it took the others to draw and cut out one. It seemed to be an uphill battle, but I thought it was not an insurmountable one. I was wrong.

Sitting at my desk in the back of the room, I started out with the letter "A," drawing it as carefully and precisely as I could. Then, using scissors, I tried to cut clean—not ragged—lines, because Miss Julian had emphasized that ragged lines were unacceptable. When I was done cutting, I unfolded the paper and discovered that I was holding a letter in each hand—they were not joined in the middle as they were supposed to be.

Almost immediately, I sensed Miss Julian hovering over me. "What did you do?" she asked in a shrill, accusatory tone of voice.

Jack D. Atchison

I looked at the letter in each of my hands. "I don't know. They aren't together."

"You didn't follow instructions," she said; her voice rising, causing the others students in the class to turn around and look in my direction.

"I made a mistake," I said; stating the obvious, shivering in my seat, not knowing what to expect.

She grabbed my hand. "Come with me." She led me to the front of the room where she pulled a big wooden ruler from her desk. Turning to the rest of the class, she held up the two detached letters for all to see. "This is what happens when you don't follow instructions. You waste paper." She turned toward me. "Maybe this will help you listen better. Hold out your hand."

Reluctantly, I held out my left hand. She grabbed my wrist and, without warning, raised the ruler and hit my knuckles. I let out a yelp of pain. The ruler had a piece of metal imbedded in the edge and, when she hit me, the metal dug into my knuckles, immediately bringing tears to my eyes. She swatted a second time, laying the ruler across my knuckles at the same point where the first blow had landed. Apparently satisfied that she'd made her point, she said: "Now go back to your seat and do it right."

I walked down the aisle, holding my sore hand, and fighting back tears. As I walked, I heard snickers coming from the other students—none of whom had I met at this point. I was humiliated and embarrassed.

Back in my seat, I grasped another piece of paper in my hands and stared at it, trying to figure out where I'd gone wrong. After a few minutes of intense concentration, I carefully folded the paper, making sure the edges were straight. Then, I drew the letter "A" and cut it out, certain that I'd followed Miss Julian's instructions to a tee. I put the scissors down on the desk and unfolded the paper, absolutely shocked when, once again, I found myself holding two separate letters.

It didn't take Miss Julian more than a couple of seconds to see my mistake. She literally ran down the aisle from her desk to mine. "Are you stupid?" She blurted out, grabbing my hand, pulling me from my seat, and leading me to the front of the classroom. Once again, she pulled out the ruler and, with me standing before the rest of the class, administered three more

Simpler Times; Better Times

cracks across the knuckles of my left hand. Then, she marched me back to my desk. On the way, I again heard snickers from my classmates.

At my desk, I asked Miss Julian to show me how to fold the paper and cut out the letter, something she hadn't really done before. Obviously irritated, she showed me how to make the joined letter "A." Once I saw how she did it, I had no trouble in repeating the operation. Unfortunately, over the next few weeks, as I moved through the alphabet, trying to catch up with the rest of the class, I occasionally ran into difficulties and made mistakes. Each mistake led to another trip to the front of the room for a few cracks across the knuckles from Miss Julian's metal-edged ruler.

As the semester continued, patterns became evident in Miss Julian's unusual disciplinary techniques. First, no girls were ever subjected to being cracked on the knuckles with a ruler nor were any of them ever called "stupid" or "dummy," that treatment was reserved for boys only. Second, she centered her attention on just a few of us—me and three others, including Johnny. But, for some reason, I was her favorite target, making almost daily trips to the front of the room where she'd smack me across the knuckles and refer to me as either "stupid" or "dumb."

The torment was not confined to the classroom. Kids being kids, some of them started to tease me about my daily confrontations with Miss Julian and started to call me "stupid" and "dummy." This was treatment I was not about to take.

During high school, in the Army, and at Michigan State, Dad had been a boxer. While we lived in East Lansing, Dad bought us boxing gloves and taught Gary and me how to throw and block a punch. We had plenty of practice fighting with each other. So, even though I was small for my age— one of the runts in the first-grade class—when I heard the teasing I reacted, getting into more than my fair share of fist fights on the way home from school.

While I successfully defended myself, and earned respect as a result of my tenacity as a fighter, continuing on in spite of a bloody nose or cut lip until the other guy called it quits, this ordeal nonetheless took its toll. I learned to conceal emotions. I realized that if you let a bully know he was getting under your skin, or if you cried, it encouraged him to continue at an even more brutal pace. On the other hand, if you showed no emotion—anger, fear, or even unhappiness—the other guy didn't know how to read you. Thus, remaining somewhat stoic became an effective defense mechanism and cut down the number of taunts and resultant fights.

Also, I started to avoid and not to trust others, keeping my own counsel and limiting my contacts to those few friends whom I knew I could rely on and trust. As a result, I became somewhat introverted, as did a number of the others who were subjected to Miss Julian's disciplinary tactics.

Finally, I dreaded failure. I associated a mistake—failure—with a trip to the front of the room where I'd be humiliated and embarrassed before my peers. So, I concentrated on trying to best the others in the class—working harder and smarter than they did. I figured if I could stay at the top of the class, there was no way a teacher could criticize or embarrass me.

Others who were the targets of Miss Julian's attacks were also affected by them. One of the guys gave up and flunked the first grade, having to repeat it the next year. Others developed stammers and stutters. All were more subdued in their behavior than they might otherwise have been. As the years passed, some got over the side effects of Miss Julian's treatment, but for others of us, the defense mechanisms that we adopted during this year became permanent parts of our personalities.

As we underwent Miss Julian's abuse, we did not discuss it with our parents. Each day, when I returned home from class, Mom asked me how school had gone. I avoided a direct answer to her question. There was the fear that, if the teacher thought I was dumb or stupid, so might my parents. It was bad enough to endure criticism and labeling at school; it would have been unbearable to experience the same thing at home. So, each of us concealed what was happening to us.

The veil of our concealment lifted over time. As the year progressed, Miss Julian became more aggressive with her ruler. Once her swats simply left a welt, but later they started to draw blood as the metal edge of the ruler split the skin. Our parents noticed the marks on our hands and their questions became more persistent. Eventually, we started to open up and told our parents what was happening.

At first, Mom and, individually, other concerned parents met with Miss Julian and confronted her with what we had reported about her behavior. She denied doing anything wrong, asserting that we were inventing things to make her look bad. Her protests might have been plausible had there been only one student who was describing her antics, but, as parents started checking with one another they learned that all of us were reporting the same things.

As the end of the school year approached, a group of parents went to the school principal, who started her own investigation into Miss Julian's conduct. The principal was appalled at what had been going on inside her school, and Miss Julian was fired—a direct result of the abuse and terror that she visited on a group of six-year-old kids.

The completion of my first-grade school year wasn't the end of this story. I passed the first grade, but my marks left something to be desired, because Miss Julian had graded many of us quite harshly. As a consequence, I was assigned to a special class in the second grade. The class was mixed—half second graders and half third-grade students. We all had one common characteristic: We were deemed to be slow learners.

It was a stigma that lasted for only one year. Once we were free of Miss Julian, all of us who had been condemned by her grades were able to demonstrate that we weren't stupid nor were we slow learners. By the third grade, we were all back in normal classes and were all above-average students.

When summer break arrived, we returned to our favorite play sites—the houses under construction in the subdivision. Each one became a temporary playground for the kids in the neighborhood—a playground that was closed when the house was completed. But since the entire area surrounding us was undergoing development—and continued to be under development for the next five years or so—we were always able to find a house where we could climb up and down the frame. As we got older, and could climb higher, we'd scale the two-by-fours from the first floor to the second and, then, onto the roofing rafters. On any given weekend day, the skeletal houses in the area looked like the monkey island in a local zoo as our little gang of boys swung from rafter to rafter.

Jack D. Atchison

The construction sites provided another benefit to the kids in the neighborhood. Each new house was the source of scrap lumber and other goodies. The area immediately west of us was acre after acre of fields, woods, and swamps. We'd pirate lumber, plywood, wood and asbestos shingles, pieces of plasterboard, and sheet-metal scraps from the various construction sites and haul it to the swamps or the woods, where we'd build forts, tree houses, and rafts.

Building a raft is not a simple process. We started by using our fathers' hand saws to cut down two or three fair-sized trees. We stripped the branches off the fallen trees to produce logs that were about six feet long and six-inches in diameter. These logs were laid parallel to one another and were joined together by two-by-fours that we had liberated from a construction site. The two-by-fours became the frame for the floor of the raft. To this frame, we nailed plywood and shingles. When we were finished, we had a reasonably seaworthy craft that was about four feet wide and six feet long.

In building a fort, we nailed two-by-fours to a series of trees that were in close proximity to one another. We placed the two-by-fours about four feet from the ground in order to form a frame for the roof and walls of the fort. Because of the placement of the trees, our forts took on some rather peculiar shapes— certainly none was a perfect square or rectangle, instead they looked like forerunners of modern architecture. We used plywood and plasterboard to build the walls and roof. The outside of the fort was completed by covering the exterior walls and roof with wooden and asbestos shingles. The interior floor was made of cardboard or plywood. When we were done, we had serviceable and reasonably waterproof structures. Within two years of moving to Canton, we'd built an extensive network of tree houses and forts, as well as a small fleet of homemade rafts.

Our fathers were veterans of World War II and each of them had brought home a collection of mess kits, canteens, and helmets. What they didn't bring home, we were able to buy at the local army-surplus stores. We stocked our forts with these items. Each time we ventured over to the swamp, we took a canteen of water, fruit, sandwiches, and candy. We camped out in our forts

Simpler Times; Better Times

with all our paraphernalia and foodstuffs and explored the swamp on our rafts—a little rag-tag army dressed in surplus war gear.

This was, in large part, the nature of play in those days. All our parents were struggling to make ends meet and fought to balance their budgets from day to day. If they were members of the emerging American middle class, they had, at best, barely reached the first rung of the middle-class ladder. There weren't any funds available to buy toys. So, we made our own from the stuff we found in the environment around us. And we were very, very happy. Nothing we could have purchased in any store came close to equaling our forts and rafts, and no arcade could ever compete with our playgrounds—the framed houses, swamps, and woods.

The field leading to the swamp was a treasure trove waiting to be explored. The field consisted of knee-high grass that was dotted with an array of small trees, milkweed plants, elderberry bushes, poison oak, sumac, and sporadic stands of maples and oaks. In the late summer, the tops of the trees were covered with silken tents woven by insects, and the air was filled with wisps of matter given off by dandelions and milkweeds. By fall, the grass turned brown and the leaves on the maples and oaks looked like an artist's palette, reflecting various shades of yellow, orange, red, and purple.

One of the most intriguing inhabitants of the field was the cinnamon snake—a small, slender, reddish-brown creature that, when mature, was about ten or twelve inches long and had the girth of a number-two pencil. The cinnamon snake lived under stones and logs and fed off insects. In our fields, there were literally hundreds of these harmless little creatures.

One day, Gary and I decided to see how many cinnamon snakes we could catch—Gary wanted to keep them as pets. We got a ball of string, and dressed in our customary blue jeans and sneakers, set off for the field. We combed through the weeds and tall grass hunting for rocks and logs that were likely refuges for cinnamon snakes. When we found a good candidate, one of us carefully lifted the object while the other got ready to grab the snake. The person who was elected to grab the snake had to have quick hands, because the snakes darted away as soon as sunlight hit them.

Jack D. Atchison

Once we caught a snake, we took a six-inch piece of string, tied a tight knot around the snake, and attached the other end of the string to one of our belt loops. Within a matter of a few hours, each of us had two dozen snakes writhing from the belt loops of our blue jeans. We were also covered from head to toe with dirt and mud.

When we got home, we headed straight for the basement. Mom had cleaned so many dirty footprints from her floors that she'd laid down the law—we had to strip in the basement before we could go anywhere else in the house. We observed her law and took off our shoes and jeans, leaving them in a heap on the basement floor. Then, before finding a suitable container for Gary's new pets, we ran upstairs to wash and get clean clothes.

Mom knew we were going to the field that day and she knew it meant we would return home with filthy clothes—we always did. She had a load of wash to do and, when she heard us clomp up the basement steps, she decided to do the wash, planning to add our stuff to the clothes she had already accumulated.

While we were in the bathroom, washing up and changing clothes, she went to the basement with her laundry basket full of dirty clothes. She filled the wash tub and placed the things from her basket into it before reaching down to the floor to retrieve our muddy jeans. When she picked up the jeans, she let out a scream that rattled the windows and walls in the house—a scream that must have startled everyone in the neighborhood, because it sure as heck got Gary's and my attention.

Dressed in our underwear, we raced from the bathroom to the basement steps to see what had caused Mom to let out such a whoop of panic. When we got to the basement, Mom, white as a sheet, was backed into a corner.

"What's the matter?" Gary and I asked in unison.

Mom pointed to our jeans, which were still piled on the floor. "What in the world is on those pants?" she asked; her voice filled with terror.

Gary reached down and picked up his jeans. He held them up—two dozen little snakes wiggling from the belt loops. "You mean these?" he asked, holding one of the cinnamon snakes.

"Yes," Mom said; her eyes wide with fear and panic.

"They're just snakes...pets," Gary said. "Why?"

"What are they doing on your pants?"

"We didn't have anything to put them in," Gary said. A logical reply. "What's the problem?"

"Get them out of this house—"

"But, Mom—"

"No, buts. Get them out! Now!"

"But, Mom," I started to say, wanting to point out that we were in our underwear and, thus, not in a position, at least as far as I was concerned, to take the snakes outside.

"No, buts," she repeated. "I want them out, right now!"

We could see that she meant business. Reluctantly, we picked up our pants, snakes and all, and trudged up the stairs. We cracked open the back door and tossed our pants into the yard, hoping none of the snakes escaped while we put on some clothes.

The swamp was a source of all kinds of creatures for us to capture and convert into pets—frogs, toads, turtles, tadpoles, salamanders, snakes, and insects of every variety. Using coat hangers; cheesecloth, potato sacks or old pillow cases; needles and thread; and sticks, we made nets to catch our prey. Bigger nets, usually ones made from pillow cases or potato sacks, were used to catch turtles and frogs. Smaller, lighter nets were used for butterflies, moths, and dragonflies.

The swamp covered several dozen acres. At its deepest point, the water was only three feet deep. The swamp was surrounded by maples and oaks, many with rotted trunks and bare branches. The water was dark and dirty, as the bottom of the swamp consisted of mud and muck. The surface of the water was, for the most part, covered with bulrushes, lily pads, and various grasses. Cattails grew along the banks. Tree stumps and logs littered the water. In short, it was paradise.

Armed with nets, we'd launch one of our rafts into the water and set off on a hunting expedition. One kid would use a pole to propel the raft, pushing off against the muddy bottom of the swamp, while the other searched for prey. Most of the rafts accommodated only two people, but even then their seaworthiness was often questionable. They leaked and occasionally sank into the murky water, forcing the tiny sailors who piloted them to abandon ship and wade through lily pads and swamp grasses to reach shore.

Jack D. Atchison

When a kid was forced to abandon his craft and had to wade to shore, he knew he was in for trouble when he got home. His shoes and clothing would be covered with mud, and the stench produced by the swamp water was truly awful. None of our mothers looked forward to washday after we'd had such an accident, sometimes claiming that it would be wiser to toss out our clothes rather than contaminate the rest of the wash. These comments were often accompanied by a threat to withhold our weekly allowance to pay for the ruined clothing. Fortunately, Mom never carried through with her threats, but she did read us the riot act every time we showed up smelling and looking like the swamp.

Frogs and turtles hid under lily pads, with just their noses showing above the water. Most of the turtles were small eastern painted turtles, but every once in a while we'd encounter a good-sized snapping turtle—mean rascals that could latch onto a finger or toe if a kid wasn't careful. The spotter on the raft scanned each lily pad. When he saw a turtle's nose or frog's head jutting out, he signaled for the pole man to slow down. We'd let the raft drift silently toward the target. When the lily pad was within the reach of our net, and if the prey hadn't been spooked by our approach, the kid with the net struck, driving the open net well below the lily pad. We learned that both turtles and frogs dive to escape attackers, so in order to catch them, the net had to be driven a foot or so below them, trapping them when they dove. After several dozen hunting expeditions, we were very proficient with the nets and caught the majority of our targets.

Tadpoles—frogs in the making—usually swam along the edge of the swamp. We used a variety of devices to catch them—nets, coffee cans with holes punched in the bottom, and Mason jars—the kind Mom used for canning. On a good day, we caught dozens of tadpoles, confining them in large Mason jars filled with swamp water. It was fascinating to watch them mature. The tail would gradually diminish, the legs emerged and the body thickened. In the end, we no longer had tadpoles, but we gained a collection of frogs.

Salamanders and newts hid under rocks and logs. Extremely fast, these lizard-like creatures darted quickly in a zigzag fashion, making them hard to catch. But, again, we were proficient hunters. Once we learned the pattern of their escape routine, we caught a good number of them. The salamanders were, perhaps, the most interesting of the critters we caught. Turtles don't do much; they just lay on the ground, moving only when hungry or disturbed. Salamanders, on the other hand, are always active. When we put flies or other insects in the jar, the salamanders ate them, nailing the bugs with their tongues.

Butterflies, moths, dragonflies, and other flying insects required more effort to catch. Once one was spotted, the hunter chased after it with his net, running through fields and across lawns as the flying critter zigzagged through the air. When the hunter got within arm's reach of his prey, he swung his light net, hopefully trapping the target inside. If the insect got in the net, the hunter quickly twisted his wrist, flopping the bottom of the net over the opening, securing the trapped insect inside. The success rate for capturing flying insects wasn't high—far more got away than got caught.

Using a net wasn't the only way to catch bugs—a jar and lid also worked well. The hunter waited until the prey landed on a flower, clover, or dandelion and then crept up on it. With the lid in one hand and jar in the other, the hunter positioned the jar on one side of the insect and the lid on the other. Then, the hunter struck, drawing the lid and jar together, trapping the insect between them. This was the preferred method for catching honey bees and yellow jackets.

Then, of course, there were our hands. The hunter sneaked up on the insect and simply grabbed it with his hands, pinching the insect's wings between thumb and forefinger. This worked well with butterflies, but with bees it was a different story. If you missed, or the grab was off center, the bee not only escaped but it became agitated and, more often than not, you got stung. But, especially with bees, this was the most exciting method of hunting. Besides, there was a side benefit to clutching an angry bee between your fingers. If your buddy wasn't paying attention, you could toss the captured bee at him and watch him run. Or better yet, you slipped the buzzing bee into the pocket of his pants. Either way, it was great sport for the hunter.

Gary became a bona fide collector of insects and swamp creatures. The rest of us caught them because we liked the thrill of the hunt. But Gary, who was fascinated by all these creatures, carefully studied them. Mom and Dad bought him books about reptiles, amphibians, and insects and Gary made a science out of it. As a result of his interests, we always had a collection of creeping, crawling critters around our house.

One day, Mom was picking up dirty clothes from the basement floor. She reached for a pair of Gary's blue jeans. Before her hands grasped them, the soiled jeans moved. They rose off the floor, flew in the air, and landed a short distance away from her outstretched hand. She reached again and, once more, they moved. On the third attempt, she grabbed them.

When she lifted the jeans up, a big gray-green bullfrog leaped out. Mom tossed the jeans across the basement and let out one of her patented shouts. Her scream drew Gary to the basement where he quickly recaptured his frog, completely mystified by Mom's reaction to the harmless little creature.

After each load of wash, water didn't automatically empty from Mom's wash tub. If the water wasn't too dirty, it was reused. Otherwise, she drained and refilled the wash tub with each load.

One day, after washing a load of blue jeans, she checked the tub to see if the water was clean enough to use for another load. When she looked into the tub, she was shocked to see a couple dozen huge, six-inch-long worms floating on top of the water. Immediately, she called us to the basement and demanded an explanation.

In springtime in Ohio, warm rains draw night-crawlers from the ground. In the morning, after a light, night rain, sidewalks are strewn with these big worms. That had been the case on this particular morning. When Gary got up and went out to explore for bugs, he found that the sidewalk outside our house was covered with night-crawlers. He didn't have a jar or a can, so he did the next best thing: He filled his pockets with as many worms as they'd hold, intending to transfer them later to a more appropriate container. But, as was typical of Gary, he got preoccupied with something else and simply forgot about the contents of his pockets, walking around the rest of the morning with the crawling creatures in his jeans. Nor did he remember them when he took off his dirty pants just before lunch.

Simpler Times; Better Times

By now, Mom was accustomed to finding strange things in our pockets, and, as a result, she usually turned them inside-out before doing the wash, usually dreading what she might find. On this day, however, she'd been in a hurry and failed to inspect Gary's pockets before washing the jeans, hence the worms in the wash.

Gary couldn't understand why she was upset. They were just worms. He walked over to the tub, reached in, and scooped up a couple handfuls of the now bleached worms, wondering why Mom hadn't simply done the same. Go figure.

Gary's fascination with nature evolved into a collection of mounted bugs and insects. He attached two parallel slats of wood to a larger board, maintaining a distance of a quarter of an inch or so between the slats. This became his mounting board. A butterfly, moth, or other winged insect's body was placed in the space between the slats; a pin was stuck through the body to hold the specimen in place; the wings were spread onto the slats; and, then, strips of paper and pins were used to tack the wings down as well.

For other bugs, he used a piece of bulletin board material. A pin was driven through the bug, so the bug rested at the top of the pin, then the point was pushed into the board. The result was that the bug was suspended on the pin, a quarter of an inch in the air.

When Gary caught a specimen, he put it in a bottle containing either DDT or chloroform, killing the butterfly or bug within a few minutes. He was careful when catching each specimen, and he used great care in handling it, so as to avoid damaging its wings or other body parts. His object was to obtain perfect, undamaged specimens and, for the most part, he was successful.

As the months passed, his collection grew. His part of the bedroom, as well as an area in the basement, contained an assortment of mounting boards. He had separate boards for butterflies, moths, dragonflies, bees, beetles, crickets and grasshoppers, and other creepy-crawlies. Each board contained a dozen or more specimens. Each insect was labeled with its common and formal name—names he took from the many books on insects that he had accumulated and which he used to identify the bugs he caught. It was an impressive undertaking for a seven-year-old kid; one that continued to expand year-after-year.

In the process of putting together his collection, Gary discovered an easy way to gather butterfly and moth specimens. In the fall, caterpillars start the process of metamorphosis, spinning a cocoon (moths) or forming a chrysalis (butterflies), in which they change into pupae, before emerging as adults. As the leaves fell off the trees and shrubs, Gary spotted cocoons on the branches. He collected these cocoons, put them in shoe boxes that had small holes punched in the top, and kept the boxes in the warmth of his room. When the insect completed its metamorphosis, Gary had another specimen for his mounting boards.

At any given point in the fall, Gary had a few dozen cocoons stored in various boxes in the bedroom. One year, he discovered a field containing praying mantis egg cases. He figured they were like a butterfly cocoon—each cocoon yielding a single butterfly. He collected dozens of these "cocoons"—all he could find—with the objective of having a number of good praying mantis specimens several months in the future. He'd run out of boxes, so he simply put the praying mantis "cocoons" in his dresser drawer, where they were largely ignored.

Weeks later, the family took a brief holiday trip. When we returned, and opened the door to the house, we were greeted by hundreds of small praying mantises—little brown sticks with wings. They were everywhere, covering the furniture and drapes, infesting rugs and closets, and climbing the walls. Gary's "cocoons" had hatched, if that's the proper term for the process, and Gary learned a new lesson. Unlike a butterfly cocoon, a praying mantis egg case produces not one, but many—maybe a hundred—young insects.

In order to make the house habitable, we set off bug bombs in every room, trying to kill the horde of praying mantises that had invaded us. When the fog from the bug bomb lifted, the floors were covered with the carcasses of praying mantises. But even after this massacre, the bothersome insects continued to pop up throughout the house for months to come.

While Gary's trips to the fields or the swamp were often for scientific purposes, the rest of us went there with less lofty ideals.

Simpler Times; Better Times

He captured creatures in order to study them; we just went after them for the thrill of the hunt. To this end, we often carried a variety of homemade weapons, intent on striking down our prey.

Some of our earliest weapons were bows and arrows. To make the bows, we cut down a sapling, trimmed off any small branches, stripped off the bark, and tied twine to each end of the now-bare stick, applying pressure to it, so that it bowed in the middle as we attached the twine. Our arrows were small, straight branches from which we had removed the bark. We cut a notch in one end of the arrow and sharpened the other end so that it formed a point. Using our crude bows and arrows, we spent hours trying to shoot rabbits, squirrels, and birds. We'd carefully stalk our prey, take aim, and let our arrows fly. Despite all our efforts, we never hit a thing. Without feathers to regulate their flight, our arrows flew on unpredictable paths, wobbling in the air, veering off in crazy angles, or merely plopping harmlessly to the ground a few feet from the would-be archer.

When our bows and arrows turned out to be ineffective, we turned to slingshots, first homemade ones and, later, store-bought models. The homemade versions were fashioned out of a forked branch, to which a piece of rubber from an inner tube was attached. When we discovered that our homemade devices lacked power, we ordered factory-made slingshots from catalogs or bought them at sporting-goods stores.

While some of our slingshots may have been crude, our ammunition was superb. Some of the men in the neighborhood worked in a factory that manufactured roller bearings and ball bearings. We were able to obtain hundreds of small bearings from these workers and the steel bearings became the ammunition used in our slingshots.

But, once again, no matter how hard we tried, no one ever hit a rabbit, squirrel, or bird with a bearing launched from a slingshot. Reluctantly, we were forced to admit that we were not cut out to be hunters. We put away our weapons and gave up trying to kill the elusive critters in the fields and swamp.

Two brothers lived a few blocks away from us. They were several years older than we were and had reputations for being "bad actors." They would steal anything that wasn't nailed down.

Jack D. Atchison

They tormented younger—and always smaller—kids. And they loved to play with matches—fire and its effects fascinated them.

On visits to the fields and the swamp, they'd catch an insect, usually a bee or butterfly, strip off its wings, and then touch a match to the insect's body, taking extreme delight in watching the bug squirm and wiggle under the heat of the match. They'd also catch a frog or turtle, put it in a box filled with dried grass or leaves, and set the box on fire, watching and laughing at the critter's futile attempts to escape. The rest of us thought these guys were sick and tended to avoid them.

One day, as a group of us were playing in the swamp at the end of our street, these two brothers joined us. They had pilfered a box of wooden matches—the kind that ignite when struck against virtually any hard or abrasive object—from a local store and had the matches with them. As we played, they struck matches on rocks, or the zippers of their jeans, and tossed the burning matches at the rest of us, laughing as we dodged their missiles.

One of the guys yelled at them: "Hey, stop it! You're going to hurt someone!"

"Oh, yeah," the older brother said, "what are you going to do about it!" Then, he tossed a lit match at the kid who had challenged him—a kid who was much smaller than he was.

The rest of us were also fed up with the brothers' actions and we came to our friend's defense, threatening to gang up on the two brothers. This seemed to work, because they stopped throwing matches. But, then, they started something that was even more worrisome.

The older of the two brothers got one of the Mason jars that we used to capture tadpoles. He took the box of matches and started breaking the heads off the matches, putting the match tops into the jar. Within a few minutes, the bottom of the jar contained a two-inch-deep layer of match tops. Then, the kid filled the rest of the bottle with dried grass.

"What are you doing?" one of the other kids asked.

"Making a bomb," the older brother replied.

"What are you going to do with it?"

"I'm going to blow you guys up." He turned to his younger brother, held out the jar, and said, "Light it!"

Simpler Times; Better Times

The younger brother struck a match and dropped it into the jar. As the dried grass ignited, the older brother tossed the jar in our direction. Before anyone could react, there was a loud "Whoosh" and flames shot from the jar, igniting the dry grass near the swamp. Within seconds, the area was on fire and we fled.

Fortunately, a neighbor called the fire department to put out the blaze. Even then, the fire consumed a sizeable portion of the field near the swamp before it was brought under control.

All our parents questioned us about the cause of the fire. None of us disclosed that the two brothers had started it. We had a code of conduct that said: Don't tattle on others. But after that incident, we avoided the two brothers and they became social lepers—shunned by all the other kids in the neighborhood until they moved a few months later.

Over the course of several years, our informal playgrounds gradually disappeared. All the houses in the subdivision were completed, eliminating our make-shift monkey bars and drying up our supply of scrap lumber and discarded building materials. The swamp at the end of the street was drained, filled in with dirt, and converted into a city playground and parking lot. The hill south of the swamp became the site of a shopping center. The fields, woods, and swamp to the west gave way to housing developments. Progress had caught up with us.

But what fun we had and what lessons we learned while they existed. One of the sad aspects of urbanization is that young boys are deprived of the opportunities to build forts, sail homemade rafts, hunt creepy-crawly critters, and explore nature's mysteries.

Jack D. Atchison

CHAPTER SIX

The summer of 1949 was a busy time. Mom was pregnant, and so another addition to the family was expected to arrive in mid to late August.

In order to make room for the new arrival, Dad completed the construction of the second floor of the house. Walls and a ceiling were built by nailing plasterboard to the studs and rafters, forming two large rooms and a storage space. To protect the stairwell, Dad built a long, double-shelved bookcase along the opening in the floor, forming a three-foot-high wall around the stair opening. When the basic carpentry was completed, he painted the walls and ceiling. In all, the conversion of the upstairs area from an unfinished attic into useable rooms took Dad several months of weekends and late nights.

In July, Gary and I moved from our quarters on the first floor into one of the big rooms on the second floor, making our old room available for the new baby. As soon as we vacated the first-floor room, Mom furnished it with a crib, Bassinette, and other baby furniture. Not knowing whether the expected new arrival would be a boy or girl, she held off on some of the decorating and furnishings. Still, by the time of her expected delivery date, she was basically ready.

On August 14, 1949, Janet Kay was born. Gary and I were appalled. We'd expected a brother, not a sister. We told Gram and Gramp, who were watching us while Mom was in the hospital: "There's no way we're giving up our room to a girl. In fact, there's no way we'll live with a girl in the house—we'll move out." And we started packing our bags, ready to leave Canton, surrender the house to the "girl," and move to East Lansing to live with Gram and Gramp.

And so it went, from the time of Jann's announced birth to the day she was brought home from the hospital. Two little male-chauvinist pigs marched around the house, chins down, frowns on their faces, anger in their voices, denouncing all females, especially the one who was about to invade their home. The protest lasted until about two seconds after Jann was in the house; then it vanished.

Jann was a beautiful baby—blonde hair, blue eyes, rosy cheeks, and an incredible smile. She immediately captured the hearts of her brothers, especially her oldest brother, who did everything possible to spoil her rotten from that point forward. Gone were the protests of "having a girl in the house," in their place were smiles, hugs, kisses, and arguments over which one of us got to rock or hold our sister.

On their visit for Jann's birth, Gram and Gramp brought Gary and me suitcases as gifts. They were really good suitcases, but we had expected toys, so we weren't too thrilled.

One day during their stay, Gary and I were wrestling in the living room. I had him down on the floor in a firm headlock, and he was screaming bloody murder. Gram came into the room and told us to break it up. I wasn't about to set him free and ignored her request.

She said to me: "If you want to wrestle, why don't you wrestle me?"

I thought the idea was ridiculous. Gram was, in my mind, an old lady and no match for a tough, young kid of seven years old. But, I thought, what the heck, why not, so I said, "Okay." I released Gary from the hold.

Before I knew what had happened, Gram had me on my back and was sitting on me. Now, Gram was not a small woman—not by a long shot. She carried a few pounds on her wide frame. As she sat on my chest, I thought she'd crush me. It felt like my spine was merging with the floor. I started to yell as loud as Gary had earlier.

"Do you say uncle?" Gram asked, wanting to know if I was giving up.

"Yes...yes...uncle!" I shouted, throwing in the towel.

When she let me up, I was furious. Both she and Gary were howling like hyenas high on laughing gas. I raced up the stairs to my bedroom, where I spent the remainder of the day sulking.

Later that night, when everyone was in bed, I sneaked down the steps and placed the suitcase she had given me outside

Jack D. Atchison

the door of the bedroom that she and Gramp were using. Attached to the suitcase was a note that read: "Go home and take this with you."

The next morning, she got a real chuckle out of the note. Over the course of the next forty years, she often referred to this incident and the note I had written. Whenever we got into an argument, she'd say: "Do you want me to knock you down to the floor and sit on you?" It was a line she used well into her eighties. And I never took her up on the challenge. I was no fool.

On October 12, 1951, the family expanded again with Mike's birth. Like Gary, Mike had a freckled face and bright red hair that, as he got older, was cut close to the scalp, earning him the nickname of "Burrhead." Mike's wide grin, coupled with his red hair, made him a likeable little character—a walking, talking replica of the children's TV star of those days, Howdy Doody—to everyone but Jann. To her, Mike was a pest, and she whacked him with the same regularity that I pounded on Gary.

Mike and Jann shared the first-floor bedroom until he was old enough to negotiate stairs safely. Then, he moved upstairs, sharing a room with Gary while I occupied the other half of the second floor by myself.

When we shared the upstairs room, Gary and I enjoyed freedom that we hadn't had when we were located next door to Mom and Dad's room. They no longer could hear our arguments, fighting, and plotting, unless we got carried away and got too loud, which was not an infrequent occurrence.

Our twin beds, which were box springs and mattresses resting on metal frames, were on opposite sides of the room. We drew an imaginary line down the center of the room. Everything on the right side of the line was my space; everything on the left was Gary's. Many of our fights and arguments started when one of us stepped into the other's territory without seeking permission to do so—permission that was only required at those times when we were already engaged in sibling warfare.

We quickly discovered that, using a pencil or some other pointed object, we could pry the hard, white grout out from between the floorboards. Pieces of grout became excellent

Simpler Times; Better Times

ammunition to throw at the other guy as he tried to fall asleep. It was like pelting him with small rocks, producing a nice sting when the hardened grout hit bare skin. So, almost every night, missiles of grout flew through the air between our beds.

One problem developed as a consequence of using grout as a weapon. The more of it that we pried from between the floorboards, the weaker the floor became. Not so weak as to cause any problems when walked on, but weak enough to cause a board to break if it was jumped on with sufficient force.

At some point in each of our nightly battles, one of us—usually me—leaped across the room and pounced on the other guy as he slept. On a couple of occasions, when I landed on Gary, one of the metal legs of his bed punched through a floorboard, each time producing a three to six-inch hole in the floor. When this happened, we had several options. We could tell Dad what had happened and face a certain spanking. Or we could cover the hole with some object and hope that neither Mom nor Dad would discover it. Discretion being the better part of valor, we opted for the second option. As a result, Gary always had a pile of junk under his bed. Mom just thought he was messy, not learning the real truth of the matter until years later.

After we moved into separate rooms, we had a similar problem with one of the walls in my room. While engaged in a particularly active scuffle on my bed, I threw Gary over my back, sending him head-first into the wall. He hit the wall between two of the studs and, to our surprise (his more than mine) his head crashed through the wallboard, leaving a ten-inch-diameter hole in the wall. After we extracted him from the wall, we again studied the problem and opted for a variation on the messy-bed defense. I got a map from a *National Geographic* magazine and tacked it on the wall, completely covering the hole. The map remained there, as did the mess under Gary's bed, until 1959, when we moved from Canton.

During one of our many fights, Gary took off in flight, running down the stairs to escape from me. For years, Mom had told us not to run in the house. Nonetheless, I ran after him. He had a good head start and was clearing the bottom step just as I reached the top step. The only way I could catch him was to jump. I launched myself off one of the upper stairs, intending to land on Gary's back, but I seriously miscalculated the move. I forgot about the top of the doorframe and banged my head on it. While my head stayed in place, my feet continued on through the door opening, causing me to crash to the floor.

When I landed, the back of my head hit the third step from the bottom and my tailbone hit the edge of the bottom step. I was out like a light. When I came to, I thought my skull was fractured and back was broken. The pain was incredible.

I yelled for Gary to go get Dad—I needed help. He was rolling around on the living-room floor, laughing at my discomfort. Tears were running down his freckled face and his laughter got louder as my pain became more intense.

Thankfully, Dad heard Gary laughing and came inside to see what kind of mischief we were up to. He picked me up off the floor and put ice packs on my head and back. It took several days before I could move without pain.

From that point forward, whenever we got in a tussle, Gary ran for the steps, knowing that if I followed, I'd do so very cautiously. He'd found an ideal escape tactic.

The incident on the steps wasn't Gary's only victory, although the others were few and far between. One day, he goaded me into a fight. I should have known something was wrong. Gary lost ninety percent of our fights. There wasn't any reason why he should want to talk me into starting one, but he did. He was dancing around, taunting and teasing, trying to get my goat. Finally, he succeeded and I came after him, hands balled into fists, intent on silencing him.

Before I could throw a punch, he nailed me flush on the chin with a roundhouse right, dropping me like a sack of potatoes. I lay on the floor, seeing stars and brilliant flashes of light, as the room spun around me. I'd never been hit so hard. It was like he'd used an axe to chop me down.

When my head started to clear, I asked: "What did you hit me with?"

"My fist and this." He opened his fist and showed me a flashlight battery clenched in his hand, a triumphant smile on his face.

Simpler Times; Better Times

From then on, I checked his hands before starting anything. I never wanted to be hit that hard again.

When our night-time battles became particularly active, the noise downstairs was deafening, causing Dad to come to the bottom of the stairs to shout: "Settle down and keep it quiet up there or I'll have to give you guys a whipping!" We'd be quiet for a few minutes and then start again, drawing Dad to the stairs a second time. "I told you guys to settle down and go to sleep! I'm not going to tell you again!" When that warning didn't work, we'd hear him climbing the stairs. "Okay, you two asked for it!"

Dad usually approached my bed first. He'd turn me onto my stomach and deliver two or three swift swats to my bottom with his bare hand. Then, he'd repeat the process with Gary. Finally, he'd step back and say: "That's just a sample of what you guys will get if you don't settle down. Now go to sleep and no more fighting."

We'd usually go to sleep. Dad was pretty strong, and it didn't take more than a few swats to get our full attention and drive any thoughts of further fighting from our minds. Unfortunately, the message didn't stick very long and, by the next night, we'd be at it again, drawing Dad back up the stairs to render another spanking.

After several weeks of nightly punishment, I decided to do something about the situation. On a visit to a house that was under construction, I picked up two pieces of one-by-six, scrap lumber, each about eight inches long. That night, as we turned into bed, I gave Gary one of the pieces of wood and told him to slide it into the seat of his pajamas. I did the same. Then, I started yelling at Gary, pretending we were fighting. He took the cue and started yelling back at me. Within minutes, it sounded like World War III had broken out in our bedroom.

Dad came to the bottom of the steps. "Stop the racket up there and get to sleep!" Our shouting continued unabated. "I'm not going to tell you again! Keep quiet up there!"

When we ignored his second command, he wasted no time. We heard his footsteps as he stomped up the stairs, frustration evident in the heavy fall of his feet on the wooden stairs. Both Gary and I were lying on our stomachs, anticipating the fall of Dad's hand on our respective rumps.

In a departure from his normal routine, Dad went to Gary's bed first. He raised his right hand high in the air and brought it down with considerable force, aiming at the center of Gary's rear end. When Dad's hand struck, he let out a loud cry of pain and started dancing around the room, alternately shaking and grasping his hand. Gary and I couldn't contain ourselves. First, we giggled. Then, laughed lightly. Finally, we roared at the sight of Dad dancing around the room.

Dad turned on the bedroom light and inspected his damaged hand. The palm was scarlet red. Still shaking his hand in a futile attempt to relieve the sting, he pulled back Gary's covers and discovered the eight-inch board in Gary's pajamas. He pulled it out and stared at it.

Gary's and my eyes opened wide in anticipation, and with palpable apprehension, as Dad turned the board over in his uninjured hand and inspected it. We wondered what kind of punishment we were going to receive now. I felt sweat trickling down my back.

Dad looked up from the board. His face broke into a sheepish grin. "You guys really got me this time." He put the board down on the floor. "Now go to sleep." He tucked us both in, turned off the light, and quietly walked down the stairs. No scolding. No spanking. No punishment. Dad knew that he'd been set up and he accepted it.

That was one thing about the punishment Dad and Mom meted out—it was consistent and fair. Gary and I both knew, at an early age, if we violated the rules or misbehaved, punishment would be swift and certain. The punishment also always fit the offense. A minor infraction drew a scolding; a somewhat more serious transgression brought a few light whacks on the fanny; and major violations resulted in a vigorous spanking and deprivation of privileges.

Spanking wasn't something either Mom or Dad enjoyed. They gave us every chance to avoid a whipping. When we'd act up, Dad would usually say: "I'm going to give you until the count of three to stop what you're doing. If you don't stop by the time I get to three, you get spanked." Then, he'd start counting. "One...two—" By the time the word "two" left his lips, we'd usually stop.

Simpler Times; Better Times

While spankings got our attention, Mom and Dad's emotional responses to our actions had more of an effect on our attitudes and future behavior, especially when they clearly let disappointment register on their faces. When they were angered by something we did, we knew the anger would pass rapidly. But disappointment was another story; it tended to last for days, even weeks. Consequently, we both tried to behave in a fashion that would never result in either of our parents being disappointed by our actions—that was an emotion both of us dreaded seeing on their faces and in their eyes.

Not long after we'd moved to our second-floor room, Gary and I found some mementoes that Dad had brought back from the War. Like many veterans, he'd collected a number of things—dress Lugers and bayonets confiscated from SS officers; dress swords taken from German Wehrmacht officers; a German Mauser; books of Bill Mauldin cartoons; and boxes of pictures. These things were put in the attic, and Dad seldom, if ever, looked at them. His service in Europe was something he was proud of, but it was also something he wanted to forget—dead and wounded friends, the aftermath of the atrocities committed by the Nazi troops, and the fear that all soldiers experience as they lay in foxholes, burying their heads to avoid shrapnel from the shells and bombs bursting overhead or the gunfire from enemy forces.

As we rummaged through the boxes in the attic storage room, we came across some huge pieces of bright red material, each one large enough to fill an entire box—big boxes. We pulled one of the red things out of its box and spread it out on our bedroom floor. It was too big. We'd only unfurled a portion of it and, already, our entire floor was covered by the red material. On the edge of the room, where the unrolled portion of the material lay, we could see pieces of white cloth emerging in the middle of the red. We didn't have any more room and our curiosity was eating at us—we had to find a way to unroll the whole thing.

After a few minutes of thinking about the problem, an idea flashed into my brain. If Gary held onto a corner of the material while we tossed the rest out the upstairs window, it would hang down the side of the house and, if that wasn't enough, I could spread the remainder out on the lawn. Gary thought it was great idea. We opened the window leading into our room. While I ran down the steps and out the door, Gary started to feed the unfurled portion of the material out the window. When the edge of the material hit my outstretched fingertips, I started to tug on it, drawing more of it out the window. It was much larger than the side of the house and, soon, I was spreading more than half of it across the lawn between our house and the neighbor's to the south.

When the thing was completely unfurled, and with Gary still grasping a corner of it in his hands as he leaned out the upstairs window, I was able to see its complete design. It was all red, with a big white circle in the middle, and in the center of the white circle was a black design I recognized—a Nazi swastika—the kind we saw every day in the papers when the War was still being fought. "Neat," I said to myself as I looked at it.

Satisfied that we had unfurled the whole thing, I ran back into the house and up the stairs to our room. "You gotta see it. It's a huge flag," I said to Gary, taking the corner from his hand. As he ran downstairs to see it, I tied the corner to the handles on the window frame—the ones we used to open and close the window. Then, I raced to join Gary outside.

After staring at the flag for a few minutes, I said, "Johnny and Chuckie have to see this."

"Right," Gary said. We ran around the corner of our house, across the back yard, and through two neighbors' yards to their house.

When Johnny opened the door, I said, "Come on. You guys have got to see this flag we found in the attic."

We waited for Johnny and his brother to put their shoes on, and then the four of us raced back to our house. When we got there, and Johnny saw the flag, he said, "Hey, that's neat. What kind of a flag is it?"

I shrugged my shoulders. "A German flag."

As we stood there looking at the flag, we heard the phone ring inside the house. Almost immediately we heard Dad say, "What?" which was amazing because the phone was in the kitchen, and the kitchen was on the other side of the house. Gary and I looked at each other. We recognized the tone of Dad's "What?" For some reason, we were in trouble.

Simpler Times; Better Times

Johnny tapped me on the back and pointed behind us. It was a Saturday morning, in the summer, and the neighborhood men—all World War II veterans—who had been out mowing their lawns and tending their gardens, were now pointing at our house, gesturing wildly with their hands, anger on their faces, their voices getting louder as they shouted back and forth to each other.

"What the heck's going on?" I asked the others. They all just shrugged; as mystified as I was as to why the neighbors were so stirred up. It couldn't be this stupid flag, I thought, as I looked back at the thing hanging out our window.

As I was contemplating the answer to the dilemma, Dad came charging around the corner of the house. "What the hell have you two done now?" Stopping in his tracks, his mouth agape, he stared at the side of the house.

Gary and I backed up a few steps. Dad never cursed around us. The use of the word "hell" was ominous. We were really in trouble—and we still didn't know why.

Within seconds, Mom also rounded the corner of the house, drawn there by the phone call, the commotion in the neighbors' yards, and Dad's reaction. When she saw the side of the house, she threw up her hands. "Oh, no!"

I finally worked up the courage to ask, "What's the problem?"

"Do you know what this is?" Dad asked, pointing to the side of the house, his tone angry.

"A flag," I said; all innocence.

"Damn right it's a flag," Dad said. "A Nazi flag!"

"What's a Nazi flag doing in our attic?" I asked, still innocent.

Before Dad could reply, Mom said, "I think that's what our neighbors are wondering."

Dad looked behind him, facing in the same direction that Mom was looking. "Geez," he sighed as he watched a half-dozen neighbors converging on our house.

"What the hell is a damn Nazi flag doing in this neighborhood?" one of the men from down the street yelled.

Dad looked at him apologetically. "It's a souvenir I brought back from Germany. The kids found it upstairs and didn't know what it was. We'll get it down."

"You do that...and quick," the neighbor growled.

I didn't need any further hints. I ran into the house, up the stairs, into our room, and untied the flag, allowing it to fall to the ground. Mom and Dad quickly folded it up. Satisfied, the neighbors returned to their own yards.

When Dad came into the house, carrying the now refolded flag, I asked him, "Why are they so upset over that stupid flag? It's just a bunch of cloth."

No longer angry or upset, Dad said, "It not the flag itself that angered them; it's what it symbolizes. They fought against the people who flew this flag and everything for which it stood. Seeing it raised old feelings...feelings they don't want to be reminded of anymore." For the next hour, we got a brief history lesson on the war in Europe. We learned why the neighbors' feelings were what they were, and, on a practical level, we also learned to stay out of the attic.

When he'd finished, Dad took the flag upstairs and put it back in the box, where it stayed, along with the other flag, undisturbed, for several years. Sometime later, the flags were cut up and the red portion of the material was used to make things like Christmas tree skirts. The white portions, with their black swastikas, were destroyed. In the end, the Nazi flags served a useful purpose, and, with their destruction, old, painful memories became more distant.

Simpler Times; Better Times

CHAPTER SEVEN

The additions of Jann and Mike to our family added to Mom's already substantial daily burdens. Under any circumstances, taking care of two infants and two rambunctious older boys would be stressful. In the summer, without the temporary relief provided when Gary and I attended school, her days became almost unbearable.

Partly as a way to ease Mom's burden and partly to satisfy our grandparents' desire to see more of "their boys," Gary and I started spending the bulk of our summer vacations with Gram and Gramp. The timing was good. Gramp had retired from the Army, and he and Gram had just purchased a cottage on Manistee Lake in the northwest corner of Michigan's Lower Peninsula. At the time of the purchase, they'd hoped that Gary and I—they viewed us more as "sons" rather than "grandsons"—would spend our summers at the cottage with them.

Our first summertime trek to Manistee Lake started in June, 1951. Jann was a toddler and Mom was pregnant with Mike. The timing was ideal for everyone.

Before we left Gram and Gramp's house in East Lansing and headed north to the cottage, we had some chores to perform. The most important was catching a full summer's supply of night crawlers—our fishing bait.

Late in the afternoon, Gramp thoroughly watered the lawn, soaking it so heavily that puddles stood in the grass. Then, just after the sun set and darkness filled the sky, Gramp, Gary, and I started our nightly hunt for night crawlers. Armed with flashlights and coffee cans filled with a mixture of black dirt and coffee grounds, we stalked the lawn in search of our prey.

Catching night crawlers is a simple thing. You walk lightly across the lawn—Gramp said vibrations alert the worms and they slip back into their holes—and train a flashlight beam on the grass in front of you. The night crawlers come out at night to feed in the wet grass. The beam of the flashlight exposes the worms, stretched out almost full length on the ground, with one end of their body anchored in their hole. Once the night crawler is spotted, you draw near, being careful not to tread too heavily, bend over, quickly reach out, snatch the worm in your hand, and pull it from its hole.

The negative aspect of hunting night crawlers is that they are slimy things. After you've grabbed a dozen of them, your hands are covered with the mucus-like substance that they secrete. This disgusting stuff didn't seem to bother either Gramp or Gary but I didn't care for it. So, if the truth be known, I caught less than my fair share of the creatures, comforted by the knowledge that my naturalist brother would more than make up for any shortfall attributable to me.

On a warm summer night, with the lawn soaked sufficiently, Gary, Gramp, and I caught ten to fifteen dozen of the six-inch-long night crawlers. We put our nightly catch in a big tub that Gramp had filled with damp black dirt, coffee grounds, and moss. By the end of a week, we had enough of the slimy things to serve as a summer's supply of fish bait.

Assured that he wouldn't run out of bait, Gramp was ready to head north. We loaded up the car with clothes, bedding, the bait tub, and other supplies and set out early in the morning.

Riding in a car when Gramp was driving was a scary proposition. He had this basic belief that the road belonged entirely to him—and no one else. He never looked in his side- or rear-view mirror for other cars. If there were other cars on the road, he expected them to get out of his way, not vice versa. From his perspective stop signs were for other people; he just cruised through them like they didn't exist, not even bothering to slow down. Thus, driving to him was a lark. He just put the car in gear, pointed it in the right direction, stepped on the gas, and drove, looking out the window at the scenery passing by and blotting everything else from his vision and mind.

Gram, on the other hand, was a Nervous Nellie. She saw everything, and, even though she had never had a driver's license, she barked out instructions to Gramp: "Jim, slow down!" "Jim, watch out for the car beside you!" "Jim, there's a stop sign ahead!" Each comment was accompanied by body English, as she pumped imaginary brakes; gestured with her hands; leaned to the right and

Simpler Times; Better Times

then the left; and glared at Gramp, who just whistled to himself and ignored every sound coming from the seat beside him.

Gramp's cars were all alike—economy models with no radios and no frills. To make up for the absence of a radio, we listened to him sing. He had a complete repertoire of folk songs; all sung in a scratchy, slightly off-key, but pleasant, style that was uniquely his. Our biggest fear was that Gram would join in with a song of her own. Gram couldn't carry a tune in a bushel basket. Her singing voice sent shivers down your spine, like when chalk screeches on a blackboard. She could awaken the dead. Unfortunately, once or twice on every trip, the spirit moved her and she broke out in song, causing the rest of us to cover our ears and pray that it was a short song—it never was.

To fill the rest of the time on the four to five-hour trip, Gary and I, with assistance from Gram, played a variety of games. We studied license plates on passing cars, trying to spot at least one from every state in the country. Using letters from billboards and road signs, we played several different word games, each one ending when one of us accused the other of cheating. And we played the traditional travel games—tic-tac-toe, hangman, battleships, and connect the dots.

The highlight of the trip was a stop in Mt. Pleasant for ice cream. Gram was an ice cream freak—she could eat gallons of the stuff—so there were no restrictions on what or how much Gary and I could order. The more we ordered, the less her conscience bothered her when she loaded up.

The local dairy in Mt. Pleasant made its own ice cream and was an ice-cream connoisseur's dream. Gram started licking her lips in anticipation at least fifty miles from the place. So, on every trip to or from the cottage, we stopped for a treat.

On one of these occasions, I couldn't decide whether I wanted a chocolate sundae—chocolate ice cream topped with chocolate syrup—a chocolate malt, or a chocolate soda. I kept vacillating between these choices, unable to choose which one to order. Gramp, anxious to get back on the road, was growing impatient with my indecisiveness and kept urging me to make up my mind, each prod getting more insistent than the one before. Gram, who was also having trouble selecting the flavor or goodie that she wanted to order, solved my problem by saying: "Order one of each if you want to."

Gramp shook his head. "The boy will get sick if he does that."

"Well, he doesn't have to finish each one," Gram said. "He can taste a little of each and save the rest for later."

"Nope," Gramp said. "That stuff will spill in the car. Whatever he orders, he has to finish before he gets into the car."

I understood what he was saying. Because of living through the Great Depression combined with his military background, he had a firm rule that stated: You have to eat everything you put on your plate. Another rule was: You can't take anything into the car that, if spilled, will cause a mess. If I ordered more than one treat, compliance with his rules meant I had to eat everything—none could be tossed out—before I got into the car.

Being stubborn, and not liking to turn down a challenge, I said to the man behind the dairy counter, "I'll have a chocolate sundae, made with chocolate ice cream, a chocolate malt, and chocolate soda."

The man looked to Gramp for confirmation that the order was acceptable. He nodded for the man to proceed. Then, he said to me: "If you get sick, I don't want to hear about it, young man."

One of the hallmarks of this particular dairy was the generous size of the portions it served. Within a few minutes, the counter man returned with my order—a huge, three-scoop sundae, a large malted, and equally large soda. Any of these concoctions would have been a challenge for a boy of my age to eat in one sitting; three was an impossible task. But I hadn't yet reached the stage in life where what my eyes saw, my stomach could handle. As Gramp put it, "Your eyes are bigger than your belly." So, undaunted, I sat down at one of the outdoor tables and dug into the treats arrayed before me.

I started with the sundae. I knew it would melt in the summer sun and, if I was to avoid dealing with a dripping mess, I'd have to polish it off rapidly. Taking inordinately large bites, I wolfed down the sundae in record time. By the time I finished, my stomach felt stuffed and bloated.

I turned to the soda. The whipping cream on top was already starting to melt, running down the side of the glass, and

Simpler Times; Better Times

forming a sticky, gooey pool on the table. Alternating between a straw and spoon, I tackled the soda, stopping frequently to belch, hoping the escaping gases would make more room available in my stomach. After much strain, and a considerable struggle, I finally was relieved to hear a sucking sound when the straw hit the bottom of the class, signaling that I'd reached the end of the soda.

Before taking on the malt, I excused myself and visited the rest room. I felt queasy, like I was about to throw up. In the rest room, I dashed water on my face, emptied my bladder, and took a few deep breaths to settle my protesting stomach before returning to the table.

When I got to the table, I discovered that all the ice cream in the malt had melted, leaving the contents of the glass almost lukewarm, accentuating the strong chocolate flavor of the drink. On the second sip, my stomach gurgled. On the third, it completely rebelled. I jumped from my seat and, with a napkin covering my mouth, ran for the rest room. As soon as I got inside, I leaned over the toilet and, with several heaving retches, tossed up the greater portion of one chocolate sundae and one soda. When I was done, and my stomach felt a little calmer, I found I was bathed in sweat and my legs were shaky. Again, I dashed water on my face and took a few deep breaths.

On wobbly legs, I made it back to the table. Gary was sitting there with a grin on his face, obviously delighted with my discomfort and looking forward to my further attempts to dispose of the malt.

Gramp pointed to the malt. "Finish up, so we can get on our way," an "I told you so" expression on his face.

As for Gram, she'd used the extra time to order another ice cream cone and was sitting there contently enjoying it.

Fighting gag reflexes, I took repeated sips of the warm malt and was gratefully relieved when I finally heard the welcome sound of straw meeting glass. I pushed the glass aside and, with my stomach rumbling in protest over the treatment it had been subjected to, and said to Gramp, "I'm done. Let's go."

I sat in the back seat of the car, holding my stomach, head resting against the door panel, choking back bile, as Gramp piloted us toward the cottage. We hadn't been on the road for more than fifteen minutes when I knew I was going to throw up again. "Gramp, I'm sick. Can we pull over for a minute?"

"Nope."

I knew from prior experience that he was not about to stop the car. He'd given me fair warning before I had placed my foolish order and I'd failed to heed his words. Now, I had to live with the consequences of my decision, and he wasn't going to make that task easy for me.

Unfortunately, the realization that I'd screwed up didn't do anything to ease my upset stomach. I knew I was about to upchuck, and I also knew that if I did it in Gramp's car, messing up its interior, I was in even deeper trouble. So, I did the only thing I could. I rolled down the back window, stuck my head out, and heaved all over the highway, decorating it with a liberal quantity of chocolate malt.

The worst part of the experience was that I had to listen to Gary's giggling and Gramp's chuckles as I lay in the back seat, holding myself, hoping I wouldn't have to lean out the window again.

It was a long, long time before I could bring myself to be in the same room with chocolate ice cream.

In its early days, the cottage was a somewhat rustic affair. It was built out of cement blocks, painted white. A sun room faced the lake, so that side of the cottage was largely glass windows.

The cottage consisted of two bedrooms, both formed by partitions that didn't quite reach the ceiling; a large, open, L-shaped room that served as a combination living room, dining area and kitchen; and an open loft, where Gary and I had our beds. There was no bathroom; instead, a combination boathouse and outhouse was located about thirty feet in back of the cottage. There was no running water; rather, a pump in the kitchen area was used to draw water from a well. Finally, the only heat for the place came from a wood-burning, cast-iron stove located in the center of the space that served as the living room.

Manistee Lake is in Kalkaska County, midway between the towns of Kalkaska and Mancelona, near the cities of Grayling and Traverse City. The lake covered several hundred acres and was about thirty feet deep at its deepest point. It was fed by springs and was the headwater of the Manistee River, one of the most popular rivers for canoeing and trout fishing in the Lower Peninsula. The lake was a natural habitat for northern pike, walleye, perch, large and smallmouth bass, bluegills, sunfish, and rock bass.

The cottage sat on the eastern shore of the lake amid a number of other private cottages and undeveloped lots. The north shore was also dotted with private cottages. The west was taken up by a summer camp for young people. And the land on the south shore, although divided into lots, was largely undeveloped—Gram and Gramp owned a couple of the south shore lots, holding them as investments and a source of firewood.

An unpaved road ran around the perimeter of the lake. It was set back about a hundred feet from the shore and served as the boundary for all the lots on the lake. The area on the non-lake side of the road was mostly a dense swamp, a home for cattails, pines, birch trees, frogs, snakes, birds, blueberries, and huckleberries.

The lake had an all-sand bottom, and, as the water rose and retreated, the sand beach bordering the cottage shrank or grew. Some years, the beach was as wide as fifteen feet, while in other years it was as shallow as three feet. We had a forty-foot, movable, wooden dock that stretched from the beach out into the water. The dock rested on wooden sawhorses and, as the shoreline moved, we had to move the dock, something we were required to do a couple of times each summer.

The cottage was surrounded by white birch and pine trees, one of which grew at a funny angle and stretched out over the beach and water. That particular tree not only offered shade on the beach, but it was ideal for climbing—one simply had to walk up its angled trunk to reach the upper branches. Green ferns and huckleberry bushes grew beneath the pines. A pine-needle-strewn path running between the cottage and the beach served as a passageway to other nearby cottages.

Because of its crude heating system, and the bitter cold of Michigan's winter days, and spring and fall nights, the cottage was useable only from May to late September. Even then, some nights were quite chilly, requiring the wood-burning stove to be lit, even on some nights in midsummer.

The snowfall in the winter was very heavy, drifting as high as the roof line by January. In order to prevent the roof from collapsing under the weight of the snow, Gramp hired people to shovel the roof several times each winter. And he covered all of the windows with wooden panels, so they wouldn't cave in from the crush of the drifts that accumulated along the cottage's exterior walls.

But for the few brief months that the cottage could be used each year, it provided an ideal environment for two young boys, especially if they had retired grandparents who were ready and willing to entertain them from morning until night.

Most mornings, Gramp got out of bed before sunrise; put wood in the pot-bellied stove; placed a big, iron pot full of water on the stove; turned the radio on to a station that played country, or hillbilly, music; plopped down into his favorite rocking chair; and immediately fell asleep, snoring loud enough to rattle the windows. Of course Gramp's morning antics woke the rest of us. When we got out of bed and staggered to the living room, rubbing our eyes and suffering from sleep deprivation, there Gramp was—eyes closed, head back, mouth open, snoring like a freight train, sound asleep in his rocking chair.

When Gram saw Gramp—as she did every morning—she banged pots and pans, sang as loud as she could in her terrible, off-key manner, and generally made as much noise as possible, intent on paying him back for waking everyone else. Her actions had absolutely no effect on him—none. He could sleep through anything. He sat in the chair, snoring contentedly, oblivious to the noise around him.

Gary's and my two primary daytime activities at the cottage were swimming and fishing, interspersed with excursions into the surrounding swamps, cattail fights, and berry picking.

Because the lake was spring fed, the water was always cold, even on the hottest of summer days. I have a low tolerance for the cold, and so my swimming sessions, while frequent in number on any given day, were fairly short ones. After fifteen minutes in the water, my lips turned blue and I'd start to shiver, teeth clicking together like castanets, goose-bumps rising on my skin.

Simpler Times; Better Times

The water depth was shallow by the shore and gradually deepened to about five feet, until you reached a point about sixty feet from the shoreline. There the lake bottom abruptly dropped off and the depth immediately increased to over ten feet. Gary and I were not permitted to pass the drop-off point.

Every time we entered the water, we were required to notify Gram or Gramp. One of them would sit on the dock or on a swing on the shore and watch to see that we were safe and observing the rules they had established. It wasn't until I was a little older that I discovered the fundamental flaw in this supervisory routine. It was okay as long as Gramp was our observer. Even though he seldom entered the water to swim, confining his entry into the lake to quick baths, he could swim. Gram was a different story. Not only could she not swim a single stroke, she was afraid to submerge herself in the water. So, if either Gary or I had encountered any difficulties while swimming—fortunately we never did—and Gram was the person watching from the shore, we would have been out of luck. All she could have done was stand and scream for help, hardly much comfort to someone in the process of drowning.

The only instance when a rescue seemed necessary occurred quite a few years after the cottage was acquired. Our cousin Jimmy, who was considerably younger than either Gray or I, was swimming with a huge beach ball, using it as a flotation device. Gramp was sitting in the swing on the shore, reading a magazine, and, ostensibly, watching over Jimmy. At one point, Gramp looked up from the pages of the magazine to see how Jimmy was doing. To his dismay, Jimmy was nowhere to be seen. All he saw was the multi-colored beach ball bobbing on the gentle waves.

In a panic, Gramp leaped out of the swing, ran down the dock and, without stopping to remove his clothes or shoes, jumped into the water and plunged toward the beach ball, shouting "Jimmy! Jimmy!" As he approached the beach ball, heart in his throat, fear permeating every fiber of his body, he was certain that Jimmy had been pulled out past the drop-off point by the lake's undertow and drowned.

Suddenly, Jimmy's towhead popped up from behind the beach ball. "Gramp, why are you in the water with your clothes on?" Jimmy asked, his voice a combination of innocence and concern over Gramp's seemingly strange behavior.

Gramp, feeling completely foolish, didn't know what to say. He just uttered a "Harumph" and waded back to shore, hoping no one had seen him. But, of course, as luck would have it, Gram had. She wasted no time in telling everyone about his botched rescue attempt.

While swimming was a source of entertainment, fishing was serious business. The first few years, we had only one boat: a red, white, and blue craft. It was designed like a speedboat with a center bridge and steering wheel; built from watertight, tongue-and-groove slats; and powered by a ten-horse Mercury outboard motor—one that sounded like a 747 on takeoff. When Gramp pulled the starter cord on the old Mercury, sound echoed all over the lake. The motor was a temperamental thing, taking a dozen or more pulls on the cord before it kicked in, stalling every fifteen minutes, and frequently coughing up a blue-gray plume of smoke from its exhaust.

Initially, Gramp believed in "still-fishing." Keeping the Mercury at a low setting in order to cut down on the noise, we'd putt-putt out to a weed bed and drop anchor. There, we each armed ourselves with ten-foot bamboo poles, complete with line, leader, lead sinker, hook, and bobber. We took a third of a night crawler and strung it on the hook, making sure the worm's body completely covered the entire hook. Then, after spitting on the worm for good luck, we swung the hook into the water, after which we sat with our eyes fixed on the bobber, waiting for it to plunge below the surface.

When Gramp first started fishing, he didn't bother to read any of the Fish and Game Department's rules. He'd bait and use five or six poles, even though the law permitted him to use only two. He reluctantly changed his practice after neighbors informed him of the rules. After Gary and I joined him in the boat, he still stretched the rules a little, and we could always be found with more than our allotted number of poles. In fact, we had so many of them that it was hard to remember which ones you were supposed to be tending.

Simpler Times; Better Times

When the bobber dropped below the surface, it meant you had a bite. You pulled your pole up rapidly, hopefully fixing the hook in the nibbling fish's mouth. If successful, you caught the fish. If not, you discovered that the bait had disappeared into the gullet of a fish more crafty than you.

Neither Gary nor I were patient fishermen. We'd fidget in our seats, yammer back and forth, and lift our hooks out of the water every few seconds to see if the bait was still there. This last bit would prompt Gramp to grumble, "You can't catch fish with the hook in the air."

In those days, when the population around the lake was limited, the supply of fish seemed endless. On a good day, the three of us caught a few dozen fish. But, even with this success rate, still-fishing had its limitations.

First, it was boring. Time seemed to stand still as you sat and watched the red-and-white bobber float on the water's surface. After an hour in the boat, your rear end was numb, eyes strained, and you were hungry and thirsty—all things that we complained to Gramp about with great frequency; the whine in our voices growing stronger as the minutes passed. As for Gramp, he ignored our complaining, oblivious to the whining, content to sit there for hours, lost in thought, taking in the sunshine, and relaxing with the rise and fall of the boat as it floated on the waves.

The only things that made the sitting bearable were the momentary interruptions in the boredom each time you pulled in a fish and Gramp's stories. He knew hundreds of folk stories and jokes. With hardly any encouragement, he'd sit in the boat and tell us one after another, repeating his favorites over and over again. Neither Gary nor I minded the repetition, because it was not the content of the stories that held our attention, it was how Gramp told them.

No one laughed harder at the punch line to one of his stories than he did. His laugh was almost silent, not a loud guffaw. When he laughed, his face turned brick-red, his eyes filled with tears, and, if he wasn't careful, his false teeth slipped from his mouth. He started to giggle halfway through a joke, anticipating the punch line, and, as it came closer, his giggle turned to laughter. In the end, the punch line, delivered in the midst of fits of wheezing laughter, was barely intelligible to anyone but him. But no one who heard one of his jokes cared that they couldn't understand the punch line, because his antics were all they needed to send them into gales of their own laughter.

Gramp would generally move from telling jokes to singing songs and yodeling. The sound of his yodeling was much like the cry that a cat makes when someone steps on its tail. After a few minutes of his screeching, your ears ached and you craved the return of the quiet boredom of the lake. Maybe that was the method to his madness. When he started to yodel, Gary and I sure settled down and became quiet. We didn't want to do anything that might encourage him to continue.

He also spent hours telling us about his boyhood or describing historical events, along with his interpretation of their significance, and explaining to us math and science concepts. Two hours on the lake with Gramp provided a better, and more practical, education than a month in any classroom. His presence made the sore rump, thirst, hunger, and boredom all worthwhile. He was, by far, the most fascinating, entertaining, colorful, and, once you penetrated his often stern exterior, thoroughly lovable character I've ever met in my seventy years on this earth.

The second problem with still-fishing is that you can only catch pan fish—little ones—perch, bluegills, sunfish, and rock bass. So, while you get quantity, after a few sessions of still-fishing the challenge is gone. This factor led Gramp to explore alternative forms of fishing.

During our second year at the cottage, Gramp decided trolling was his preferred method of fishing. In trolling, you move slowly around the lake, dragging a line and hook behind you, rather than sitting in one place as you do in still-fishing. The equipment is also different. Instead of a bamboo pole, you use either a casting rod and reel or a spinning rod and reel. The line is a hundred to a hundred and fifty feet long, not the fifteen feet or so that a still-fisherman uses. In place of a single hook, sinker, and bobber, you use a harness—a series of three hooks, arranged in a straight line along a piece of clear leader, with a small propeller-like device and a string of red plastic beads placed directly in front of the hooks. The fisherman skewers the head of a night crawler on the first hook, buries the second hook into the center of the worm, and places the last hook about an inch or so from the end of the worm, leaving the remainder of the night crawler dangling behind that last hook. Then, the fisherman tosses the worm in the water, slowly lets out line as the boat moves ahead, stops the release of line when the bait is about a hundred feet behind the boat, and sits back as the bait is dragged through the water. The fisherman hopes a fish, drawn by the movement of the little propeller, the color of the beads, and the offer of a meal, will strike at the night crawler, snagging itself on one of the three hooks.

When we first started trolling, we had a problem. The ten-horse Mercury wouldn't run slow enough. Every time Gramp tried to throttle it down to a good trolling speed, the motor stalled. Forced to operate the motor at higher settings, he tried to the slow down the boat by dragging a collection of buckets and anchors behind us. This improvised solution was, at best, only moderately successful. Our fishing lines got entangled in the junk dragging behind the boat and the motor still stalled out with maddening frequency.

Gramp inherited the frame of a boat from a friend who died before he could finish building the boat. He, Gary, and I completed the boat by covering the frame with a plywood skin, which we painted red, white, and blue, just like the speedboat. Gramp bought a motor with less horsepower than the Mercury, and we thought we had our trolling problems licked; until we cornered the boat at higher speeds, that is. If we turned the boat at high speeds, water poured over the sides. It turned out that the sides were too shallow and the boat rode too low in the water. This was just one more example of Gramp's carpentry gone astray.

The object of trolling on Manistee Lake was to catch walleye and northern pike. In those days, in order to be a legal catch, a walleye had to be at least thirteen inches in length, anything shorter had to be tossed back in the water or the fisherman faced a fine from the local game warden. It is easy to tell, without measuring it, if a walleye is of legal size. The immature fish—one less than thirteen inches long—has a yellow belly and resembles a perch. When the walleye hits its mature size, the belly turns from yellow to white. Thus, all one has to do is to look at the fish's belly in order to know whether it is a keeper or not.

Jack D. Atchison

In addition to size limits, the law stated that the daily limit on walleyes was five per person. Gramp always complied with the size limit, but he thought the daily limit was unduly harsh. So, we'd go out fishing once in the morning and again in the evening. We'd troll around the various weed beds in the lake, following Gramp's favorite routes—ones that he'd named Walleye Boulevard, Walleye Lane, Walleye Alley, and so on. On many outings, especially in the early years when the population (and thus the fishing) around the lake was limited we caught our limit—fifteen walleyes among the three of us. As soon as we hit shore, Gramp cleaned and skinned the fish, cutting them into fillets. Then, when we went out in the evening, we started over again, following Gramp's belief that the limit ought to be five fish per person per trip rather than five per day.

His stretching of the rules didn't end there. When we came in at night, he left a line out in the water—a practice severely frowned upon by game wardens. The nightline contained six treble hooks, each one loaded up with a huge night crawler. Early in the morning, as the sun was rising, he reeled in his nightline and, invariably, caught two or three good-sized fish.

Now, when we caught fish, Gramp had a rule that he lived by—every fish was to be eaten by someone, either our own family or friends. He viewed fishing as a way of obtaining nutritious food, not just a form of entertainment. After he cleaned the fish, he even buried the heads and guts in his garden, where they served as a natural fertilizer. So, even though he may have caught more than the legal limit permitted, nothing went to waste.

In fact, his insistence on eating what we caught was a real problem. He was one of those people who could eat the same thing at every meal, every day. It didn't bother him if every meal he ate consisted of nothing but fish, bread, and a vegetable—the same vegetable—day after day, week after week.

In that regard, he'd go to a local farmer and buy a couple bushels of sweet corn—enough to get a good price break on his purchase. Then, we had fish and corn-on-the-cob every day for weeks on end. By the end of a summer, I couldn't stand to look at a fish fillet or an ear of corn. I was sick of the stuff. But not Gramp. Each meal was fine with him. If we complained or asked for a

Simpler Times; Better Times

change of fare, he'd say: "What's the problem? Corn and walleye taste good, and they're good for you."

And so it was. Every day, twice a day, we set off on a trolling expedition to catch our limit of walleyes.

Strangers to the area didn't know how to distinguish the difference between a keeper and a fish that had to be tossed back.

One day, I walked to a local bait shop, which also sold candy bars and soft drinks—the objects of my trip. The six-ounce, glass bottles of soft drinks sat in a big chest filled with ice or, later in the day, ice water. A nickel bought a bottle of Coca-Cola, orange soda or root beer and, once the drink was done and you returned the bottle to the store, you got a penny refund of the bottle deposit. The ultimate in effective recycling and a much more practical alternative to today's recycling of cans and plastic containers. Moreover, the beverage was always ice cold and thoroughly refreshing.

That day, a couple of city-types from Detroit, dressed in chinos and sports shirts, entered the shop while I was getting a Coke from the cooler. They were extremely excited, slapping each other on the back, and hooting and hollering about what great fishermen they were.

"Hey," one of them said to the bait shop owner, "can you clean a bunch of big perch and put them on ice for us?"

"Yep. How many have you got?"

"We got a whole tub full...maybe fifty or sixty...twelve-inch perch...nicest fish you've ever seen," the city dweller answered.

"Hmmm...where'd you catch them?" the bait shop owner asked.

"Right out there," the city dweller said, pointing to Manistee Lake.

"Hmmm," the bait shop owner scratched his chin.

"What's the matter?"

"Nothing," the bait shop owner said. Then, after a brief hesitation added, "'Cept the perch in our lake don't generally get to be much bigger than eight or nine inches."

"Well," the city dweller said, smiling to his buddy, chest swelled up with pride, "I guess you just have to know how to fish."

Jack D. Atchison

"Right," the bait shop owner said; still skeptical. "Why don't you bring that tub of fish in here?"

As the two city-types left to get the fish, the local game warden entered the shop through the back door. He'd spent the morning patrolling the lake and had just tied his boat to the bait shop's dock, so he could grab a little lunch. As he walked over to the cooler containing the soda pop, where I was still standing, drinking my second Coca-Cola, he asked me, "What's happening?"

"Nothing much. Just getting a Coke."

The bait shop owner strolled over and said to the game warden, who was taking a deep pull from a Coke bottle, "got a couple guys outside who caught a tub full of twelve-inch perch. They want me to clean them and put them on ice."

The game warden looked at the shop owner. "They catch them here?" He pointed to the lake behind us.

"That's what they claim."

"No way," the game warden said. "The perch in this lake don't get that big."

Just then, the city-types reentered the store, struggling to carry a heavy metal tub that was packed to overflowing with fish. As they set the tub down, the game warden strolled over to them. He leaned down and started pulling fish from the tub, plunking them on the floor beside him. When the first fish hit the floor, he said, "twenty-five bucks," with the second, "fifty bucks," with the third, "seventy-five bucks," and so on, the amount he uttered increasing by twenty-five dollars increments every time a fish hit the floor.

As the two city-types watched this guy, who was dressed in faded Levis and a tattered work shirt, toss their prizes onto the floor, they started to get agitated. Finally, when the amount of money uttered was about five hundred bucks, and the tub was still half full of fish, one of them said, anger in his voice, "Who the hell do you think you are and what the hell are you doing with our fish?"

Barely looking up from where he was squatted in front of the tub, the game warden said, "I'm the game warden for Kalkaska County and I'm figuring out your fine...looks like we might have a record here."

Simpler Times; Better Times

The city dweller staggered back a step or two, his mouth agape. "What fine? We just caught a bunch of perch. There's no limit on perch."

"Yep," the warden said, "but these ain't perch."

"They're not?" the city dweller said, amazement in his voice and on his face.

"Nope. These are walleye—walleye that are about an inch or so below the legal limit." The warden straightened up. "Besides, even if they were of legal size, the daily limit is five per person...you're way over that." He winked at the shop owner and me, and then turned back to the two guys from the city. "You two should have read your game books, 'cause it looks like this haul," pointing to the tub, "is going to cost you a least a grand."

With that, the crestfallen fishermen blanched, all color left their faces, and they looked as dead as the stack of fish on the floor.

Allen and Beth, year-round residents of the nearby town of Mancelona, were our next door neighbors. Allen drove a truck for a local refinery, delivering fuel oil and gasoline to homes and businesses in a two-county area. Occasionally, Gary and I rode along with him on portions of his route.

Allen was an avid trout fisherman. He viewed people like Gramp, who fished in lakes, with disdain. He'd say to Gramp: "How can you spend the whole day putt-putting around in a boat, feeling your ass grow dead, drowning a poor worm, and catching fish that don't offer any fight after you've dragged them through a hundred yards of water? You could be walking a stream, using a fly rod, which requires skill, and catching trout, the best tasting fish on earth."

Gramp answered: "Walleye are the best tasting fish you can catch. Trout can't hold a candle to walleye. And the best way to catch walleyes is by trolling. Besides, you don't get eaten to death by mosquitoes when you're out on the lake. Trout fishermen have to bathe in insect repellent before they can get near a river."

The debate raged on, with each defending his particular brand of fishing and neither giving an inch.

Allen took Gary and me to the river with him one morning to show us how much better trout fishing was than lake fishing.

Jack D. Atchison

We watched him don chest-high rubber waders, get his rod and creel, and douse himself with a liberal dose of insect repellant. Before entering the stream, he fired up the pipe that was his constant companion—he claimed it warded off mosquitoes and, on chilly nights, kept his nose warm.

Gary and I stood on the river bank as Allen slowly made his way upstream, casting out the fly on the end of his line every step or so, letting it drift for a few seconds on top of the water, propelled by the river's current. Within fifteen minutes, Allen caught his first trout—a nine-inch rainbow. He held it up for us to see before he opened the lid on his creel and put the colorful fish inside.

I wasn't impressed with his catch. The trout was much smaller than the twenty-five-inch walleyes we were accustomed to catching in the lake. Allen's trout was puny by comparison.

For the next hour, we trailed along on the bank, watching Allen as he cast his fly and caught a series of speckled and rainbow trout. It was boring, and I was getting tired of slapping at the bird-sized mosquitoes that were feasting on my blood. Gary, on the other hand, a naturalist at heart, found the walk along the river exciting. He picked at flowers and weeds, chased after bullfrogs and butterflies, skipped rocks off the water, and generally was having a good time.

Allen saw that I had lost all enthusiasm for trout fishing and decided to do something to perk me up. "Hey, guys," he shouted, "why don't you come out here in the river with me?"

I looked at him like he was crazy. "We don't have waders."

"Don't worry about it. The water's only a few feet deep."

He was right. The water was just barely above his knees. Still, we were wearing tennis shoes and Levis, and I didn't want to get them wet.

"Don't worry about your clothes," Allen added, apparently aware of my concern. "They'll dry out."

While I was debating whether to enter the water or not, Gary plunged in and waded over to where Allen was standing. The water came up to Gary's waist, but it didn't seem to bother him. What the heck, I thought, anything is better than staying on the river bank and being lunch for a swarm of mosquitoes. I entered

Simpler Times; Better Times

the water and, fighting the rapid current, waded over to Gary and Allen.

Now, river bottoms are not level. A shallow part of the river can rapidly give way to a deep hole—a hole carved by the water's force when the current is diverted downward by some object in its path, like a log or a rock. Gary and I didn't know this. Allen did.

We'd waded along for about fifty yards in water that was waist deep when Allen said, "There's a log up ahead. Why don't you two go stand on it and you'll dry off a little before we continue upstream?"

That sounded like sensible advice. Gary and I climbed on top of the slippery log and waited for Allen to catch up to us. When he drew abreast, he said, "Okay, it's time to move on. Get off the log." He pointed straight into the stream.

Simultaneously, Gary and I leaped off the log. We hit a hole of ice-cold water that had to be six-feet deep. Both of us plunged below the surface, the water a couple feet over our heads before we started kicking for the surface. When we broke through the water, spitting and sputtering, Allen stood there laughing. "What's the matter, guys, did the water get a little deep for you?"

Over the course of the next hour, Gary and I stepped into every hole in that stretch of the river—guided into them by our practical-joking neighbor. By the time Allen had caught his limit, both Gary and I were thoroughly soaked, cold, and shivering. The river water, especially in the deeper holes, was much, much colder than lake water. My skin was turning blue, my teeth were chattering, and I wanted to get back to the cottage where I could remove the wet clothes.

When we got to Allen's car, he put his gear into the trunk. As soon as it looked like he was finished, Gary and I started to get into the back seat. "Whoa, guys. Where are you going with those wet and muddy clothes?"

"Into the car," I said.

"You can't do that," Allen said. "You'll mess up the car."

"So, what are we supposed to do?"

"You'll have to take off those clothes and put them in the trunk."

"What?" Gary and I said in unison.

"You have to take off the clothes. I don't want the car messed up."

Gary and I looked at each other. The thought of stripping off our clothes didn't appeal to either of us. But it didn't look like we had much choice in the matter. Allen seemed to be pretty firm in his position.

Reluctantly, we took off our tennis shoes and socks, Levis, and shirts and pitched them into Allen's trunk. As we started for the car, in nothing but our Jockey shorts, Allen said, "Didn't you forget something?"

"What?" we asked.

"Your underwear. It's wet. It'll have to go into the trunk, too."

"Yeah, but we'll be naked if we do that," Gary said.

"You got that figured out right," Allen said. "But don't worry; no one is going to see you. You can duck down behind the seat while we drive back to the lake. Now, off with the underwear."

Embarrassed as heck, Gary and I stripped off our underwear, tossed it into the trunk, and scrambled into the back seat of the car as fast as we could.

About a half mile or so from the cottage, there was a little country store—one of Allen's customers—that served the lake community. As we approached the store, Allen signaled to turn and started to pull into the parking area.

"What are you doing?" I asked, panic in my voice, as I saw other cars in the parking area.

"I've got to get some pipe tobacco. Just take me a minute."

"But someone might see us," I protested.

"Don't worry." When had we heard that before? "I'll be right back."

Before we could protest further, he was out of the car and heading for the store. Gary and I slunk down as low as we could in the back seat, covering our vital parts with our hands, praying that no one would look into the car.

After what seemed an eternity, Allen hadn't returned to the car. I worked up the courage to look over the seat and out the front window to see what he was doing. I could see him in the store. He was carrying on an animated conversation with the store's owner, gesturing with his hands and, to my dismay, pointing toward the car. Just as I was about to duck back down behind the seat, Allen spotted me looking at him. He said something to the owner, laughed heartily, and started walking toward the store's door, bringing the owner with him. I was shocked, trembling in fear and panic. The store's owner was a woman!

As they emerged from the store, Allen had an ear-to-ear grin on his face, as did the store's owner. They came down the steps and moved closer to the car. By this time, Gary knew something was wrong and he, too, was looking at the two of them as they walked toward us. When they were about ten feet away, both Gary and I started waving our hands and shaking our heads, signally for them to stop. Allen was, again, laughing hard, his face red, tears streaming down his cheeks. So was the store's owner.

Gary and I ducked down behind the seat, curled into fetal positions, and covered ourselves as best we could. The car door on the driver's side opened and we heard Allen deposit his rear end on the seat. "You guys aren't very sociable. I was going to introduce you to the store's owner, but you didn't seem to want to meet her."

"Where is she?" Gary and I asked.

"She went back to the store. I think her feelings are hurt, because you didn't want to say hello." He started to laugh again.

"Allen," I said, "drive us home. No more stops, please."

"Okay."

A few minutes later, Gary and I, still crouched down behind the back seat, felt the car slow down. I looked over the seat. We were starting to turn into Allen's driveway.

"Allen," I said, "go into our drive. Pull in right next to our cottage."

Allen ignored my request and pulled in next to his place. He opened his door, got out of the car, and pulled our door open. "Okay, guys, we're home. You can get out."

I saw Gramp standing in his garden. He was leaning on his hoe and looking in our direction, curious as to why Allen was laughing so hard.

It was least seventy-five feet from Allen's car to the back door of our cottage. There was nothing Gary and I could do except make a run for it. It meant that we had to run over little stones, pine needles, weeds, and twigs in our bare feet, but we had no choice. Like two rockets, we shot from the back seat of Allen's car and, with our little, bare, white butts exposed and our hands cupped in front of us to cover our privates, we streaked across Allen's lot to the back door of the cottage, disappearing inside in a flash.

As we put on clean clothes, we could hear laughter as Allen told Gramp about our experiences that day. We vowed the next joke would be on Allen.

Practical jokes were a large part of the entertainment for the people who lived around the lake. Everyone played them on each other.

Both Allen and his wife, Beth, had a deep fear of snakes. A harmless little garter snake could send them both running and screaming. Apparently they thought a garter snake could miraculously transform itself into a rattler or king cobra.

In plotting our revenge against Allen, Gary and I turned to the swamps. Gary could find and catch any kind of snake. The swamps were well populated with garters, harmless water snakes, and black snakes—ones that resembled a rattler because of their size and coloring. It didn't take us long to catch a large garter snake, a two-and-a-half-footer. A quick smack on the head with a fist-sized rock rendered the snake dead.

That night, we sneaked out of the cottage and fetched our dead garter snake. We placed it on the floor of Beth's and Allen's outhouse, right near the hole with the toilet seat on it. We coiled the dead snake's body to make it look like a rattler that was ready to strike. Then, we returned to the cottage.

Allen was an early riser, getting up at the crack of dawn, so he could go trout fishing. The first thing he did when he awakened was to grab a hot cup of coffee and head for the outhouse to take care of his morning business.

That morning, Gary and I got up early and stood by the kitchen window, waiting for Allen to make his trip to the outhouse. We didn't have to wait long. With the first rays of morning sun, Allen opened the back door of the cottage. Dressed in a red-plaid robe and slippers, steaming coffee cup in hand, he casually strolled to the outhouse and opened the door.

In seconds, we heard a blood-curdling scream and saw Allen fly out of the outhouse. With arms and legs pumping like an Olympic sprinter's, open robe flapping in the wind, Allen ran down his drive and out to the road, yelling "Snake! Snake!"

Gary and I were laughing so hard our sides hurt. Gram and Gramp, awakened by the combination of our laughter and Allen's screams, came out to see what was wrong.

"I think that Allen saw a snake in his outhouse," I said innocently to Gramp.

"Wonder how it got there?" Gramp said, with a gleam in his eye.

"Beats me," Gary and I said, shrugging our shoulders.

"I'll bet," Gram said. "You rascals better go get that snake before Beth comes out."

Too late. We heard another, and even louder, scream coming from the direction of the outhouse. Beth had gone to the outhouse to see what was wrong with Allen, who was still trying to break the world record for the hundred-yard dash as he ran down the road. Beth opened the outhouse door and immediately saw the snake. She let out one good scream and darn near passed out in fear.

When Gary and I ran over to the outhouse, she was just standing there, as pale as a sheet, shaking like a leaf, and mumbling "Snake. Snake," as she pointed toward the outhouse door.

Gary went inside and picked up the dead snake. Grasping it behind the head, so its full body length was evident, he carried the snake outside. As soon as Beth saw it in his hands, she let out another terrified scream.

Very solemnly, Gary said, "I think that it's dead." He held it up, so she could see that it wasn't alive. But it didn't matter to Beth whether it was dead or alive, she just screamed again. "We'll take it away," Gary told her.

While Gram settled Beth down, we walked back toward our cottage. As we got to our drive, we saw Allen walking toward his cottage, completely exhausted by his spirited sprint—more exercise than he'd had in years. Gary was holding the snake behind his back.

"It's alright, Allen," Gary said, "the snake's dead."

"Are you sure?" Allen asked; his voice still tinged with fear.

"Yeah," Gary said. "See." He removed the snake from behind his back.

Allen's eyes got the size of dinner plates and he started backing up. "Get that thing away from me!"

"Geez," Gary said. "It's just a little garter snake. Can't hurt a flea."

"I don't care! Get it away," Allen said, as he continued to back-pedal, his voice on the edge of panic.

"Okay." We walked away, taking the snake with us. As soon as we rounded the corner of our cottage, we broke out in uncontrollable laughter. Revenge is, indeed, sweet.

When Mom and Dad visited the cottage, it signaled the start of snipe-hunting season. Dad and Allen were the organizers of the annual snipe hunt.

Their first order of business was to recruit that year's honorary snipe hunter. The recruit was usually a kid who was visiting the lake for the first time, but that wasn't always the case. Over the years, honorary snipe hunters included a middle-aged woman who lived a few cottages down the lake from us, college students, and a retiree or two.

Before setting off on the hunt, Dad always explained to the recruit the nature of snipes, as well as the art of hunting them. As he put it, snipes are a rare mix of several species—part bird and part mammal. They live only in the woods surrounding Manistee Lake. They have beaks and bird-like feet, but are wingless and incapable of flight. Instead of feathers, their bodies are covered with fur—a fur more precious than sable or mink. To compensate for their lack of flight, snipes are blessed with tremendous speed. To escape their enemies, they run at breakneck speed down paths in the woods. Finally, they are nocturnal creatures, emerging from their underground nests only after the sun has set.

Because of the nocturnal nature of the beasts, snipe hunts occur only at night. The hunting team scouts the woods in search of snipe paths. When a suitable path is located, the honorary hunter is given a gunnysack and is positioned on the path. The hunter lays the sack on the ground and opens it, with the mouth of the sack

Simpler Times; Better Times

facing down the path. The rest of the hunting team spreads out into the woods and starts beating the ground, yelling "Here snipe! Here snipe!" for good measure. The object is to scare the snipes, causing them to flee down the path, right into the gunnysack. The hunter is cautioned to close the sack quickly when he or she feels a snipe enter it, because a snipe can change direction in a flash and escape or, worse, attack the hunter with its sharp beak.

The hunting party usually consisted of Allen, Gramp, Dad, Gary, me, a few people who had already experienced the thrill of hunting snipes, and that year's honorary hunter. We drove to the woods just as darkness arrived. Using flashlights, we searched for an ideal path. Dad or Allen always found a suitable path, usually one located deep in the woods. Then, we helped the hunter get into position. When the hunter had his or her sack open, we spread out into the woods, banged on trees with sticks and yelled. We always told the hunter that we might have to cover a good deal of ground before we scared up a snipe, so the hunter shouldn't worry if he or she couldn't hear the rest of us.

As was normal for these hunting expeditions, the hunter heard our voices gradually fade off into the distance. The woods grew quiet—the only sounds were the chirping of insects, the rustling of leaves, the croaking of bullfrogs, and the beating of the hunter's own heart. After a half-hour or so, the woods resonated with the mournful, and often frightening, cry of a wolf. Then, the fearsome growl of a black bear, a creature indigenous to the woods of Manistee Lake, filled the night. Suddenly, Allen would burst out of the trees and sprint past the now frightened hunter, screaming "Wolf! Wolf!" And then would disappear into the darkness. Immediately, the woods would return to silence.

By this time, the hunter usually didn't know whether to run or stand his or her ground—a decision made more complicated by the fact that he or she didn't have a flashlight and the woods were darker than the inside of a coal mine, so dark that it was difficult to see your hand in front of your face.

The silence would last another five minutes, then Dad would come running down the path screaming "Bear! Bear!" He'd flash by the hunter before the hunter could react. And then, again, silence.

Now, as for the rest of us, we were back in the cottage enjoying soft drinks, popcorn, and a good game of canasta, awaiting the return of Allen, Dad, and the hapless hunter.

After an hour or so of standing alone in the woods, even the most gullible of people usually caught on to the fact that they'd been set up as the victim of a practical joke. At that point, Dad and Allen would emerge from their hiding places in the trees and put the poor soul out of his or her misery. Laughing so hard that tears ran down their cheeks, the two jokers would lead the sheepish person back to the car.

When the person showed up at the cottage, the rest of us joined in the heckling, asking the person to describe for us in detail the nature of a snipe, taking great delight in the person's embarrassment over believing that such a creature existed.

The strange part of snipe hunting is that as soon as the hunter recovered from his or her embarrassment, he or she would always be the first to volunteer to lead the next year's hunt. It must be that snipe hunting gets in your blood.

Gram and Gramp were generous with the cottage, sharing it with their friends and relatives. As a result, we had guests almost every week. Some were Gram's and Gramp's nieces and nephews and their families, but most were retired friends from the East Lansing area.

Gary and I enjoyed the company of these older folks. Most were real characters who would tell us stories and participate in our practical jokes. All treated us as their own kids.

One of the most memorable characters was an old boxer, named Joe, who was in his late sixties when I first met him. Even at that age, Joe was an energetic, barrel-chested guy with huge biceps and forearms that would have put Popeye to shame. Dad had gone to high school and boxed with Joe's son, Jack. So, our family members knew Joe's family.

Every time Joe visited the cottage, he'd greet me by saying: "How ya doin', Champ." Then he'd give me a little love tap on the shoulder—a punch that traveled about three inches and had enough force to darn near knock me into the next county. Then, Joe would ask, "How ya doin' with the push-ups and sit-ups?"

"Fine."

Simpler Times; Better Times

"Let me see."

I'd get down on the floor and do about thirty push-ups before collapsing.

"That ain't so good," Joe would say. Then, he'd lower himself to the floor and, with me counting he'd rip off a hundred push-ups without breaking into a sweat or showing any sign of labored breathing.

"Want to see another hundred?" He'd always ask.

"No thanks," I'd answer, knowing he was capable of doing several hundred of the darn things.

We'd then repeat the drill with sit-ups. I could do fifty or so. Joe could do hundreds. It was embarrassing, because Joe was still doing this when he was well into his seventies. At seventy, the man was as strong as a bull, with the stamina of a man half his age.

After his strength demonstration, I'd sit next to him and he'd give me round-by-round, blow-by-blow descriptions of every bout he ever fought, many of them with world-ranked boxers, including a sparring session with the great Joe Louis. As he told his stories, he fired up the most foul-smelling cigar you can imagine. Because of the cigar, Gram always banished us to the outdoors. We'd sit outside on a bench by the lake for hours as he told his tales. I never tired of them, even though, over the course of several years, I heard most of them many times.

Joe's wife, Becky, liked the color purple—really liked it. Everything in their house was purple—carpet; drapes, walls; dishes; furniture coverings; towels—everything. Her clothes and shoes were purple. And the darnedest thing; so was her hair. And when Old Joe fired up a cigar in the house, it didn't take long for her face to turn purple, too.

The biggest character among all our visitors was a retired taxidermist from East Lansing, who went by the nickname Parkie. He was a slender, bespectacled leprechaun, with false teeth and thinning white hair, who had a wicked sense of humor and a penchant for mischief.

One day, when a group of older women was staying in the cottage to the south of us, Parkie decided to play a joke on them. Gramp kept a lot of old clothes out in the combination boathouse/outhouse—old coveralls, work shirts, hats, fatigue jackets, and boots. Parkie's plan included using some of these clothes to make a life-sized dummy.

Gary and I collected old newspapers and, following Parkie's instructions, stuffed them into the legs of an old pair of bib-top coveralls. Next, we stuffed a tattered work shirt. A pair of work gloves served as hands. Parkie took the stuffed shirt and put it into the bibbed overalls, using the bib straps to hold the shirt in place. The legs of the coveralls were stuffed into a pair of knee-length, black, rubber boots. Then, a coffee can, filled with newspaper, was painted white and mounted on a pole, which Parkie stuck down through the neck of the shirt, making the can into a head for our dummy. Finally, we put a droopy, wide-brimmed hat on the coffee can. From a distance, this apparition looked like a man—a grungy one at that.

That night, the ladies next door walked to a neighboring cottage to play bridge. After they'd been gone for an hour or so, Parkie told Gary and me haul his homemade dummy over to their front porch—the one facing the lake. He instructed us to lay the dummy on its back, with the head resting on the ladies' front doorstep. He put an empty whiskey bottle in one of the dummy's hands. Then, he stuck a big butcher's knife in the dummy's chest, surrounding the knife with a liberal dose of ketchup. Finally, we overturned some of the outdoor furniture, making it look like a fight had taken place in the yard.

Standing at a distance, the scene looked real. The yard was lit by a single light over the front door. In the dim light, the dummy looked just like a dead man lying on the doorstep.

Back in our own cottage, Parkie, Gary, and I squatted below one of the bedroom windows, waiting for the ladies to return down the dark path leading to their cottage. A few minutes after eleven o'clock, we saw the beam from a flashlight bobbing up and down. The first lady emerged from the darkness. She had the flashlight in her right hand and her left arm was encased in a sling—she'd broken her arm in a fall a few weeks earlier. When the beam of her light played on the porch step and illuminated the dummy, she let out a panicked scream and spun around, crashing into the women trailing behind her.

All heck broke loose. Women were knocked to the ground as they tried to abruptly reverse direction. All were screaming like

Simpler Times; Better Times

banshees. Soon, they regained their footing and ran down the path, continuing to scream.

Parkie was rolling on the floor in laughter. His trick was more effective than even he had dreamed it would be. When he regained a little of his composure, he motioned for Gary and me to follow him. We went to the ladies' cottage, straightened up the yard furniture, and carried the dummy away, stashing it in our outhouse.

About a half-hour later, a car entered the neighbor's driveway. The local constable, his gun drawn, exited the car and walked to the front of the cottage. The ladies stayed in the police car. The constable rounded the corner of the cottage, stopped, and scratched his head. He turned around, took a few steps, and shouted, "Are you sure this is the right cottage?"

One of the women cautiously stepped out of the car. "Yes! This is our cottage!"

"Well," the constable shouted, "there's nothing here!"

All three women walked to meet him. "There was a body on our porch," one of them said.

"There isn't now. See for yourselves."

Parkie had watched all of this from our window. "You boys stay here," he said and walked out our door. Approaching the women and the constable, he asked, "What's the problem?"

The constable looked at him. "These ladies say there was a body on the porch...a drunk from the tavern at the end of the lake."

Parkie turned to the lady who owned the cottage. "Have you gals been drinking again?"

"What—"

Parkie didn't let her finish. "Officer," he said to the constable, "I think I can straighten this out. When the girls have a nip or two at the bottle...which they're prone to do...they see all kinds of things. A few nights ago, it was a bear in the outhouse." He put his skinny arm around the constable. "I'll handle it from here. Sorry, they disturbed you."

The constable looked at the women, who were fuming, madder than wet hens, and just shook his head before walking back to his car.

"We haven't been drinking and we weren't imagining things!" one of the ladies yelled after him.

"Yeah, yeah," the constable said over his shoulder, before getting into his car and driving away.

"Have a good night, girls," Parkie said to the ladies, his face split by a wide grin, a gleam in his eyes.

"You—," one of the ladies said, starting after Parkie as he scampered back to the cottage.

The next morning there was knock on the cottage door. When the door was opened, one of the ladies from next door, a seventy-year-old farm lady from Indiana, who could out-hunt, out-fish, and out-cuss any man on the lake, now armed with a shotgun, pushed her way into the cottage. "Where's that miserable excuse for a man?"

Gramp, who had opened the door, eyed the shotgun in her hands. "Do you mean, Parkie?"

"Darn right. Where is he?"

"Why do you want to see him?" Gramp asked, concerned about the anger in her eyes and the gun in her hands.

"I'm going to fill the little devil's butt full of buckshot for what he did to us last night. Now, where is he?" She started moving toward our guest bedroom, shotgun at the ready, eyes blazing with anger.

When Parkie heard her enter the cottage, he peeked through the curtains that served as the bedroom door and saw the shotgun she was carrying. He darn near died. He was convinced she was about to shoot him for the embarrassment he had caused the night before. He quietly opened the bedroom window and started to crawl out.

Just as he was swinging his leg through the window frame, the lady burst into the bedroom. "Got you," she cried, raising the shotgun.

Parkie, dressed in baggy pajamas and slippers, dropped to the ground and started running through the birch and pine trees as fast as his spindly legs would carry him. Looking back over his shoulder, he saw the barrel of the shotgun being thrust out the window. His legs pumped even harder as he cleared the trees and hit the road. He turned right and fled.

Inside the cottage, the lady with the shotgun started to laugh. With a big grin on his face, Gramp pointed to the shotgun. "That thing ain't loaded, is it?"

Simpler Times; Better Times

"Heck no," the lady said, wiping tears from her cheeks. "But that old fool," pointing in the direction of the fleeing Parkie, "don't know it. Guess we're even for last night."

About fifteen minutes later, an exhausted and thoroughly disheveled Parkie sheepishly poked his nose into the cottage. "Is she gone?"

"Yes," Gramp said, "but I'd steer clear of those gals if I was you. They'd like nothing better than to pepper your seat with buckshot."

Over the next two days, Parkie slunk around the cottage like a fugitive in hiding, running for cover every time he heard a female voice. Finally, we couldn't take it anymore and told him that he'd been had. He laughed harder than anyone over the poetic justice of the ladies' revenge.

Over the next few years, Parkie's dummy made frequent appearances—mostly in outhouses and boats—but none compared to its debut that night.

During one of Parkie's visits, Beth and Allen invited all the neighbors to take part in a Saturday afternoon potluck picnic in their yard. On Wednesday morning, Parkie started acting strangely. He stopped shaving and refused to go outside, opting instead to stay indoors with his nose buried in a book. He behaved the same way on both Thursday and Friday. On Saturday, as the rest of us prepared for the picnic, Parkie claimed he had a headache and stayed in bed, saying he felt too poorly to attend a picnic.

A little after noon, we carried salads and other dishes that Gram had prepared to the picnic tables in Beth's and Allen's front yard, where neighbors were beginning to assemble. We tried one last time to get Parkie to join us, but met with no success. He planned to stay in bed until his headache abated.

Midway through our picnic lunch, Allen pointed toward the beach. An old man, dressed in torn and dirty clothes, was walking along the edge of the water. Every few feet, he'd stop, bend over, and pick up an object—a shell, a piece of driftwood, and even a dead fish or two—and put them into a gunnysack he was carrying.

When he drew abreast of Beth's and Allen's yard, he stopped and flashed a toothless grin to the people seated around the picnic tables. Then, to our amazement, the old bum started walking toward the table. As he neared, the smell of whiskey was overpowering. He walked over to where Allen was seated and said, in a voice hoarse from too much drinking, his words slightly slurred, "say, mate, could you spare an old man a meal?"

Allen looked quizzically at Beth, who seemed embarrassed by the old bum's presence, then turned back to the man. "This is a private gathering. I'm afraid we can't help you."

The old man's face dropped, his shoulders sagged. "I haven't eaten in a couple days, mate. Are you sure you can't spare just a bite?"

Allen, who was, by nature, a very generous person, was obviously affected by the old man's plight. "Well, maybe we can get you something."

"Bless you, mate," the old man said, flashing Allen another big, toothless grin. He put his foul-smelling sack on the ground and sat on the end of the bench, right next to Allen, who reluctantly handed the old man a paper plate. As dishes were passed in his direction, the old man helped himself to large portions from each dish. Soon, his plate was heaped with food. He reached in front of Allen, took Allen's fork from his plate, licked it once with a loud smacking sound, and dug into the mound of food.

The old man literally had no teeth, just pink gums. Each time the fork entered his mouth, a little of the food dribbled down his chin. Without teeth, he gummed each bite, creating a sickening, smacking sound when he moved his jaws. By the time he'd taken a half-dozen bites, rivulets of food and drool were streaming off his whiskered chin. The sight was so repugnant, and the stench from the sack sitting at his feet so overpowering, people were forced to excuse themselves from the table, retreating to chairs spread around the yard. It wasn't long until just Allen and the old man remained at the table.

The old man never looked up. He sat with head bowed, shoveling food into his toothless mouth. When his plate was about half empty, the old man finally raised his head and let out a loud belch. He patted his stomach. "It's been so long since my last meal that my belly's shrunk. I can't finish this now," pointing to the food left on his plate. "Mind if I take it with me."

"Not at all," Allen said, anxious for the old man to leave.

Simpler Times; Better Times

"Good." The old man reached out and took a napkin from the table. He unfolded it and, using his fork, scrapped the remaining food off his plate and into the napkin. Then, he reached down and picked up the sack full of driftwood and dead fish. "I'll put it in here and eat it later." He folded the napkin full of food and dropped it into the smelly sack. The idea that this guy would pull the food out later and actually eat it made everyone in the yard gag.

The old man stood, hitched up his baggy trousers, grasped the sack in his hand, and said to Allen, "Well, mate, thanks for the grub. I'll be getting along now." He walked to the edge of the water and, within minutes, was out of sight, having rounded a bend in the lake.

None of us could believe what had happened. When people returned to their seats and we started dessert, the tables buzzed with comments about the old man and his behavior.

We were just finishing dessert, when Parkie, dressed in a new golf shirt and Bermuda shorts joined the picnic, sitting down between his wife and Gram. "Boy, I'm glad that I got rid of my headache," Parkie said. "I'm famished." He filled a plate with food and, as the rest of us continued to talk about the old man, Parkie quietly ate his meal.

When Parkie pushed his plate aside, Allen asked him if he wanted some dessert. Parkie smiled at Allen, belched loudly, and said, "Not now. But thanks for the grub, mate. I think I'll be getting along."

With those words, Allen sputtered, "You old son of a bitch," and we all knew the true identity of the beachcomber.

Later, Parkie told me how he'd set Allen up for the joke. When we left for the picnic, he took out his false teeth, shoved cotton balls into his cheeks, rubbed some of his wife's mascara under his eyes, and messed up his hair. He put on some old clothes that he'd stored in the boathouse and walked down the road to the tavern at the end of the lake. There, he ordered a couple shots of whiskey and, to the bartender's shock, dumped the whiskey on his clothes, never drinking a drop. Smelling like a distillery, he waded along the shore picking up junk and putting it into a sack that he'd taken from the boathouse.

His act was so good that his wife of over thirty-five years, who was seated at one of the picnic tables, never recognized him.

Jack D. Atchison

It was a masterpiece practical joke and one we talked about for years.

Not all of our practical jokes turned out well, some backfired.

Gary was often the first one to get up in the morning. While the rest of us continued to sleep—Gram and me in our beds and Gramp in his rocking chair—Gary would fix himself a bowl of cereal.

One night, while the others were sound asleep, I crept down the stairs from the loft. I got the sugar bowl from over the stove and emptied its contents into the sugar bag. Then, I refilled the bowl with salt. Satisfied that no one had detected me, I climbed back up the stairs to the loft and returned to my bed.

In the morning, I awoke as soon as I heard the first sounds from the kitchen, anticipating that Gary was about to receive a big surprise. But, to my amazement, Gary was still asleep in the bed beside me. I wondered: Who is in the kitchen? I peered over the edge of the loft and saw Gramp.

It was drizzling outside and Gramp had decided to bypass his second snooze in the rocking chair in order to go fishing. He believed that fishing was at its best when there was a light rain. He claimed that the clouds eliminated any reflections on the water—reflections that would otherwise distract the fish. So, anytime it rained, he was anxious to start fishing. He also knew that both Gary and I hated to fish in the rain, so on rainy days, he went by himself, avoiding the whines he knew he would hear if he took us with him.

Now, Gramp was usually a stickler about breakfast, believing it was the most important meal of the day. On most mornings, he waited until Gram fried bacon and eggs, made pancakes and toast, and brewed the coffee. Then, he'd eat a breakfast big enough to choke a horse.

The only exception to his breakfast routine came on those days when he wanted to hit the lake early. Then, he was content to fix himself a bowl of cereal and a glass of milk, making up for the deficient breakfast with a larger than usual lunch.

I watched as he heaped spoon after spoon of the white substance from the sugar bowl onto his cereal, inwardly cringing

Simpler Times; Better Times

each time he dipped into the bowl, knowing my planned joke on Gary had gone dreadfully astray.

Gramp shoveled a huge bite into his mouth. He chewed once. Twice. Then, he spit, spraying the kitchen with milk, cornflakes, and salt. He roared. "Jack and Gary, get down here!"

Gramp's blast woke Gary up. He rubbed his eyes. "What's the matter with Gramp? Why does he want us?"

"Never mind. Go back to sleep. It's me he wants to see." I got out of bed and started down the stairs. Gramp was waiting for me at the bottom. His face was as red as a beet.

"Did you do this?" he asked, pointing to the sugar bowl.

"Yes." No use not admitting it, I thought.

"Haven't I told you two not to mess with the salt?"

"Yes." He had—repeatedly. One of our favorite tricks was to unscrew the top of the salt or pepper shaker and wait for the other guy to use it. Rewarded when the other guy dumped a big pile of salt or pepper on his plate. Each time we got a stiff lecture from Gramp, who hated to see any food go to waste.

Gramp was fuming. "Well, this time you're going to learn to listen. Go out to the boathouse and stay there until I come in off the lake"

Oh, no, I groaned. No punishment was worse than the boathouse. Whippings I could handle, but not the boathouse. The boathouse was also the outhouse. On the best of days, it was a terrible place. It smelled something awful; was full of horseflies and mosquitoes; and there was nothing to do in there—nothing. On a wet day like this, it was even worse. The odor intensified and the flies and mosquitoes multiplied.

With my chin down, I headed for the boathouse. When Gramp was upset, there was no reasoning with him, any appeal of this harsh sentence would fall on deaf ears. I knew that I was in for a long stay. Gramp would intentionally extend his fishing from the customary hour, or so, to well over two hours. He did. It was three hours later when he finally returned.

For those three hours, I sat in the boathouse, choking back gag reflexes and swatting at the hundreds of flies and mosquitoes that were feasting on my blood. But the worst part was listening to Gary prance around outside, as he celebrated my misery. No joke

Jack D. Atchison

was worth having to listen to him. Lesson learned: I resolved to keep my hands off the salt in the future.

We really didn't need practical jokes to get our fill of laughs. Gramp supplied enough just through his own antics.

When he was at the cottage, no one would have guessed that he had spent thirty-three years in the Army, wearing immaculately clean and sharply pressed uniforms and shoes that shined like mirrors. While at the lake, his normal attire was faded khaki trousers, a plaid shirt, and old, military-style shoes. He donned a fresh change of clothes every Sunday and, if Gram didn't intercede, he proceeded to wear the same trousers and shirt for the rest of the week. By Saturday, the clothes were thoroughly soiled, reflecting the long hours he spent fishing and working in his garden, as well as displaying stains from more than one meal. Maybe it was a form of rebellion against years of forced neatness and conformity to a stringent dress code.

His fishing attire was even worse. He wore an old, battered hat that was stained with paint and tattered and torn at the crown and along the brim. His bulky army fatigue jacket was also stained with paint and oil. In place of shoes, he wore knee-high, black rubber boots.

Adding to the overall effect of his clothing was the fact that if Gramp bothered to shave, he did so in the afternoon. In the morning, his chin reflected a healthy stubble of whiskers. And with each passing year, his trousers tended to ride a little lower on his hips—and his hips appeared to hang lower on his body. In all, when Gramp got ready to head out for a morning fishing trip, he looked like a refugee from skid row.

Before we could go fishing, we had to load the boat. Gary and I carried life preservers, rods and reels, tackle boxes, and bait out to the dock and Gramp loaded it into the boat. He was usually impatient to get going, so he'd untie the boat from the dock before he loaded it. To keep the boat in place after he'd untied it, he'd put one foot in the boat and the other on the dock. With this straddle-posture, he kept the boat still—sometimes.

If the wind was from the southeast, the waves tended to shove the boat away from the dock. On really windy days, the waves were white-capped and powerful, generating considerable force. Gary and I waited for days like these.

We'd look down the dock and see Gramp, dressed in his boots, fatigue jacket, and battered hat, straddling between the dock and the boat. As the waves pounded in, the boat would drift away from the dock, forcing Gramp to use the leg that was anchored in the boat to pull it back. But he often had his mind on other matters, like where he was going to stow our gear or which route he was going to use on the trip, and wasn't aware of when or how far the boat was drifting. We'd see his legs spread farther and farther apart.

Suddenly, Gramp would find himself in a position where his legs couldn't generate enough force to draw the boat back to the dock. The boat would continue to drift away. As it did, he was forced to do the splits. When his legs were as far apart as nature allowed, he'd fall into the water. Each time he'd get up spitting water and cursing. Then, he'd sheepishly wade back to shore.

Over time, he became a little more cautious about untying the boat too early. He'd wait until it was loaded, then he'd untie it and push off from the dock by forcefully jumping into the boat. One day, as he did this maneuver, he forgot to untie the boat. When he jumped into the boat with his push-off step, the rope drew taut and the boat stopped abruptly, but he kept going forward, through the boat and into the lake, hitting the water with a world-class belly flop. When his head rose from under the water, he got to his feet and, without saying a word, calmly walked to the cottage to change clothes, leaving Gary and me in the boat, where we were rolling in laughter.

Gary and I got to watch this sight a couple of times every summer. Even Gram sat at the window on windy days, waiting to see him take an unplanned belly flop in the lake.

Then, there was the search for Tilly Lake. Gramp was always searching for new fishing holes. Allen told him about a little lake—Tilly Lake—which he described as being located on an old logging road somewhere between our cottage and the town of Mancelona. The lake was isolated and small, so few people knew of its existence. Because no one fished it, Allen said that Tilly Lake was so full of bass you could catch them with your bare hands. Allen told Gramp he'd only been to Tilly Lake one time and couldn't remember exactly where it was located—Gramp would have to search for it.

One morning we set off to find Tilly Lake. We loaded the trunk of Gramp's 1952 Plymouth with our fishing gear and an assortment of other paraphernalia that he thought might come in handy. We drove to the highway leading from the lake to Mancelona and looked for the first logging road. It didn't take long to find one, because the area was laced with them. Each logging road broke off into several forks, resulting in a maze of abandoned dirt roads that blanketed the county. They were everywhere. Most were just a couple of worn out ruts covered with weeds.

We wound our way down the road until we came to the first fork, presenting Gramp with a decision to make: Did he go to the right or the left? He opted for the right and we started down a weed-covered road. About three hundred yards later, the road dead-ended in a thicket of pine and birch trees. We got out of the car and hiked through the trees, trying to see if the road continued on the other side of the thicket. Finding no sign of the road, we returned to the car. Because of the trees and brush on the side of the road, Gramp wasn't able to turn around and had to drive in reverse until we hit the fork.

At the fork, we tried the left-hand road. Again, we hit a dead end. This time we got stuck in sand when the road petered out. We all pushed the car until the tires were freed from the sand. Then, again driving in reverse, we headed back to the fork in the road.

We returned to the highway and found another logging road. We turned down it and within minutes were once again at a dead end. And so it went all day long. Dead end after dead end. No Tilly Lake.

But the search wasn't entirely for naught. We did find wild raspberries, blueberries, and blackberries, and we picked a couple quarts of each. We also saw a number of deer, porcupines, beaver, rabbits, turkey buzzards, and hawks. And we had a great picnic in the woods.

On one of these searches for Tilly Lake, Gramp drove the old Plymouth down a tree-lined path that, with a great many twists and turns, climbed up a rather steep hill. Because of the sharpness

Simpler Times; Better Times

of the bends in the path, and the lack of visibility caused by the dense trees, every turn was a blind one. As we negotiated one such turn, Gramp suddenly slammed on the brakes, bringing the car to an abrupt, shuddering halt. With trees brushing against the car on both sides, we looked out the front window and saw nothing but open air. The path, without warning, ended at the edge of a severe cliff—a cliff that plunged downward some fifty feet or so. The car was resting a mere three feet from the edge of the precipice.

While the rest of us in the car were scared out of our wits by thoughts of what could have occurred had we not stopped when we had, Gramp appeared totally at ease with the situation, seeming not to have a concern in the world. Calmly, he said, "Hmm...guess we have to back up." With that, he coughed several times, cleared his throat, turned his head slightly to the left, and spit.

"It helps to roll down the window, Jim," Gram said.

As we watched the yellowish gob of spit run down the still-closed car window, we realized that he was not as calm as he had appeared to be.

Over the course of the next fifteen years, the search for Tilly Lake continued. A few times each summer, we'd travel through the maze of logging roads looking for the elusive lake. After our enrollment in college prevented Gary and me from spending our summers at the cottage, Jann and Mike went with Gramp on these annual searches. We never found Tilly Lake.

To this day, I don't know if there is or was such a lake or whether it was just another of Allen's practical jokes. But I do know that the days we spent searching for Tilly Lake were always among the best of each summer.

A few times each summer, Gram would leave the cottage for several days to visit friends. When this happened, Gramp took over her cooking duties. He had unusual cooking habits, to say the least. Gary and I never knew what to expect.

One time, he got a huge pot and filled it with white beans and chunks of pork. The pot bubbled on the stove for hours as he cooked his concoction of pork and beans. Then, Gary and I had to eat beans for several meals, necessitating far more trips to the outhouse than usual.

Jack D. Atchison

Another time, he got on a cabbage kick. I think he was trying to make sauerkraut. Again, the huge iron pot bubbled on the stove for an entire day. The odor inside the cottage was so overwhelming that Gary and I spent all the time outside.

Then there was the time when he got a good deal on turnips. Meal after meal, we were treated to a plateful of turnips and fish. It was enough to make anyone give up on food. It was never a treat when Gram was away from the kitchen.

When Gram was home, she tended to serve larger portions of food than either Gary or I could eat. About halfway through each meal, we were stuffed. But, with Gramp's rules against waste, we had to finish everything on the plate. To do so, Gram told us to run around the exterior of the cottage, claiming the activity would make room in our stomachs for more food. By the end of each summer, there was a well-worn path around the cottage, the result of the countless laps we ran in order to clean our plates.

Then, there was the process of doing the dishes. One of us had to help after each meal. Gramp boiled a large pot of water to use as rinse water. The water was so hot that we had to use a spatula-like stick to remove the dishes from the water. Even then, wiping them was a painful experience. We'd ask Gramp to go easy on the boiling, but he ignored us or said, "Gotta kill all the germs." I still think he did it just to see us squirm.

One summer Gramp decided to modernize the cottage. He wanted to install indoor plumbing and upgrade the heating.

The old wood stove was replaced with an oil heater. That phase of the project was no big deal because an outside contractor did the work. The rest of the project was a different story.

In order to have indoor plumbing, we needed to build a bathroom. Gramp had a plumbing contractor lay out all the water lines, but decided to build the room himself, with Gary and me assisting. It was an exercise that permitted us to witness, first-hand, his approach to construction.

First, we built the forms for the floor. We didn't use any plans or drawings. Gramp just took a stick and drew the outline for the floor in the dirt surrounding the pipes that the plumber had already installed. Using this outline, we dug down about four feet and laid cement blocks for the foundation. Then, we leveled the

Simpler Times; Better Times

area within the perimeter of the foundation to a depth of six inches to form the floor area.

Gramp had a cement truck come and pour the concrete for the floor. While the concrete was being poured, he shoveled it around and Gary and I used planks and trowels to level it out. In the end, we had a reasonably level floor.

Next, we built the walls. Gary and I carried cement blocks and mixed cement while Gramp laid the blocks. With each tier of blocks, he'd use his trusty plumb line, a T-square, and level to make sure the walls were straight and the corners square. It sounded good in theory but, when the walls were nearly complete, I could stand at the corners and see that they were as crooked as a dog's hind leg—just like the chimney he built in the Gunson Street house. When I pointed this out to him, he didn't seem too worried. He thought it was a visual aberration caused by irregularities in the size of the blocks. He was certain the inside walls were straight and the corners were square.

With the walls complete, we started building the roof. Rafters were attached to the top of the walls and then crossbeams were added. It was in this operation that Gramp finally realized his walls weren't straight or square. We had to do a considerable amount of improvising to get the rafters and the walls to join together.

We then covered the crossbeams with roofing planks; the planks with plywood; the plywood with tarpaper; and, finally, the tarpaper with shingles. Since we only worked between fishing trips on the lake, the whole process took most of the summer to complete. When we were finished, we had a pretty solid room, even with Gramp's unusual construction techniques.

While Gramp laid tile floors in the interior and installed the sinks and toilet, Gary and I painted the outside. It was a labor of love because each of us knew that when we completed the room addition, we'd never have to use the outhouse again. It was all the incentive we needed.

This project was one of many. Over the years, the cottage was upgraded, expanded, and modernized by the combined efforts of Gramp, Mom and Dad, Gary, and me. With each project, the cottage became more than a physical structure—it became an important and treasured part of each of our memories.

Jack D. Atchison

Evenings at the cottage were filled by hotly contested games of canasta. The critical point of each game occurred when we first sat down and partners were selected. Whoever got stuck with Gram was in deep, deep trouble.

Gramp was a crafty card player. He'd change his strategy with each hand. He played with a complete poker face, never changing his expression throughout the game. One never knew whether he had a good hand or a bad one. And, if you weren't vigilant when it was his turn to deal, he wasn't above stacking the deck.

Gram was a different kettle of fish. She played virtually every hand the same way. There were certain cards—queens and aces—that she never discarded and there were others—fours and fives—that she never held. She was impatient, always acting before the pot had built to a reasonable level, prematurely stripping her hand of good cards. She grinned from ear to ear, leaned back in her chair, and chanted "Oh, ho, ho" when she had good cards and pouted when her hand was bad. As such, she was easier to read than an open book.

Somehow, I usually managed to stick Gary with Gram. Gramp, wise old bird that he was, never had her as his partner. With partners established, the outcome of the game was reasonably predictable—Gramp and I won nine times out of ten. The one time in ten that we lost, however, was painful. Gram gloated over her victories, reminding Gramp and me on almost an hourly basis, from the close of that night's play to the opening of the next day's game, who had won.

The games themselves were filled with taunts, barbs, and baiting. In this aspect of the game, Gram was in her element. She had an extremely quick wit and knew how to get under your skin. With one subtle dig after another, she'd goad you into making a dumb play. Were it not for this ability, all the games would have been routs. But Gram's table talk always kept her team in the game. It usually wasn't enough to overcome her predictable play, but it kept every game interesting.

When Gram and Gary grew tired of losing, they'd ask to change the night's game to either hearts or Rook. But, even though they changed the game, the outcome was the same. Gram's skill at these games was no better than with canasta. Once she and Gary realized this, we'd switch back to canasta.

There were few nights at the cottage when we didn't play cards. Even when we had guests, the game was played. We just added a few more decks and expanded the size of the teams. The canasta game was an unavoidable part of anyone's visit to the cottage.

Not every summer at the cottage was an entirely pleasant one. One spring Gramp's father died. At the time, he was well into his nineties. According to Gramp, he got sick and, for the first time was placed in a hospital. He was a gruff, crusty, independent man, and, after one day of hospital food and being subjected to probes and tests by doctors and nurses, he left the hospital—sneaked out without telling anyone. Later that same day he died on his farm.

His death left Gramp's mother—Gary's and my great-grandmother—alone. She, too, was over ninety years old and in poor health. Quite senile and incontinent, she was unable to care for herself. In fact, she was not able to recognize the people around her, nor did she have any real sense of time or place.

Gramp didn't want to place his mother in a nursing home or hire someone to care for her. He believed a family should care for its own. So, he had his mother come live with Gram and him in the cottage that summer.

Because of his mother's physical and mental condition, Gramp had to spend the better part of each day with her. He carried her to and from the bathroom; changed her soiled garments and bedding; fed her; bathed and combed her hair; read to her for hours on end; and talked to her, even when her responses made absolutely no sense. He was with her almost every minute of every day that summer. When he needed some relief, Gram, Gary, or I took over, reading and talking to her. Gram also helped with her bathing or feeding and washed her clothing and bedding. But, for the most part, Gramp insisted on caring for her.

As a result of caring for his mother, Gramp did virtually no fishing that year, nor were there any searches for Tilly Lake or similar activities. Through it all, he never complained and never showed any sign that caring for his mother was a burden; nor did Gram.

Jack D. Atchison

As for me, I saw my great-grandmother as almost a shadow or a ghost. While she was physically there, mentally she was in another world, lost in thoughts that only she understood. Each day, she'd think I was someone else. One day she'd think I was Gramp, as a boy, or she'd think I was Dad or my Uncle Bill.

And, like a child, she threw temper tantrums. If she didn't like what she was being fed, she spit it out. If she was in a bad mood, she swung her cane at you when you walked past her. If she didn't want to listen to you, she just closed her eyes and ignored you. In all, she was pretty difficult to handle, even for Gramp. But, again, he never complained nor did he let her ill-tempered outbursts bother him.

There were times, however, when Gramp didn't know anyone was watching him as he tended his mother. On some of these occasions, I watched him as he sat quietly and just stared at her. Perhaps he was wondering if she would ever be lucid again; knowing she would not. Then, uncharacteristically for this stoic man with the gruff exterior that had been formed by years of military service, I'd hear him sob and watch tears stream down his cheeks. At those moments, he was no longer Gramp; he was simply a son who deeply loved his mother and cared about her health and welfare.

My great-grandmother died later that year. Gramp did everything he could to make her last few months as comfortable as possible. No son could have done more than he did.

Gary and I stopped spending our entire summer vacations at the cottage when we entered high school. But neither of us ever experienced better times than we enjoyed on Manistee Lake with Gram and Gramp.

We met a wide range of colorful characters, most of whom were in their sixties or older. As we fished with them, listened to their stories, played practical jokes, engaged in contests of Canasta, Rook, and Hearts; or simply observed them, we gained a great deal of respect and admiration for our elders. We found they were creative, imaginative, wise, energetic, interesting, and fun to be around. Every day we learned something new—some piece of information or advice drawn from their past experiences—

Simpler Times; Better Times

information and advice they were more than willing to share with two young boys.

As a result of spending so many summers with these "senior citizens," as they now would be labeled, I became extremely comfortable being in the presence of my elders. In many respects, I preferred their company to that of people nearer my own age. I found that by asking a few questions, I could learn more practical knowledge in two hours of discussion with one of them than I could in a week's worth of classes in school. More importantly, they used humor and real-life examples to impart this knowledge, making the learning experience highly entertaining.

Gary and I were fortunate to have had the special privilege of spending time with folks like Beth, Allen, Parkie, and all the others who visited us over the course of these memorable summers.

Jack D. Atchison

CHAPTER EIGHT

As with any generation of children, when not in school, play is an important part of a child's day, and my generation was no exception. When we first moved to Canton, the country was still recovering from World War II. All the kids in the neighborhood had been affected by the war. We'd watched the newsreels, listened to radio reports, read letters from our fathers, and seen pictures in magazines. As a result of these sources of information, we, like the adults in the country, strongly identified with and supported the country's war efforts. An outgrowth of our knowledge of and interest in the war was that war games were a part of our play.

On weekends, a band of boys wearing helmets, canteens, and other bits and pieces of battlefield garb, and armed with cap guns, gathered near the swamp at the end of our street. Two boys were selected to be generals and one-by-one on an alternating basis they selected their troops from the rest of the group. After sides were drawn, a coin was tossed to determine which group would be designated "Americans" and which had to play the role of the "Germans."

The Americans always were given the high ground—the hill on the other side of the swamp—while the Germans had to dig into positions in or near the swamp. The rules of the game were simple. The Americans attacked and the Germans defended. A person was removed from the game if he was deemed to have been killed. There were two ways a person could be killed. First, if an opponent spotted a person, pointed his cap gun at him, fired, and yelled "You're dead" before the person could conceal himself, the person was deemed to have been killed. Second, if a person was struck by a "grenade" he was deemed dead. For this purpose, a grenade was a rock about the size of an egg. The winner was the army with the most people left in the game at the conclusion of the Americans' attack.

Of course, since we were all patriotic and gave the Americans the high ground, that team held a distinct advantage

Simpler Times; Better Times

when it came to the use of grenades. It is a heck of a lot easier to toss a good-sized rock downhill than it is to hurl it uphill. Consequently, the Germans were constantly bombarded with a hailstorm of rocks during these battles, while the Americans seldom had to duck to avoid a German-launched grenade. This, of course, made it highly desirable to be selected as a member of the American forces.

Only one helmet was included in the gear that Dad brought home with him when he was discharged from the Army. As a consequence, when Gary and I set out to play in these war games, only one of us was able to wear a helmet. The other was stuck wearing a soft field cap, which was made of cloth and, as such, offered the wearer scant protection from flying rocks.

On the day of one of our more eventful battles, Gary had the misfortune of drawing the imaginary short straw and had to wear the field cap. His bad luck was compounded when he was selected to join the German forces.

The American forces climbed the hill behind the swamp and armed themselves with pockets full of rocks. One of the Americans, a cousin of one of our neighbors, was new to our game. When he selected the rocks that he intended to use as grenades, he picked out ones that were considerably larger than those we normally used. Instead of being egg size, his rocks were the size of a baseball.

In the meantime, the Germans took up positions below the hill. They hid behind fallen trees and in "foxholes" that had been dug specifically for these conflicts. While the foxholes offered more cover than the fallen trees, they were located on higher ground and were closer to the hill (had they been closer to the swamp, water would have seeped into them). So, the people in the foxholes were the first targets in the grenade attacks.

The American forces started their assault by bombarding the Germans with their complete arsenal of grenades. The sounds of rocks thudding into the dirt and splashing into the swamp water were punctuated by the "crack!" of cap guns and the occasional "bonk!" of a rock meeting a helmet.

As rocks rained down on the Germans who were dug in below the hill, the new kid yelled out, "I think I just killed the red-haired kid!"

Jack D. Atchison

Big deal, the rest of us thought. Gary was always one of the first to be eliminated from the game. With his bright red hair, he was an easy target, even when he was wearing a field cap or helmet.

"Really," the new kid yelled, panic in his voice, "the guy's lying on the ground and bleeding! I think he's dead!"

That got our attention. Another of the guys, one who was hiding near Gary's position, shouted: "Hey! He is bleeding!"

We stopped our battle and ran toward Gary. He was stretched out the ground, half in and half out of the foxhole in which he had been hiding, and wasn't moving. Just as we got to him, however, he started to sit up. His face was pale. He acted woozy. Blood soaked his field cap. On inspection, we found that he had a big gash on his head, the product of the baseball-size rock that lay on the ground next to him.

We picked Gary up and, while Johnny pressed a cloth to the wound, helped him walk home. We couldn't move very fast, because Gary's legs were pretty wobbly and he was still fairly dazed.

As soon as we got home, Dad didn't waste any time. He loaded Gary into the car and took him to the hospital for stitches—over a half-dozen of them.

Later that night, Dad issued an order that affected our war games. Gary's injury, the first anyone had suffered in our battles, was used as evidence that our games were potentially dangerous. We were instructed to permanently cancel any further grenade battles. The other parents in the neighborhood issued similar orders to their sons.

With our war games ruled off-limits, we turned to a variation of the old game of cowboys and Indians.

We raided the scrap heaps of homes that were under construction and retrieved long sticks of one-by-one wood that were used for trim and molding. Using penknives, which all of us carried in the pockets of our jeans, we converted these sticks into spears by whittling one end of the stick into a point. Then, we purloined the lids off of neighborhood garbage cans to serve as shields.

Simpler Times; Better Times

Armed with spears and shields, we went to war. The object was to hurl spears at the opponent and for him to ward them off with his shield. The unspoken rule was that you only aimed at the other guy's legs and torso.

One day, Gary and I were engaged in a private spear fight—just the two of us. After our initial throws—tentative tests of the other guy's reaction time with his shield—the action picked up and spear after spear clanged off our shields. As fast as we could pick up a spear, we hurled it at the other guy, hoping to catch him with his shield down.

I was straightening up from retrieving a spear, when Gary fired one of his. It sailed high and nailed me just below the left eye, opening an inch long cut and darn near tearing off the bottom eyelid. While I tried to stop the bleeding, Gary jumped up and down with joy—finally someone instead of him was going to make a trip to the hospital for stitches.

Mom and Dad didn't share Gary's thrill of victory. Like our other war games, we were banned from using spears. We also got one heck of a lecture about the dangers of throwing objects at another person's head—one in a long series of such lectures.

Because we did not have the money to buy games, we used materials that were at hand and that didn't cost us anything. A lack of funds made kick-the-can one of our favorite games. All we needed was an empty coffee can and a field.

We started by selecting two teams, making sure that the members of the teams changed with each game. The object of the game was for one team to capture all the members of the other team. A player was captured when he was tagged by an opponent. Once captured, the player was placed in jail—a circle drawn in the dirt. An empty coffee can was placed on the ground, directly in front of the jail. If a player kicked the can without first being tagged, all his captured teammates were set free. Thus, one or more players were assigned to guard the can. Their job was to ward off attacks on the jail by tagging any opponent who made a run at the can. If a player was able to elude the guards and kicked the can, no freed prisoners could be recaptured until the can was put back in place, so another objective was to kick the can as hard as possible, driving it as far as you could.

Jack D. Atchison

We used two types of playing fields. In the daytime version of the game, we usually used a big field or parking lot. All players had to stay within the designated boundaries of the playing field. If someone stepped outside the boundaries, they were considered to be captured. In the night version of the game, we always used the back and side yards of a half-dozen houses. We could do that because none of the yards in the neighborhood had fences. The only things separating one yard from another were small hedges and flower beds. As long as we didn't trample on flowers or damage the hedges, none of the neighbors objected to our using their yards as a play area.

In the daytime games, speed was the primary factor that teams relied upon in their strategies. The faster members of the team that was attacking the can hung around the far perimeters of the playing area, making it difficult for their opponents to chase them down and tag them. As slower members were captured and placed in jail, two or more of the faster members converged on the can. One player feinted to draw the attention of those guarding the can. When the guards chased after the decoy, as they invariably did, the others charged the can. More often than not, one player got through the other team's protective screen and kicked the can, freeing his teammates.

After watching the can get kicked away a few times, the team guarding the can usually adjusted its strategies. It ignored the slower members of the attacking team and concentrated on capturing the faster ones—the ones who were quick enough to penetrate the screen around the can. Two or more of the better players went after and boxed in one of the attacker's faster players. If they succeeded, and put the faster opponents in jail, it was just a matter of time before the slower ones were nabbed, because none of the slower ones had the necessary speed to get through the screen to kick the can. This strategy reduced the odds that any of the captured opponents would get released.

If traditional measures failed, and one's opponents kept kicking the can with regularity, there were other tactics a team could, and often did, employ to turn the tide. First, the can could be filled with egg-sized rocks. Alternatively, a stake could be driven into the ground and the can placed over it. In either event, the next kicker-of-the-can was in for one heck of a surprise. Nothing

Simpler Times; Better Times

stopped an opposing team faster than having them watch one of their teammates as he danced around on one tennis-shoed foot while he held the other foot in both hands, swearing he had a bunch of broken toes. After one such occurrence, every opponent approached the can with extreme caution and kicked it feebly, if at all, even after repeated assurances that the can was no longer rigged.

Night games were different from those played in the daytime. Stealth replaced speed as a team's primary strength. Attacking players concealed themselves behind trees, garages, and the like, using darkness as a cover, making it difficult for their opponents to find and capture them.

The players on the team guarding the can were armed with flashlights, enabling them to search for the hidden attackers. The capturers also used the cover of darkness to set traps and ambushes. Players positioned themselves along the better escape paths while others made noise in an attempt to make an attacking player bolt from his concealed position, a process much like using a beater in a safari hunt. When the attacker spooked and started to change positions, those waiting in ambush sprang the trap and tagged him.

Some of the slower players, ones who were at a disadvantage during daytime games, were especially sneaky. Faster players continued to believe in their speed and became overly confident and easy to trap. Slower ones were more patient. They'd burrow into a hedge and lie there silently, ignoring the noise around them. Then, after the capturers got frustrated with their futile attempts to find his place of concealment, the attacker emerged from hiding and crept toward the can, using darkness as his friend. If he could crawl, undetected, to within ten feet or so of the can, even the slowest player had a good shot at kicking the can. So, a player who normally was one of the last ones selected during daytime games was often one of the first selected at night.

Some of these games took hours to play. During the course of the games, players from each side huddled in order to rethink strategies. Before a game concluded, dozens of plans were put in motion by both sides, as each team tried to outthink and outmaneuver its opponent.

Jack D. Atchison

This simple game was not only fun; it was a great learning experience for all involved. Evaluating the relative strengths and weaknesses of teammates; formulating strategies; learning that patience can be the key to victory; and, working with others to achieve a common objective were just a few of the skills this simple game helped the participants develop and build upon. And it didn't cost a dime to play.

Capture-the-flag was a close relative of kick-the-can and, again, was a contest between two teams. Each team had a goal—a flag (actually just an old rag) attached to a pole. The goals were located at opposite ends of a playing field. The object of the game was to capture the other team's flag before they captured yours.

Each team divided itself into two units. An offensive unit, usually consisting of the fastest runners and smallest team members, attacked the other team's goal and a defensive unit, made up of the bigger players, defended the team's own goal by knocking down or tackling any opponent who approached the flag.

The offense of each team devised various plays to penetrate the other side's defenses. For example, the offense tried to overload one side of the field. Three offensive players would make a run at one or two defenders, hoping a mismatch in numbers would allow one player to get a free run at the flag. In order to counteract overloading, the defense employed rovers to hover near the flag in order to intercept any player who broke through the perimeter defenses. Knowing there were rovers, the offense would send in players from the other side of the field to distract or tie up the rovers when an overload attack was launched. And so it went, each team trying to outguess the other.

There were no rules limiting the number of players that a team could assign to either its defensive or offensive unit. Conservative teams kept more defenders near their own goal and limited the number of players who were sent against the other team's flag. On the other hand, more daring teams held back very few defenders and hoped that their offensive players could storm the other side's flag before their own minimal defenses were penetrated. The game was fast moving and, because play was at both goals, all members of both teams were constantly involved in the action.

Simpler Times; Better Times

On those occasions when we had an insufficient number of people to form two teams, we altered the rules. One team defended a single goal, while the other attacked. A time limit was established for a team to be on offense. At the end of the time limit, the teams reversed roles. A team scored one point each time it captured the flag. The object was to capture the flag as many times as possible during the team's available time on offense. The team with the most points was the winner.

Unlike kick-the-can, capture-the-flag was a rough game. There was a lot of tackling and blocking involved and players were knocked to the ground with considerable frequency. Yet, in all the years that we played this game, no one was ever seriously injured. There were a few bumps and bruises, but nothing worse.

We also played flashlight tag. This was a simple game that was always played after the sun set for the night.

One player was designated as being "it." He was given a flashlight. With his eyes closed, he counted out loud to one hundred while the other players scattered around the various yards that were used as the playing area and concealed themselves. When the person who was "it" reached one hundred, he opened his eyes and started searching for a concealed player. If he spotted one, he shined the light on them, yelled "You're it!" and dropped the flashlight.

The person who was now "it" had to run to the flashlight, pick it up, close his eyes, and count to one hundred. While he did, all the other players changed positions.

In playing this simple game, a person had to know the locations of the hedges, holes, garbage cans, and other obstacles in the playing field. If he didn't, he could receive a real surprise.

One night Gary and I had to stay in and finish our homework and, therefore, were unable to participate in that night's game of flashlight tag. While we were seated at the table with our books open, we heard this loud "Twang!" in our backyard. It sounded like someone was tearing down the wall to our house. I turned on the light above the back porch and saw one of our friends, Larry, lying on his back in the middle of the yard.

I went outside to see what his problem was. By the time I reached him, he was trying to sit up. "What happened?" I asked.

He seemed confused. "I don't know. I was running through your yard when suddenly everything just went black."

He was rubbing his neck. "What's wrong with your neck?" I asked.

"I don't know. It's really sore."

I looked where he was rubbing and saw a big red welt under his chin. Looking up, I realized what had happened. "Did you remember the clotheslines?"

"Huh?"

He hadn't. The real hazards at night were the clotheslines in everyone's yard. Most of us were so short that the lines were well above our heads. But Larry was one of the tallest kids in our group. When he raced through our yard to find a hiding place, he forgot about the clothesline that was strung down the center of the yard. It must have caught him right under the chin, stopping him dead in his tracks.

In the years that followed, and as more of us gained added height, being strung up by a clothesline became a more frequent occurrence and was about the only way a kid could get hurt in this game. To this day, the term "clothes-lined" has a place in sports lexicon.

When we grew tired of playing flashlight tag, we could end the game by simply agreeing to quit. But another ending was much more entertaining. We waited until one of the more gullible members of the group was it. As he counted to one hundred, the rest of us quietly retreated to our respective homes, calling it a night, secure in the knowledge that our victim would comb the neighborhood with his flashlight for another half-hour before he came to the realization that he was all alone. To our great delight, Gary, the most gullible in the group, fell for this trick every time we pulled it on him.

In the winter, when there was snow on the ground, the preferred game was fox-and-geese. We'd create an elaborate maze of crisscrossing paths in the snow. The paths ran through eight to ten contiguous yards in the neighborhood and became our game board. One person was designated to be the "Fox" and all others were "Geese." The geese positioned themselves in the maze, usually as far away from the fox as they could get. When the game

Simpler Times; Better Times

started, the fox chased after one of the geese, trying to tag him. If he did, the tagged person became the new fox and the game continued. The only real rule was that if anyone ran outside the paths when he was being chased by the fox, he was considered to have been tagged and became the fox.

After hours of kids running back and forth on the paths, the snow turned to slush. Overnight, the wet slush froze into ice. When we played the next day, the paths were slick and slippery, causing players to lose their balance and fall as they tried to negotiate sharp turns or evade the fox. Thus, the real fun in the game of fox-and-geese didn't start until the paths had been used for a day or two.

The drawback in the game came when the weather turned warmer. Then the slush didn't freeze into ice. Instead, the paths turned into trails of mud. At this point, the adults in the neighborhood complained that continued use of the paths would destroy their lawns and, almost always, the game was canceled until the temperature dropped or the next snow fell.

There was one time, however, when the father of two of our playmates ran into resistance when he tried to bring a game to a close.

Early one Saturday morning, a large group was playing a fairly raucous game, shouting and yelling as we ran up and down the paths in the snow. This particular father had been out partying the evening before and was suffering from a painful hangover. The noise from our game exacerbated his splitting headache and played on his frayed nerves. He came out of his house, dressed only in pajama bottoms and slippers, and yelled at us to "quiet down and stay out of my yard!"

As kids are prone to do, we didn't immediately respond to his demands and continued to play, acting as if we hadn't heard him at all. Our indifference to his demands infuriated him, especially since he was standing half-naked in twenty-degree weather. He started to curse at us. The sight was pretty funny. Here was this guy, standing there freezing his rear end off, yelling like a madman, his language deteriorating rapidly, his face beet-red, and no one—no one—was paying the least bit of attention to him. One by one, we started to laugh.

As our laughter increased, he really lost it. He started to chase the nearest kid down a path, shouting one invective after another, intent on grabbing the kid by the scruff of his neck. He'd only taken a few strides when his slippers hit a slick spot. His feet flew out from beneath him, and he landed in a heap in six-inch-deep snow. As he rose shakily to his feet, he was greeted by the unrestrained laughter of a dozen kids, further feeding his anger.

He took off after another kid, more mindful of his footing this time. As he started to gain, the kid did the natural thing. He turned sharply down another path, gained a little distance, stopped, and made a snowball. When the man got close enough, the kid threw the snowball and took off. In ducking away from the snowball, the man's feet lost their purchase on the icy path and he fell again.

The rest of us figured this latest fall would make the man even more determined to catch the kid who had thrown the snowball, so we came to the aid of our playmate. As the man tried to regain his feet, he was pelted with a barrage of snowballs that stung his bare chest and back. Warding off snowballs, he retreated to his house.

Believing the incident over, we returned to our game. But, within minutes, angry parents started calling for their respective kids to "Come home, right now!" It seems that as soon as the man got to the safety of his home, he called all our parents and complained about the snowball attack.

When Gary and I got inside, Dad started to chew us out. But when he heard the full story, he laughed as hard as we had earlier. The threat of punishment disappeared. Nonetheless, our game was canceled and we got a lecture on showing more respect to adults, even if they were hung over and a little irrational in their behavior.

Three years after we moved to Canton, the area at the end of our street changed dramatically. A shopping center was built on the hill and the swamp gave way to a parking lot on one side of the street and a city-built playground on the other. Our play areas were no longer fields, hills and swamps; they were ball fields and basketball courts. The games changed from mock wars and cowboys and Indians to the traditional sporting games of football, baseball, and basketball, among others.

Simpler Times; Better Times

Even before the playground at the end of the street was built, we started learning the basic skills required to play each major sport. Dad was our primary teacher. Every night, after he got home from work, and every weekend day, he'd spend an hour or more teaching us basic skills.

This was a change for all three of us. It wasn't until we moved to Canton, that Gary and I really had a chance to spend any time with Dad. He was in Europe and didn't return home until I was four and Gary was three. Then, he was gone all the time, either attending classes or working in the tractor factory. So, these sessions in which he taught us various sporting skills was the first real "bonding" that any of us had really had a chance to experience.

In the spring, as soon as the snow started to melt, we got out a baseball and our gloves and played catch in the front yard. Our gloves were nearly twenty years old. One had belonged to Gramp before it was passed down to Dad and, finally, to us. Dad had gotten others from secondhand stores when he was a kid. The gloves were basically shot—the leather cracked and the padding gone—but we didn't care; they seemed fine to us. Nor were the balls in very good shape. The covers were gone from most of them and, in order to keep them from unwinding, they were wrapped with sticky, black, friction tape. But, again, they served their purpose.

With infinite patience, Dad showed us how to grasp the ball and how to coordinate our hands, arms, shoulders, hips and legs to get a proper throwing motion. After each toss, he offered advice on how to improve the throw—change the way we held the ball, widen our stance, put more rotation in the shoulders, or release the ball differently.

He did the same in teaching us how to catch. He instructed us on how to hold our hands, position our bodies, and track the ball. He started out by tossing us a ball from a distance of just a few feet. When we were able to handle these tosses, he backed up, making the throws longer and harder. Next, he moved the ball around, making us reach for it rather than aiming it into our mitts. One toss to the right, one to the left, one short, the next high, and so on.

Jack D. Atchison

In order to add mystery and excitement to the game, Dad stayed in the front yard and Gary and I went to the backyard. Dad threw the ball over the roof, yelling "ally-ally-over" when the ball cleared the roof and "pigtail" when it fell short. When we heard, "ally-ally-over," we looked skyward for the ball. Dad varied his throws and, to catch the ball, we had to cover the entire backyard. Once we caught, or retrieved, the ball, we threw it over the roof to him, yelling either "ally-ally-over" or "pigtail."

In the summer, our attention also turned to basketball. Johnny's dad constructed a backboard and hoop in their backyard. At first, it was all we could do just to toss the ball high enough to hit the rim. Day after day, we stood in Johnny's backyard and shot the basketball—lucky if one out of fifty cleared the rim, ecstatic when one actually fell through the hoop. As time passed, our strength and technique improved and more and more of our shots found the mark.

Before long, we were shooting running lay-ups, set shots, and shots from where a regulation foul line would be located. Johnny had an innate talent for and appreciation of the game of basketball. His natural eye-hand coordination quickly made him a better player than the rest of us. But it wasn't just natural talent; he worked harder at mastering the game. Every day, no matter what the weather—rain, snow, sub-zero temperature—from the age of eight until he was in high school, he spent an hour or more shooting baskets in his backyard.

As our skills improved, we played a variety of games on the backyard court—P-I-G, H-O-R-S-E, twenty-one, one-on-one, and around-the-clock. All of these games primarily focused on shooting skills, but we didn't ignore the other aspects of the game. Whenever we had a few minutes, we worked on dribbling or passing skills.

Fall was football season. Once again, Dad taught Gary and me the basic skills of the game. He showed us how to throw a tight spiral pass. He had us work on catching mechanics, just as he had when he taught us the fundamentals of baseball.

Again, we lacked most of the equipment generally associated with the game. We had an odd assortment of somewhat ancient helmets and shoulder pads, but none of them fit us nor were any of them in any condition to be very useful. So, when it

Simpler Times; Better Times

came time for Dad to show us how to block and tackle, we simply put on a couple of extra shirts for protection.

Dad took us to the backyard and demonstrated the proper posture and body position for launching and sustaining effective blocks. He helped us work on spacing our feet, squaring our shoulders, positioning our heads, increasing our leverage, and improving the force and driving power of the blocks. We worked on blocks that were used on the line of scrimmage as well as down-field blocks.

With respect to tackling, he again focused on technique. We learned when and how to make below-the-waist tackles, concentrating on making sure that we controlled the opponent's legs. We also worked on open-field tackles.

Unlike throwing and catching, blocking and tackling lessons were rough. A good, properly executed tackle or block left a sore shoulder or impressive bruise. A bad one often resulted in a bloody nose. But even though it was rough and, frankly not a heck of a lot of fun, we understood the importance of learning the right way to tackle and block.

In the winter, we taught ourselves how to skate. Gary and I each had a pair of old hockey skates. Neither pair was the right size. In order to make them fit, we wore extra socks and stuffed newspaper into the toes.

During our first attempt to skate, we spent most of the time on the seat of our pants. Each time we got to our feet and attempted to move, the skates shot out from under us. Even standing still was a trick. We couldn't balance ourselves on the slender blades and, after wobbling for a few moments, crashed to the ice.

Two things happened when we fell. First, depending on how we landed, it hurt like heck. Second, after a couple falls, our clothes were soaked from water that had formed as the ice melted, making the cold, winter air even more uncomfortable. So, after a half-dozen rather spectacular falls, something had to give. I was sore, wet, and shivering from the cold. Not my idea of a good time. We had to figure how to stay on our feet.

After some experimentation, I announced to Gary and the other first-time skaters who were with us that I had solved the problem. Instead of standing directly on the blades, I found that when I turned both of my feet in an outward direction and balanced my weight on my ankles I could stand up and slowly move forward without falling.

Soon, all of us were shuffling around the ice on our ankles, the blades of our skates barely touching the ice. We were quite a sight. Six eight-year-old boys, dressed in wet Levis, noses running, checks red, stumbling around the ice with our skates at right angles to our legs. No one moved faster than a snail's pace as we shuffled along, drawing stares and smiles from everyone else who was on the ice that day.

After a half hour of this novel form of skating, Gary asked: "Are you sure we're doing this right?"

"Why?"

"We're not moving very fast and my ankles are killing me."

"Have you fallen down?"

"No."

"Well, it must be right then."

"I guess so," Gary conceded and continued to shuffle around on his sore ankles.

When Dad came to pick us up, he burst into laughter.

"What are you laughing at?" I asked.

"You guys."

"Why? What's so funny?" I asked; somewhat upset by his laughter.

"Look at the way you're skating."

"What's wrong with it? We're not falling down."

"Yeah," he laughed, "but if you keep it up, you'll all be crippled. You have to straighten up. Get off your ankles."

I felt everyone's eyes on me, especially Gary's. "It's the only way we can keep from falling."

"Yes, but you're not even using your skates. You'd do just as well if you took them off." He had me there. It was one of the possibilities I'd considered earlier when I kept hitting the ice. "Here, let me show you how to do it." He walked out on the ice and, in the matter of a half hour, showed us the right way to stand on the skates.

Following his instructions, we gradually improved. We still fell a lot, but by the end of that winter, we all could skate.

Simpler Times; Better Times

In the years that followed, Gary took great delight in telling others how I almost destroyed the ankles of every kid in the neighborhood.

The city playground contained a baseball diamond; asphalt basketball court; horseshoe pits; swings, monkey bars, and a slide; lavatories; and an equipment storage room. The entire playground was enclosed by a chain-link fence that had two-inch, X-shaped barbs on the top. Two gates, which were locked during the hours the playground was closed, provided access to the area. The playground opened in June and closed in September. During the open season, the gates opened at eight o'clock in the morning and closed at nine o'clock at night. The city hired college students to serve as playground supervisors.

For the most part, we ignored the playground's official hours. If the gates were locked and we wanted to use the ball diamond or basketball court, we just climbed the fence. Because of the barbs on top, it was no easy task, especially for the younger, shorter, or weaker members of our circle of friends.

Not long after the playground was built, and before it officially opened, a bunch of us wanted to use the ball field. Some of us had already scaled the fence a few times and had developed techniques for handling the problem of the barbs. But others hadn't climbed it before, and they were a little apprehensive about lifting themselves over the sharp, X-shaped pieces of metal.

One kid in particular was frightened by the fence. He wasn't part of our regular group. He lived in a housing project a few blocks away—on the other side of West Tusc, the main street that was on the other side of the shopping center—thus, only occasionally did he venture over to our side of West Tusc. The kid was overweight, physically weak, and not very tall. As the rest of us scampered up and over the fence, he stood looking at it, afraid to climb.

"Hey," one of the other kids yelled to him, "do you want some help with the fence?"

Seemingly embarrassed by the thought that he might need help, he said, "No. I'll climb over in a minute." As the rest of us set up the ball diamond, he stared at the fence, trying to work up his courage.

By the time we started choosing teams, he still hadn't climbed the fence.

"If you don't get over here by the time we're done picking sides, you aren't on a team," one of the guys yelled to him.

"No...no, I'll be there. Put me on a team," the kid shouted back.

As we were making our selections, we heard him scream. The fence he was climbing served as the right field boundary, so it was more than one hundred feet from home plate, where we were standing as we chose sides. We used that particular fence to enter the playground because shorter guys could stand on a neighbor's garbage can to start their climb. When we heard the screams and looked up, we saw that he was hanging by his outstretched arms from the top of the fence. We figured that he didn't have the strength to pull himself up and over the top.

"Geez," I said. "Let's go help him get over the fence." Two other guys and I trotted out to right field to give him a hand. "Get down," I shouted to him as we ran, "we'll give you a boost."

"I can't!" he screamed. "I'm caught...it hurts...hurry!"

He was now crying and screaming louder than ever, so we ran faster. When we got to the fence, it looked like he'd caught his shirt on some of the barbs. We scaled the fence and jumped over to his side. Another kid and I grasped his waist to lift him up, so the third guy could shove the garbage can under his feet. As soon as our hands touched him, he screamed in pain. We pulled back. I looked down at my hands and was surprised to see that they were covered with blood. Looking at the kid's shirt, I realized, for the first time, blood was soaking through it.

"Geez," I said. "His wrists must be caught on the barbs. We need help!"

Just then, a police car was driving past the playground, apparently headed for the shopping center. We yelled for the cops to stop. Fortunately, they heard us and turned their car in our direction. I ran over to meet them.

"What's the matter?" one cop asked as he got out of the car.

I pointed to the fence. "That kid must have slipped and caught his wrists on the fence. He's bleeding and we can't get him down."

Simpler Times; Better Times

The two cops hurried over to where the kid was hanging. The kid's shirt was now bright red, completely soaked with blood. One cop looked at the kid's wrists. "He's impaled on the barbs, but that's not where all the blood is coming from. Lift up his shirt," he told the other cop.

When the cop lifted the kid's shirt, blood poured everywhere. There were huge openings under each of his armpits and blood was flowing out of them. "Christ," the cop said, "he's split wide open!" Quickly, they freed the groaning kid's wrists from the fence and lowered him to the ground. "This kid is losing blood fast. We don't have time to call an ambulance, let's get him to the car." The two cops put their arms under the kid's torso and the three of us took his legs. We carried him to the cops' car and carefully laid him on the back seat. He was very pale, his eyes were closed, and he was no longer moaning. Without saying another word, the bloodstained cops jumped into the car and took off for the hospital.

Later, we learned that when the kid had tried to pull himself up on top of the fence, he slipped and fell. He grabbed out and both wrists came down on the barbs. The weight of his body, combined with his falling motion, created too much stress on the skin under his arms and it popped open. In the hospital, the kid received several pints of blood and it took literally hundreds of stitches to close his wounds. The injuries were severe enough to force him to spend several weeks in the hospital. More significantly, had the cops not gotten him to the hospital when they did, the kid probably would have died.

While the accident shook us up pretty badly, it didn't stop us from climbing the fence in the future. Nor did any of us make a big deal about the accident with our parents. Had we, we all knew they'd stop us from climbing over the fence. But, when we did climb the fence, we always remembered the kid's accident and each of us was more cautious than we otherwise would have been.

As for the kid, we rarely saw him. Either because of fear or embarrassment, he completely avoided the playground.

There was a major flaw in the layout of the playground. Because of the way the ball diamond was positioned, right field was very shallow—the fence was only a little over one hundred feet from home plate. Left field, one the other hand, was wide open, as the fence forming that end of the playground was over a thousand feet away.

Calling our playing field a "ball diamond" is gilding the lily a little. The city put up a backstop and mowed the weeds—that was it. We built a pitcher's mound by hauling dirt from what would become our horseshoe pits and we put in all of the base lines. Each morning we pounded in some homemade bases that we stored in the equipment room. While the set-up was fairly crude, for a bunch of kids who were accustomed to playing ball in backyards and fields, it was like having our own Yankee Stadium.

When we lined up to play ball, we were a sight to behold. Dressed in faded and patched Levis, white tee shirts, and sneakers, we looked like anything but baseball players. Even our caps weren't traditional. A few wore baseball caps. But others donned army fatigue caps, painters' hats, and the like.

If you had a regular baseball cap, there was a correct and incorrect way to wear it. Geeks left the bill of the cap the way it came from the store—sticking out like a duck's bill. Cool guys carefully molded the bill until it gently curved in from the sides, forming a perfect arc. In order to obtain the proper curve, you needed to spend hours rolling it tightly. If the curve was uneven, or if a crease developed in the bill, the cap was "ruined" and had to be discarded.

So, with our curved caps and mismatched "uniforms," we showed up every morning to choose sides and play ball. Each captain tried to make his selections so that he'd have a good balance between hitters and fielders. Because scoring was important, the hitters were usually taken first. In this regard, Johnny was normally the first player picked.

Johnny was the only left-hander in our group. It didn't take long for us to realize that this gave him a huge advantage. Lefties naturally hit the ball to right field, while right-handed batters tend to hit to left field. Even as young and puny as we were, a solid blast, hit high enough, cleared the fence in right. Thus, Johnny hit automatic home runs with relative ease. The only way the rest of us could hit a homer was either to slice the ball to right field—not so easy for a young kid—or drive it over the outfielder's head into

Simpler Times; Better Times

left or center and dash around the bases before the ball was thrown into home plate.

Tired of watching Johnny's home-run trots around the bases, the rest of us took aim at the right field fence. And, as we got older and stronger, we all routinely popped the ball over that fence. At that point, we changed our rules and decided that a ball hit over the right-field fence was a double, not a home run. We also switched from using a baseball to playing with a softball. Some of the softballs were so soft they resembled overripe peaches. The softballs didn't fly as far as a baseball, thereby reducing the number of home runs. With those decisions, Johnny's left-hand stance was no longer a big advantage.

There was one other problem with the short right-field fence. A house stood about twenty feet past the fence. The house had three windows facing the playground—one upstairs and two downstairs. As we started peppering hits over the fence, we broke a window at least once a week. At first, we chipped in and paid the neighbors for each broken pane of glass. But that wasn't a very good solution to our problem. It became expensive; the glass had to be constantly replaced; and the neighbors hardly felt secure in any room on that side of their house—a ball and broken glass could hit them at any time. Finally, the neighbors got fed up with the situation and placed plywood over the most vulnerable windows. Even then, they had to listen to the sound of balls crashing off the side of their house.

Before each game, we chose new sides. Our group was relatively small, and even when everyone showed up, we barely had enough players to field two baseball teams. We had the same problem when we played football.

In baseball, we solved the problem by making some players permanent fielders for a given game. Three or four guys simply didn't get a turn at bat. It wasn't an ideal solution, because none of us looked forward to spending an entire game in the field. But, if we wanted the game to be challenging, we had no other option.

On weekends or later in the evenings, our problem of too few players was partially solved by Dad and a few of the other men in the neighborhood. They came to the playground and played with us. When they did, they were treated just like any of the other guys. That is, they were chosen on teams like anyone else, played

Jack D. Atchison

the position the team captain assigned to them, and were given a place in the batting order just like any of the kids. And if they failed to catch a ball or goofed up at the plate, they were jeered just as loudly as anyone else.

Over the years, we played a lot of softball with Dad as our teammate. Dad, Gary, Johnny, and I played together on several softball teams sponsored by our church. We played in both slow-pitch and fast-pitch leagues. And, in each case, we viewed ourselves, not so much as father and sons, but as teammates. It was a great experience for all of us.

In football, we played with six- or seven-man teams. Instead of tackling, a runner was down if an opponent tapped, or tagged, him. With six-man teams, the tag could be with one hand anywhere on the runner's body. With seven or more players, the tag had to be with two hands and both hands had to hit the runner below the waist. Again, not an ideal solution.

There was another playground on the other side of West Tusc. It was used by the kids who lived in the "Projects." The Projects were low-income, apartment-style dwelling units. Many of the fathers of these kids didn't serve in the War and, therefore, they didn't qualify for low-down-payment, low-interest government mortgages. Thus, they had to rent rather than buy their living unit. Some of the kids in the Projects attended our school, but most went to another elementary school—one on their side of West Tusc.

They had the same problem we did—not enough players for either baseball or football. So, we started to arrange weekend games between our two groups. One week we'd visit their field, the next week they came to ours. These games were more spirited than our own intra-group games, because neighborhood pride was at stake. But, even with our reputations on the line, the primary purpose of each game was to have fun. If we were short a player or two, some of their guys joined our team and vice versa.

The football games were especially spirited contests. We had enough people for each side to field a full team of eleven players. So, we played tackle football. Neither side had any equipment, except for a few old leather helmets and some ancient shoulder pads. Our only protection was the three or four sweatshirts that each of us wore. As a consequence, bloody noses, split lips, cuts, and impressive bruises were commonplace.

The age differential between the youngest and oldest player was about three years. During the years these contests were held, we were all between the ages of eight and twelve. The age differential, combined with the fact that some kids mature earlier than others, resulted in big differences in the height and weight of the players. At any given time, you could find yourself lined up across from a kid who was six inches taller and fifty pounds heavier than you were (because of my size in those days, the converse was never true). When you did, it was a given that you were going to be knocked on your can by a forearm to the chops. These forearm blasts were known as "mucus makers" or "snot snarfers," because after the blast your nose ran and eyes watered for a half hour. One big kid could make a dozen little guys snarf snot for a whole game. It wasn't all bad. If you somehow survived the blast without too much damage, it was a great confidence booster. As a result of these frequent mismatches, most of us became fearless of physical confrontations, making us bully proof.

If anyone had kept score of the victories and defeats in these contests, and no one did, the guys from the Projects won more than their fair share of the football games; we had the edge in baseball; and, because of Johnny's shooting ability and ball-handling skills, we also probably came out on top in basketball. But all the games were close—one team never dominated the other.

By the time we reached the seventh grade, we all played on school teams. Here we had coaches, practice sessions, and spectators. While our skills improved as a result of participating on "organized" teams, the level of enjoyment didn't necessarily go up. Winning, rather than fun, became the prime objective. Practice sessions were work—drill, drill, and more drill. If you screwed up and made a mistake, you had a coach climbing down your throat. Oh, we still had a good time, and we actively sought to participate on these teams, but it wasn't the same as our informal pick-up games.

During the first year the playground was open, we discovered the game of horseshoes. It was an unlikely game for a group of young city kids to play, as it's usually associated with older, rural people. But we were fascinated by the game.

Every day, we rushed to the equipment room and got out the stakes and shoes. Traditional horseshoe pits are made from clay; our pits were just sand and dirt. The stakes were pounded in at a prescribed distance and, to make the dirt more receptive to the shoes, we watered it frequently, keeping it in a semi-mud form.

Horseshoes is a simple game. Each player has two shoes. The object is to toss them as close to the stake as possible. A ringer, where the shoe surrounds the stake, scores three points. A leaner, where the shoe leans against the stake, is worth two points. And a non-ringer, non-leaner is worth a single point, provided it lands within one span of a shoe from the stake and an opponent has no closer shoe. Thus, close does count in horseshoes.

When we started to play this game, none of us knew how to hold a shoe in order to control its flight or landing. We did know that in order to get a ringer the open end of the shoe had to face the stake when the shoe landed. If the closed end of the shoe hit first, the shoe just clanged off the stake and bounced too far away to count as a point. With this in mind, we experimented with all kinds of grips and throwing motions.

Our first attempts to toss the shoes were pretty pathetic. Some flew straight up in the air and landed halfway between the stakes. Others were thrown wildly to the right or the left, forcing onlookers to run for cover. A few even sailed over the playground fence and landed in the middle of Whipple Road. But we didn't give up. Hour after hour, we stuck with it. In the end, each of us settled on our own, individual style, one that we thought was effective. And after several weeks of intense play, we could usually get a leaner or ringer out of our two tosses.

One aspect of the game that made it especially entertaining was that it was ideal for wagering. We'd bet each other a nickel or dime per game. Because we were pretty evenly matched, no one ever walked away at the end of a day winning or losing more than a dime or so, but the exchange of nickels after each game made the contests more intense and exciting.

The adults in the neighborhood hated the game. First, when you played horseshoes as we did, you got covered with dirt. The pits were made of sand thoroughly soaked with water. Before each

Simpler Times; Better Times

toss, a player had to wipe his hands on his shirt or pants to remove any sand that might cause the shoe to slip from his grasp. By the end of the day, all players looked like they'd taken a mud bath. None of our mothers appreciated the impact of this game on their daily laundry requirements.

Then, from morning until night, they had to listen to the sound of horseshoes clanging together or banging against the stakes. Surprisingly, very few of the adults ever chose to join in these games. Maybe the reason that most of them stayed away from the game was that the few adults who tried their hand at it were usually soundly thrashed by an eight-year-old kid—not exactly an ego booster.

The adults celebrated the day that the playground closed for the season, because the closing silenced the horseshoes, meaning all was quiet until the start of the next summer.

Another thing about horseshoes. When Gary and I left Canton to go to Manistee Lake in the summer, we started playing horseshoes at the cottage. Gramp bought us some stakes and shoes and we set up pits between the cottage and the lake.

When we first started playing, the games were just between Gramp, Gary, and me. But it didn't take long for the clang of the shoes to draw our neighbors to the horseshoe pits. Many of the neighbors were wheat and corn farmers from Indiana. They came to the lake and spent the time between planting and harvesting the crops as a vacation. Being rural folks, they knew all about horseshoes and were avid fans of the game. They were also surprised that two young city kids were playing horseshoes.

We set up a few benches facing the pits. Anyone who wanted to play took a seat on the benches and waited for their turn. When one team lost, another took its place. The winners continued to play until they were defeated.

Gary and I took our places on the benches with the rest of the players—most of whom were men in their sixties—and were treated as their equals in the game of horseshoes. As the games progressed, the assembled group talked politics, traded stories, teased and taunted one another, and told fishing tales. The horseshoe pits became the gathering point and social center for all the men on our side of the lake.

Jack D. Atchison

Over the years, all of these older men became Gary's and my good friends. They didn't treat us like kids, but as worthy competitors—as we managed to win our fair share of games. In the process, we learned a great deal about a whole host of subjects—knowledge imparted to us by our more worldly and experienced "friends." And both Gary and I were comfortable in their presence. We came to appreciate their humor, wisdom, and good cheer.

In the winter, we had to find other sports and other venues. A string of city-owned parks runs through the middle of Canton. One of these parks features a good-sized lagoon. In the winter, the lagoon and Meyers Lake, a small local lake that had an amusement park on one of its shores, became our ice rinks—venues for ice tag and our bastardized version of hockey.

Most of our makeshift hockey games were played on Meyers Lake. Friends of our neighbor, Jack, lived at the lake and we used their house as home base for meeting, changing clothes, and using the bathroom.

The lake was actively used by ice fishermen, who cut holes in the ice and put little shanty-like structures over them. Using their shanties to shelter them from the cold and wind, the fishermen sat at a given hole watching their bobbers and drinking hot coffee, probably with a little alcohol added to compensate for the boring nature of ice fishing. After a day or two at a given hole, they changed locations, abandoning the old fishing hole. When we skated on the lake, we had to dodge the shanties and half-drunk fishermen who were scattered all over the lake's surface.

As with most of the games we played, our hockey equipment left a great deal to be desired. We had a few hockey sticks and a puck. Those who didn't have hockey sticks used brooms and tree branches as substitutes. No one had any pads or hockey gloves. Nor did we have real goals, instead a couple of garbage cans set at each end of the playing area served as goal markers.

After we chose up sides, the slowest, least accomplished skater on each side was designated to be goalie. This was incentive enough to practice your skating. The goalie's job was one to avoid at all cost. Without pads, and wearing only wool-knit mittens or gloves, it stung like heck when you blocked a shot, especially if it was launched by a guy wielding a real hockey stick. Nor was it a rare occurrence for a goalie to get whacked in the head by the hard-rubber puck or by a stick. And when several players converged on the goal, the goalie often was driven into one of the two metal garbage cans that made up the goal.

Just being a player in this game was no great shakes either. In the afternoon, the sun warmed the ice, which was then covered by a thin layer of water. Every time someone knocked you down, you slid through the water and your clothes got a little wetter. As the day progressed, and the intensity of the sun's rays diminished, the temperature dropped and your wet clothes started to freeze. By the end of the day, you walked stiff-legged because your pants were caked with ice.

If that wasn't enough, everyone got nicked-up playing the game. Each check and each whack with a stick produced a nice bruise or bump. But the worst bumps and bruises, and occasional cuts, came from skates.

We wore an odd collection of skates. Some had hockey skates; others wore figure skates; and two of the guys in our group used racing skates with their long, pointed blades. During a game, you invariably got kicked with a skate. Without any padding, it stung when the hit came from a hockey or figure skate, but those racing skates were darn near lethal. Once you got struck by one of them, you learned to give their wearer a wide berth.

If the truth be known, none of us liked to play hockey. But we felt obligated to give it a try each year. It was a traditional winter sport, and you felt like you were a sissy if you didn't at least take a stab at it.

One day, we showed up at Meyers Lake for our annual attempt to play hockey. Two of the guys, both practical jokers, had arrived early and set up the playing area. They shoveled snow off the ice, clearing a rectangular space that was about eighty-feet long by forty-feet wide. Garbage-can goals were placed at each end of the cleared area.

As we laced up our skates, these two guys seemed especially anxious for us to take to the ice. They had big grins on their faces and exhibited unusually good cheer. This should have served as a warning, because neither of them liked the game and

Jack D. Atchison

constantly complained every time we played. But it didn't. We all put on our skates and hit the ice.

We were warming up—remembering how to stand on our skates and getting a feel for the ice—when I discovered the reason behind their grins. As I skated across the center of the playing area, intent on keeping my balance, the ice gave way beneath me. Suddenly, I found myself in ice-cold water. I'd had the good sense to throw my arms out when I felt the ice crack and, as I fell downward into the water, my outstretched arms hit the ice, keeping my head from going under the water's surface.

When I hit the water, I let out a war whoop that could be heard miles away. God, the water was cold. In a reaction that only males experience, my testicles immediately sought protection from the cold and retreated into my body. I was afraid that if I didn't get out of the water fast, the darn things would end up in my throat.

The other guys reacted to my situation and skated over to pull me from the water. I yelled to them to be careful, because they too could fall in if the ice cracked any further. If that happened, I'd lose my hold on the edges of the hole in which I found myself and I'd sink under the water. Dad had warned both Gary and me that the biggest hazard in falling through the ice is that a person can go under and, when he comes to the surface, finds that he's under the ice and can't locate the hole in the surface again. If that occurs, the person will drown.

The others listened to me and stopped hurrying toward the edge of the hole. I asked one of the guys to lie down and shove his hockey stick in my direction. He did. I grabbed one end of the stick and, as two guys held the other end, used it to drag myself out of the icy water. As soon as I hit the air, I started to shiver, and, by the time I reached Jack's friend's house, I was starting to turn blue. After I removed the wet clothes, it took better than an hour before the shivering stopped and my body temperature returned to normal.

Later, I learned from the, now sheepish, practical jokers that the hole was no accident. They thought it would be funny to build the hockey area around an abandoned fishing hole. They found one with barely an inch of new ice formed over it. They shoveled the snow from the area around the hole, leaving it dead center in the middle of the playing area. Without any awareness of the potentially serious consequences that could occur, they hoped

Simpler Times; Better Times

someone would fall through the hole, thinking it would be a great joke. After they learned what could happen, that a person could easily drown, they were sorry.

The good part about the incident was that we canceled the hockey game and didn't reschedule another one that year.

When the shopping center at the end of the street opened, it included a small, twenty-four-lane bowling alley on the lower level. In order to attract business in the off hours, the proprietor started a league for kids. Our group of guys immediately signed up. In fact, we were the only members of the league. As league members, we could bowl as many games as we wanted during the hours from eight o'clock to noon on Saturday mornings for twenty-five cents a game.

In those days, there were no automatic pin setters in bowling alleys. Instead, a person—a pin-boy—stood between two lanes and set the pins. After a player threw his or her ball, the pin-boy picked up the ball and sent it back to the bowler. Then, he picked up the fallen pins and loaded them in a rack. The rack had a slot for each pin position. A mechanism mechanically inserted the pins into a slot as the pin-boy dropped them into the rack. Assuming the player didn't throw a strike with the first ball, after the second ball, the rest of the pins—a total of ten—were loaded and the rack was lowered by pulling a lanyard, resetting the pins for the next player. In the case of our league, if one of us set the pins, the price was reduced to twenty cents a game. So, naturally, we took turns setting pins.

When we first started bowling, setting pins was hard work. The pins were fairly heavy for an eight- or nine-year-old kid, and we had to keep hopping back and forth between two lanes. Older pin-boys could lift two pins in each hand, but our hands weren't big enough for us to do that, so we had to lift one pin at a time. As such, we needed to move twice as fast if we were to keep pace with the older guys and not slow the game down. By the time we set an entire game—ten frames for each of up to four players per lane—we worked up a pretty good sweat and our arms were dead tired.

As for our bowling, initially, we stank. More balls ran down the gutters than stayed on the lane. Part of the problem was

Jack D. Atchison

that we were barely strong enough to roll the ball. The other part of the problem was our tendency to plunge into things without taking any lessons or receiving any instructions. We just experimented with different balls, grips, and throwing motions until something worked and the ball stayed on the lane. Later, as we sought to improve, we learned from older, experienced bowlers, and our form got better and our scores improved.

One reason we sought to improve was that it didn't take us long to start betting against each other. If you didn't get better, you either had to steer clear of the bowling alley or you had to be prepared to lose all your money. So, improvement it had to be.

All of us worked hard on our game, bowling as many frames as we could afford. In order to earn money to pay for these games, we set pins. Setting pins for adult leagues was a real experience. The stronger male bowlers threw their bowling balls with a lot of power, causing pins to fly all over the pit when the ball struck. If a pin-boy wasn't careful, he got nailed by a flying pin, some of which careened all the way out of the pit. And the adults demanded that the pins be set without delay, meaning the pin-boy had to work at a fast and constant pace.

Offsetting the demand to work fast, and the flying pins, were the rewards. A pin-boy received ten cents a game. For setting pins for three games for eight bowlers—the standard for a league—the pin-boy earned two dollars and forty cents for about three hours of work—not bad when you consider that the minimum wage was about fifty cents per hour at the time. A good pin-boy earned another couple bucks in tips from the league bowlers, bringing his total take for the three hours to over four dollars. In our case, that meant our earnings from a single night paid for twenty games of bowling.

We also learned how to take care of good tippers and to get even with stingy ones. We always had a clothes hanger with us in the pit. When it was a good tipper's turn to bowl, we used the clothes hanger, which was invisible to the bowlers because it blended in with the black background of the pit, to knock over reluctant pins, improving the good tipper's score. With a poor tipper, a wad of chewing gum stuffed into the thumb hole of the bowling ball after the last frame was sweet revenge.

Simpler Times; Better Times

We spent a lot of time in the bowling alley. Because it was just at the end of the street, our parents didn't worry about us hanging out there, even when it was well after dark. With all the practice we got, each of us became better-than-average bowlers, even when measured by adult standards. By the time we were in the eighth or ninth grade, most of us had our own bowling balls and shoes, and bowling became an important part of our wintertime and summer-break activities.

Jann was about six or seven years old. A group of kids were playing in a neighbor's yard. One of Jann's favorite games involved either Gary or me lying on our backs with our knees drawn up to our chests. Jann sat on our feet and we kicked forward, straightened our legs, and propelled her into the air. If we got enough thrust from our legs, Jann soared a distance of six to seven feet before hitting the ground. If things worked out the way they were supposed to, she landed on her feet, laughed with glee, and rushed back for another "rocket ride."

Each time Jann positioned herself for a rocket ride, she encouraged us to "push harder," so that she could "fly farther." On one of her rides, she soared high into the air, did more or less a somersault, and, rather than landing on her feet, hit the ground at an awkward angle, hands forward. Instead of hearing her cheerful peal of laughter, we heard a wail of pain as she rolled on the ground clutching her arm.

Gary and I ran to her side. Tears were streaming down her cheeks and she cried that her arm hurt. Gary said: "I think her arm might be broken. We should get Mom and Dad."

At the time, Mom and Dad were down the street at the bowling alley participating in their weekly league. Gary and I were supposed to be baby-sitting Jann and Mike.

"Okay," I said to Gary. "You hold Jann's arm and I'll go get Mom and Dad." I carefully transferred her arm from my hands to Gary's and ran down the street toward the shopping center where the bowling alley was located.

When I entered the bowling alley, I spotted Mom and Dad's team. As I approached them, Mom was on one lane and Dad on the other, both getting ready to deliver their bowling balls. I walked up and glanced at their score sheet. They were in the fourth frame of their third, and last, game. The score sheet indicated that their team had won the first game and their opponents had been victors in the second. Thus, the third game would decide who won the match. I could tell that the match had been hotly contested, as members of both teams were urging their teammates on, cheering or moaning with each roll of a ball. Moreover, Dad's score was one of his best of the year, as was Mom's.

Now, I really loved my little sister and was truly concerned about her arm, but this was bowling. As a bowler myself, I knew I wouldn't want someone to interrupt a good score. So, as any good sport would do, I took a seat in the back of the bowling alley and watched the remainder of the game.

When the game ended—Mom's and Dad's team victorious—as Mom was changing her shoes, she glanced up to see me approaching her. "What are you doing here? You're supposed to be baby-sitting the kids."

"Well," I said, shifting back-and-forth from foot-to-foot, "we had a little accident."

"What?" Concern was evident on Mom's face.

"Uh...Jann might have a broken arm."

"Oh, no," Mom said, grabbing me by the arm and dragging me toward where Dad was standing. "Where is she?"

Mom was darn near pulling my arm out of the socket. If she didn't slow down, I'd have a broken arm, too. "Don't worry, Mom. Jann is with Gary."

Mom grabbed Dad by one his arms and propelled both of us out the door of the bowling alley, explaining the situation to a somewhat confused Dad as we walked. We made record time from the bowling alley to the neighbor's yard.

When we reached Jann and Gary, Jann's tears had dried, but she still appeared to be experiencing quite a bit of pain.

"What took so long?" Gary asked.

Mom shot me a look that was both inquisitive and withering.

I shrugged my shoulders. "They were in the middle of a game."

"You waited until your game was over?" Gary asked Mom, amazement in his voice. "Didn't Jack tell you that her arm might be broken."

Simpler Times; Better Times

"No...no," I said before Mom could respond. "I didn't want to spoil their game, so I didn't tell them until they were finished."

"When did you get to the bowling alley?" Mom asked, fixing me with a look that could kill.

I shrugged. "Fourth frame...last game."

"You just sat there for six frames while your sister was lying here hurt?" Mom asked, shaking her head in disbelief.

"Yeah," I said sheepishly. "It seemed like a good idea at the time." I was going to add that a broken arm isn't exactly life-threatening, but thought better of it.

As we led Jann to the car for a trip to the hospital, Mom said, "We'll talk about this later, young man."

Jann's arm was broken. She returned home in a cast, which she wore with pride, like a badge of courage—a true tomboy.

As for me, I made no headway in convincing either Mom or Dad that it wasn't proper to interrupt a good bowling score for something as trivial as a broken arm.

By the time we reached the third grade, a great deal of our sporting activities, particularly swimming, occurred at the YMCA.

The YMCA was an old, brick building with a cafeteria in the basement; a gymnasium, auditorium, swimming pool, and lockers on the first floor; and, a running track, weight room, and general purpose rooms on the second. The rest of the building had rooms where transient guests could stay and other facilities that were of no interest or use to kids. On Saturdays, and certain weekdays in the summer, the primary facilities of the YMCA were reserved for kids under the age of eighteen.

The annual fee for a family to use the YMCA's facilities was around twenty-five dollars. For another twenty-five cents a month, a kid was given a locker—actually a wire basket that fit into a non-reserved locker—for storing shoes and gym gear, a combination lock for the locker, and towels. When we entered the YMCA, we went to a counter, surrendered our membership card, fetched our basket and a towel from an attendant, and then found an open locker which we used for the day. We got our card back when we returned the towel to the attendant.

If a kid's family couldn't afford the annual membership fee, or the monthly locker fee, the YMCA had provisions for waiving such charges. Thus, the YMCA was an affordable facility for every kid in the city. As such, it was always packed.

The swimming pool was the YMCA's biggest attraction. It was an indoor, twenty-five-yard pool. The water was always warm and heavily chlorinated; so much so that if you were in the water more than a few minutes, your eyes became bloodshot and burned as a result of the chlorine. The YMCA was for males only and the policy was that suits were not worn in the pool. Instead, all swimmers swam in the nude. During the times that kids used the pool, you'd see a small army of boys running back and forth from the locker room to the pool, their bodies bare to the world.

Before entering the pool, everyone had to shower. When we left the shower room, one of the YMCA instructors rubbed our wrists and ankles with his thumb to see if we were clean enough to enter the pool. If his rubbing produced small dirt balls—and with many of the guys it did—it meant another trip to the showers. Neatness and cleanliness were not our strong suits.

In order to use the swimming pool, a kid first had to prove that he could swim one length of the pool and jump off the diving board and reach the side of the pool. The YMCA offered lessons to teach kids basic swimming skills. One hour each day was reserved for these lessons.

Even if a kid knew how to swim, he had to attend one of these sessions and pass the benchmark requirements. If he did, he was designated a "minnow," allowing him restricted access to the pool. In order to remove restrictions, and to get to the point where you could swim without intense supervision, you had to pass other skill tests. As each test was passed, you received a new designation, moving from minnow, to sunfish, to dolphin, and so on, up to shark, the highest designation, allowing the least restrictive access to the pool.

The beginners' classes were real panic sessions for kids who had not previously learned how to swim. The first trick was to get them to put their faces under water. It took many of them weeks to overcome their fear and get past this fundamental first stage. Even then, many continued to swim in dog-paddle fashion, holding their heads up, so their faces would stay out of the water. Because of the strong chlorine, kids who knew how to swim also tended to keep their eyes clear of the water. The result was that

Simpler Times; Better Times

many of us developed rather unorthodox swimming strokes—ones that made it difficult, if not impossible, to swim more than a few lengths of the pool without becoming fatigued.

Fear of the water became most dangerous when kids had to pass the test of jumping off the diving board and reaching the side of the pool. In order to cut down the distance they had to swim, kids tried to jump as near to the pool's edge as they could. They planned their jump in order to land about a foot from the edge, allowing them to grab the side of the pool without actually swimming a single stroke. More than one kid misjudged his jump and clipped his chin on the tiled edge of the pool. A few misjudged so much that they actually landed out of the water, crashing onto the pool deck.

The length-of-the-pool swim test also saw its fair share of miscues. In order to remove the temptation to walk the last few yards, the test started in the shallow end and ended in the deep end of the pool. A lot of kids did alright until they reached the point where, if they stood upright, the water was over their head. When they hit this point, they panicked. Some simply stopped swimming and grabbed onto the side of the pool. Others, however, overcome with panic, hyperventilated, lost their breath, and started sinking, causing a lifeguard to jump in and pull them out. If this happened to a kid, and it was not an infrequent occurrence, the kid's fear of water not only returned, it intensified. One of our friends had it happen to him and, despite words of encouragement from the rest of us; it took him months to get to the point where he could negotiate a single length of the pool.

Like many of the kids, I disliked the burning sensation the chlorine produced in my eyes. To avoid the chlorine, I stopped using the freestyle, or crawl, stroke and almost exclusively used a backstroke, allowing me to keep my face out of the water. This worked out okay until it came time to pass the requirements of the lifesaving designation, a credential needed to qualify as a lifeguard. One of the requirements was the ability to swim, nonstop, for a mile, or about seventy lengths of the YMCA's pool.

In order to test my ability to pass this requirement, I took a practice shot at swimming a mile. Using my rather poor imitation of the freestyle stroke, I was exhausted before I hit the half-mile mark. I knew I couldn't make an entire mile swimming freestyle without drastically altering my stroke, something that would take months to do. I didn't want to wait months to get the lifesaving designation.

On the day of my official test, I walked up to the instructor who was conducting the test and asked: "Do the rules say you have to swim freestyle the entire way?"

"I don't know. No one's ever asked me before. Let me check the rule book."

He got the book and found the section dealing with the test requirements.

"It just says you have to swim a mile without touching bottom. It's silent about the stroke that you can use. So, I guess any stroke is acceptable as long as you don't touch bottom."

"What about stopping along the way?" I asked.

"You can't touch bottom."

"I know that. But what if I float or tread water along the way. Is that alright?"

He looked in the rule book again. "It doesn't say anything about floating or treading water."

"So, am I allowed to do both of those things?" I wanted to be sure of the rules.

"It appears so."

When I got into the pool, I swam the first few laps freestyle then turned over onto my back and started using a backstroke, which I used for the rest of the mile. Throughout the mile swim, I stopped frequently and would either float or tread water for awhile, so I wouldn't get fatigued. The only problem with this approach was that it slowed down the time that it took to complete the entire mile. In fact, it took me more than twice as long as the next slowest swimmer.

When I finished, the instructor wasn't very happy—he'd had to sit there the entire time. He said: "If I'm ever drowning, I hope you're not the kid who has lifeguard duty that day. I'll be fish bait before you get to me." That was probably true, but I still passed all the requirements.

When I was about eight years old, Johnny got a bike—an affair that was rigged with training wheels—and he spent his after-school hours riding up and down the sidewalk on our street (his

Simpler Times; Better Times

street didn't have sidewalks). As we watched him pedal his way down the street, a smile of superiority on his face, Gary and I wanted bikes of our own. Each night, we bugged Dad to buy us bicycles.

Apparently fed up with our incessant whining, Dad announced one Saturday morning that he was going out to buy us bikes. I sat on the porch and watched as he drove down the street and headed for the store to purchase the objects of our desires. As I waited for Dad to return, my head was filled with images of a brand new bicycle—brilliant-red, with white pinstripes, bright chrome handlebars, and no training wheels.

Well, Dad's idea of what constituted a "new bike" was somewhat different from mine. Always frugal, he visited a secondhand store where he was able to buy two bicycles—a little one and big one—for twenty bucks. Not twenty bucks each; twenty bucks for both. They were dented and dinged. The handlebars were more rust than chrome. The tires were flat. The little one was red. The big one was a hodgepodge of colors and no two parts were from the same bike.

When Dad unloaded these relics from the trunk of the car, my heart dropped into my shoes. He must have seen the disappointment in my eyes. He pounded me on the back and said: "Hey, cheer up. With a little elbow grease and a fresh coat of paint, these bikes will look like they came off a showroom floor."

Yeah, sure, I thought, none too convinced. I'd seen Dad's handiwork before. Our baseball bats were held together with nails and friction tape. The webbing in our gloves consisted of shoelaces; instead of leather. Our basketballs and footballs had more patches than a teenager has zits. All were advertised to be "just like they came off a showroom floor."

During the next week, Dad spent every night in the basement working on the bicycles. He repaired the chains, popped out dents in the fenders, sanded the rust off the handlebars, patched the tires, and painted both bikes barn-red. In the end, they sure as heck weren't pretty, but they would do. Not that Gary and I had any real choice in the matter. It was these two contraptions or nothing.

There was another problem with the bikes. The little one was too small—the kind of thing a baby would ride, or so I thought. Gary thought the little bike was fine and it became his. The other bike was big enough. In fact, it was too big. When I sat on the seat, my feet dangled a good two inches away from the pedals. No matter how much I stretched, I couldn't touch the pedals. This was a real problem. Gary had laid claim to the little bike and wouldn't let me touch it. The big one was mine, whether I could reach the pedals or not.

What a mess! I had a bike, but I couldn't get on the darn thing. Every time I put one foot on a pedal and tried to swing my other foot over the seat, the bike fell, sending me sprawling onto the ground. My legs just weren't long enough. Now, I had to watch Johnny ride back and forth, with Gary wobbling along behind him, as I sat on the ground and watched the wheels of my fallen bike spin in the air.

Houses were still being constructed on our street. A flatbed trailer that was used to transport a bulldozer was parked halfway up the hill, three houses away from ours. I walked my bike up the hill, propped it against the side of the trailer, and climbed onto the trailer's bed. The trailer bed was about level with the seat of the bicycle. I grabbed the handlebars, straightened the bike, and jumped from the trailer onto the bicycle. Suddenly, I was rocketing down the hill, trying to maintain my balance—as this was my first time on a bike—with my feet dangling two inches away from either pedal. Well, I didn't go more than twenty yards before I crashed in the middle of the street.

Undaunted, I returned to the trailer and tried again. Same result. Twenty yards; then crash.

On about the fifteenth attempt, having made some progress on each preceding try, I maintained my balance and sped down the street, picking up speed as I went. It was at this point that another problem reared its ugly head. With my feet two inches away from the pedals, there was no way to apply the darn brakes. Here I was, setting a new neighborhood speed record on a bicycle, the rock-filled swamp at the end of the street looming ever closer, and no brakes. Geez!

Before I knew what was happening, the road came to an abrupt end. The bike, with me aboard, soared into the air and crashed in the swamp. When I got to my feet, and after determining that my arms and legs were still attached to my body, something I was none too confident about when the bike hit the rocks in the swamp, I knew I had to figure out a way to stop the darned bike. Many more crashes like the one I had just experienced, and my bike-riding days would soon be over.

I walked the bike back up the hill. On my next trip, I waited until I was one house away from the swamp and then turned sharply to the right. The bike shot off the street and into the neighbor's front yard, at which point, I jumped. I landed in the relatively soft grass and the bike crashed some ten feet away. Not an ideal solution, but better than the rocks in the swamp.

After several of these maneuvers, I got pretty good at jumping off the bike before it crashed. I did discover one real hazard in this approach, however. A nasty little bar runs from the seat to the handlebars on a boy's bike. If you don't clear this bar when you jump, you're in for a heck of a surprise. With no warning you land on the bar and find that your testicles are about to be driven up around your shoulders—not a pleasant sensation. When that happens, you're pretty sure you're about to die. The air leaves your body. Your stomach turns a thousand flip-flops. Sweat breaks out on your forehead. You desperately need to puke. And you realize that the high, soprano scream that is filling the air is coming from you.

I guarantee you that a guy only needs to land on that bar once before he develops some amazing skills. I found I could leap off a bicycle seat and achieve a cruising altitude of ten feet or more, even with both hands grabbing my crotch in a protective fashion, every time I even thought of that bar.

Anyway, after my first day with the bike, I decided Dad and I needed to talk. Covered with an impressive array of colorful bruises and cuts, I greeted him as soon as he got home from work.

"About that bike, Dad?"

"What about it?"

"Let me show you something."

We walked to the drive where the bike was lying on its side. I motioned for him to follow me to the parked trailer. When we got there, I said: "Watch what happens when I get on the bike."

I climbed up on the trailer, jumped on the bike, sped down the street, and leaped high into the air as the bike crashed into the neighbor's front yard. After I walked back up the hill, I asked Dad: "Did you notice anything about that ride?"

Dad laughed. "Yeah, you don't know how to stop the bike."

"Do you think the fact that my feet don't reach the pedals might have something to do with that?" I asked; the picture of innocence and reason.

Dad scratched his head. "Get back on the bike." He held it as I did. He laughed again. "I see what you mean." My feet were swinging in the air—a good two inches from the pedals.

"I can fix that," Dad said.

He went to the basement where he puttered around for a good hour. When he emerged from the basement, his hands were full of pieces of wood, nuts, and bolts. We went to the bike where, using nuts and bolts, he proceeded to affix the pieces of wood to the pedals of the bike. When he was finished, the pedals were about six inches thick.

"Try it now," Dad said, holding the bike for me. I put my foot on one of the pedals and swung onto the bike. It took several tries, and some spectacular falls, but the pedals worked. I finally could ride the bike without using the trailer and without crashing to stop it.

A few years later, Gary and I did get new bicycles. But the old red monsters weren't thrown out. Both Jann and Mike learned to ride on the little one. And many years later, Dad could be seen pedaling around the neighborhood on the bigger bike—sans wooden pedals. One thing about Dad, he always got his money's worth with every purchase—even from secondhand stores.

While our purpose in playing games was to simply have fun, we indirectly benefited in other ways.

All the games were organized and conducted by the kids who participated in them. We made up and enforced the rules of the game; found and defined the playing field; rounded up the players; and selected the teams—all without any input or interference from adults.

Many of the contests involved twenty or more players. Each one of us had the opportunity to assemble a group and take the leadership role in organizing and conducting a given game. None of us had to wait around for someone else to take the initiative. Thus, as we conducted these games, every one of us developed good organizational and leadership skills.

Most of the games involved teams. The nature of these games was such that no one player, or even a couple of exceptionally skilled players, could carry a team. We rapidly realized, if our team had a weak point, our opponents would discover and exploit it, sending our team down in defeat. So, we learned to analyze the skills and capabilities of each of our teammates and to support the weakest among us. We knew, if we shored up our weak spots with good teamwork, we would increase our chances of prevailing in the game. These simple games taught us the real meaning and essence of teamwork and the need to be a good team member.

Each of the games employed strategies. In order to win, a team had to anticipate its opponent's moves and devise means of counteracting them. If a team was on offense, it had to develop plans for overcoming the other side's defense. Our attack plans were amazingly elaborate, involving decoys, flanking moves, feints, massing of troops, and other gambits. On defense, we developed a variety of formations and complex schemes to block an opponent's attacks. Because the composition of the teams changed every game, so did the strategies. We learned that what worked against one group of guys failed against another. Through the planning and execution of hundreds of these game plans, we learned to analyze a problem logically, and each of us became skilled in gaming strategy.

Each game required different skills. A kid's strength in one game was his weakness in the next. As such, no one was a winner all the time nor was anyone a constant loser. Everyone had his chance to savor victory and we all had to endure defeat. Thus, we learned to be resilient. While none of us liked to lose, we accepted our losses, because we knew the tide would turn and, sooner or later, we'd again taste success. This simple lesson served all of us well in later years, because none of us had the tendency to let momentary setbacks get us down.

We also teased everyone. If a ball flew over your head or bounced through your legs, you heard the chant "no glove, no glove" from all your teammates and opponents. A strikeout or pop fly brought shouts of "no stick, no stick" from everyone on the field. By teasing both the best and worst player, no one was singled out and everyone received equal treatment.

So, while our basic purpose for playing games was to have fun, it was through games that we learned many of our most important life skills. If we had not had the opportunity to play informal games with our peers, it would have been more difficult, maybe impossible, to learn leadership, teamwork, resiliency, and gamesmanship—skills critical to our future success as adults. Moreover, play was perhaps the best way for us to learn that by exerting sufficient effort and with support from others, we always have a chance to win—no matter what the challenges we must face.

CHAPTER NINE

Passive activities, like watching television or listening to records, did not factor into our schedules or occupy our time, because, until sometime in 1952, no one in our neighborhood even owned a television or stereo. And when we finally got our own television in 1954, it was still not much of a factor because the reception was terrible, the screen small, and the scheduling of programs for children limited.

We did listen to the radio. During the day, we followed the Cleveland Indians and Cleveland Browns, listening to almost every game, especially in 1954 when the Indians beat the hated Yankees during the regular season and met the New York Giants in the World Series. We would meet at someone's house, gather around the radio, and listen to the play-by-play broadcast. While the game was on, we would trade baseball cards, guzzle down sodas or lemonade, and clown around.

In those days, players stayed with one team for most of their career, as trades were infrequent, and we followed the same players year-after-year. As such, a great bond of loyalty grew between the fans and players. Ask almost any male who grew up during the forties and fifties and chances are he will still know the names of the players on his favorite team. The 1954 Indians were:

Relief pitchers: Don Mossi and Ray Narleski.

Starting Pitchers: Bob Feller, Bob Lemon, Early Wynn, and Mike Garcia.

Catcher: Jim Hegan.

Infield: Luke Easter, Bobby Avila, Lou Boudreau, Al Rosen.

Outfield: Larry Doby, Vic Wertz, Minnie Minoso.

The 1954 Indians had the best record in the American League. We all thought they would easily win the World Series that year. When the Series started, on game days, every boy in our school was stricken with a serious malady that kept us home sick, and we had excuse notes from our parents to prove it.

Jack D. Atchison

As it was, the Series made us truly sick. Our Indians were swept by the New York Giants, losing four games to none. The symbol of the Series was Willie Mays' over-the-shoulder-catch that robbed Vic Wertz of an extra-base hit in the first game. The catch was, and still is, regarded as one of the best ever in World Series history, and serves as constant thorn in the side of all Indians' fans. Every kid in the neighborhood walked around dazed by the speed with which the Giants dispatched our team.

Collecting baseball cards was a big deal. If you didn't have a good stock of cards, you were shutout of the trading that occurred every day during the summer and early fall. And our trading skills would have put any used car salesman to shame.

Baseball cards were packaged with bubblegum. To get the cards, you had to buy the gum. For a nickel, you got a rock-hard, square piece of gum and about five cards. The gum was pretty nasty stuff, but since you had forked out a hard-earned nickel to buy it, you chewed it. It is probably one of the reasons all us had more cavities than we had teeth. As for the cards, you never knew which cards you were going to get, which was part of the excitement of the whole process. The card company stuffed the packs with lots of cards of utility players and has-beens, but provided a much lesser number of cards featuring the top stars. So, if you wanted a Mantle, Mays, Feller, or Ted Williams card, you had to buy lots of bubblegum.

The object of trading was to assemble a complete set of cards for each of your favorite teams—a card for every player on the roster. To do that, you needed a lot of trading bait, so you started out buying as many packs of gum as you could afford. You really didn't care which cards you got at the onset, because you needed them all. When you got duplicates—as you surly would—you set them aside for future trades. Because none of us had much money, it took months before you were in a position to negotiate a trade. That was okay, because in the meantime you were still filling in the numerous holes in your collection.

When you finally got a somewhat complete collection of most of the top teams—a process that took most kids a year to accomplish—you were ready for the real fun. Suppose you needed a Bob Feller card to complete your collection of the Indians roster.

Simpler Times; Better Times

You knew Larry had an extra Feller card, but he wouldn't trade it for anything but a Mantle card. You didn't have a duplicate Mantle, but you knew Pete had one. You went to Pete and asked him what he wanted for a Mantle and he said he would trade it for a Mays and a Reese. You had an extra Mays card, but no Reese. Lee had a Reese and he wanted a Berra for it. You traded Lee one of your extra Berra cards for his Reese. Then you traded the Reese and Mays to Pete for his Mantle. Finally, you traded the Mantle to Larry for the Feller that you initially wanted. It could take days to complete that one round of trades. And, as occurred more often than not, the next time you bought a pack of gum, it contained a Feller card.

    The real art of the trading game was not letting the other guys know which duplicate cards you held and which ones you needed. If they knew one of your cards was a duplicate, its value plunged to rock bottom. If they knew you desperately needed a given card, its value skyrocketed, even if they had several duplicates of that card. So sometimes you traded for a card you really didn't want or need and other times you acted totally disinterested in a card that you would have willingly traded your left testicle for. The whole object was to keep everyone guessing.

    Card trading consumed hours and hours of our time every season and we never tired of it. There's nothing better than palming off a useless, duplicate card for a valued gem. One trade like that could make a whole summer worthwhile.

    While we didn't have television, we did have movie theaters. The two main theaters—the Palace and Ohio—were located just off the city square in downtown Canton. Every Saturday they featured matinees for kids.

    It was a little over three miles from our house to the downtown square. For a dime we could get a round-trip pass on the city bus. We could catch the bus at the edge of the shopping center parking lot and it would drop us off at the square. Another dime got us into the theater and a nickel bought a bag of popcorn or box of candy. Therein was the rub. Our weekly allowance was a quarter. If we took the bus, bought a theater ticket, and a box of popcorn, we shot our whole allowance in one day. That was okay if we had some work that would add a few coins to our pockets, but when there was no work, or if we were just cheap, blowing a quarter in one day didn't make a lot of sense. When we analyzed the whole deal, there was only one logical answer—skip the bus and walk.

With that in mind, we told our parents we needed to catch an early bus so we wouldn't miss the previews and started hoofing it downtown. When we started out on these Saturday morning treks, it was just Johnny, Gary and me. But along the way others joined us and by the time we cleared the boundaries of the school district we would have anywhere from ten to fifteen guys in the group—and that was important.

First, walking three-plus miles is quite a hike for an eight- to nine-year-old kid and the more guys in the group; the easier the walk seemed to be. Second, and more importantly, the more guys in the group the sweeter the day would be.

By skipping the bus, each guy in the group saved a dime. With fifteen guys, we collectively saved a buck-fifty. If each of us chipped in two cents out of our dime savings, we had thirty cents. With that, we could buy six boxes of candy or popcorn and split it among us. Since the boxes were pretty big, we each got a good amount. Even better, we got several kinds of candy, which was way better than eating a whole box of the same stuff. And we each had eight cents, plus the additional five cents we did not individually spend on candy, making our total cost for the day twelve cents each rather than a quarter, leaving each of us with thirteen cents to spend later in the week—one sweet deal.

It didn't matter what time we arrived at the Ohio; but when we were going to the Palace, it was imperative to get there a little early. The Palace had a balcony and the best seats were in the balcony—seats the early arrivals got. The balcony seats held two advantages. First, you got a better view of the screen. Second, you weren't in the floor-level seats.

If you sat on the floor-level, below the balcony, you could count on being bombed with popcorn and candy several times during the movies. Any time there was a kissing scene—and unfortunately every movie, even westerns, seemed to have at least one—a balcony full of boys would boo and hiss and launch popcorn and candy at the screen. Of course none of the missiles ever hit the screen; instead, they rained down on the hapless chumps sitting in floor-level seats. Thus, when headed for the Palace, we ran the last half-mile—it was better to be a little winded than it was to dig sticky Milk Duds out of your hair.

In the early days, all films were in black-and-white. Most matinees started with a serial film of a western—a new episode every week, which was the hook to keep you coming back Saturday after Saturday. The serial was followed by a couple short films—Our Gang or Abbott and Costello—and several obligatory newsreels. In all, the matinee lasted about two hours—not bad for a dime.

When the show was over, it was the long walk back home. Somehow the return trip always seemed to be twice as long.

While most of our play involved teams or large groups, not all of it did. There were plenty of things to do with two or three people or just by your lonesome. Hopscotch. Jacks. Spinning a yo-yo. Mumblety-peg. Card games—War, crazy eights, Old Maid, or even solitaire.

By the time we were in the fourth grade, however, most of our small-group games revolved around betting. By then, we all had a few coins in our pockets—from setting pins, mowing lawns, or delivering papers—and we were willing to risk a portion of it. We would bet on almost anything and played dozens of games that were intended to separate our buddies from their money.

The simplest games involved tossing coins.

Two guys would each simultaneously toss a penny into the air and, before either coin hit the ground one guy would yell "odd" or "even." If he yelled even and both coins showed heads or both coins showed tails, he picked up the coins and pocketed them. On the other hand, if one coin showed heads and the other tails, the opponent won. The process could go on for an hour or more, toss-after-toss, and in the end neither guy would win or lose more than a dime.

Pitching coins was a variation of coin tossing, but could accommodate more than two players. Two parallel lines, about eight feet apart, would be drawn on the ground—usually the infield of the ball diamond or in one of the horseshoe pits. Everyone would line up with their toes touching one of the lines. Everyone would then pitch a coin—usually a penny—at the other line. The coin that landed closest to the line, without going over it, won all the coins. Again, we played this simple game for hours at a time and no one ever won or lost more than a quarter in any given session and, over time, it is doubtful than anyone's cumulative winnings exceeded two bucks.

On cold or rainy days, when we were forced to stay inside, we tossed cards at a hat. Each person got his turn with a standard, fifty-two-card deck of playing cards. A hat was placed on a basement floor about fifteen feet away from where the player was seated. The player then tossed the cards, one at a time, toward the hat. For every card that landed in the hat, the player collected a penny from each of the other guys. Everyone got a turn tossing the cards and collecting from his buddies. At the end of a round, after collecting once and paying out several times, you might win or lose a nickel or so. On a real rainy day, and with nothing else to do, the game could go on for hours.

The five-and-dime store in the shopping center sold a box of salt-coated roasted pumpkin seeds for a nickel. Each box contained maybe seventy-five seeds. Five or six guys would all chip in a few pennies to buy two or three boxes of seeds. Each guy would be given a handful of seeds. We would draw a line on the ground and stand with our toes touching the line. After sucking the salt coating off a seed, each guy would spit his seed as far as he could. The guy whose seed landed the farthest away from the line collected a penny from each of the other guys in the game.

When we first started spitting seeds, the winner's seed would land about ten feet away. But after losing a few pennies, the worst of us could launch a seed a good twenty feet or more. Seems that the fewer the pennies in your pocket the more powerful the spit.

Another rainy day game involved cards and four players were needed to play it. Each player claimed a suit—spades, hearts, diamonds or clubs. Then each player placed fifteen pennies in front of him on the table. The cards were shuffled by a player and the deck was cut by the person to his immediate right. Then the player on the shuffler's left drew one card from the deck and turned it face up on the table. Three losing players then handed the player whose suit appeared a penny. The deck then passed to the next player on the left and the process was repeated. The game lasted

Simpler Times; Better Times

until one player lost his entire stack of fifteen pennies or an hour elapsed, whichever occurred first. At that point some players might leave the table, others would take their place and a new game would start.

With any of the indoor games, a bunch of guys who were not actively involved in the active game would be in the room. As they waited there turn, they'd read comic books or heckle the guys who were playing. The end result was we could get in several hours of solid entertainment at a cost of usually less than a dime—not a bad deal.

Most of the games were played just for the fun of it, but in the process, without necessarily being aware of it, we actually learned a lot about problem solving. Take pitching coins as an example. When you started playing the game, you rapidly learned that if couldn't get your coin to land near and short of the line, you soon would be separated from your money. So you began to analyze the variables that represented the difference between success and failure.

First, you learned that if a coin was to stick on impact, it had to hit the ground in a flat position. If it landed on edge, it would roll and likely cross over the line. So, how did you make it land flat? Well, you knew if it rotated in flight, it had a good chance of landing on edge, so you need to eliminate in-flight rotation. By experimentation, you found out that if it was flipped by your fingers, it would spin or rotate, just like a baseball spun when you allowed it to slide off your fingers. To keep from flipping it, you learned to keep your fingers rigid and you more-or-less "pushed" rather than "flipped" the coin into the air. You soon learned that the pushing motion eliminated the spin and the coin remained flat—parallel to the ground—throughout its flight and when it landed, it did so softly and stuck right where it hit the ground. But that was but one piece of the puzzle.

You also had to control the velocity—speed—of flight. If the coin was launched too fast, it likely soared past the line. When launched without enough speed, the coin fell short. Either way, you lost your coin. So you had to practice, by tossing coin-after-coin, until you had a sufficient "feel" of the speed with which you tossed the coin.

Finally, you had to determine the appropriate trajectory. If the arc of flight was too flat, the coin would skid when it landed and slide across the line. If the arc of flight was too high, the coin would land short of its mark. Again, practice was required—but practice with a knowledge or awareness of what you were trying to accomplish.

By focusing on and practicing to control three primary variables—rotation, or more precisely the lack thereof, velocity and trajectory—every kid in the group could make a coin hit and stick within an inch of a line located ten feet away—and do it consistently. When we started, the distance between a winning coin and losing coins would often be a foot, but after several weeks of constant play, that margin was reduced to an inch or less.

The same held true for tossing cards into a hat. At first blush, it was a simple game—just throw a card toward the hat. But again, success depended on analyzing the way a card flew through the air in order to gain control over spin, speed, and trajectory. When we started, a guy was lucky to get two or three out of fifty-two cards to land in the hat. But after a little thought and a lot of practice, most of us could stick more than half the deck in the hat and do it time-after-time.

Success at these simple games wasn't the product of luck. It resulted from a lot of thinking and lots of practice. Later, when we reached high school and college, we came to realize that these crude games actually qualified as lab experiments in applied physics. Not bad for a bunch of kids who just wanted to kill a few hours during the day.

For most families in the area, dinnertime was around six o'clock. By then we had finished our required homework, as the rule in our household was no dinner until all schoolwork was done.

Dinner was usually over by seven, giving us an hour to eat and enjoy a little family conversation. In the winter, it was dark by the time we left the table and we usually spent the rest of the evening inside. We went to bed at nine o'clock, so each night we had two hours to kill.

A few nights a week, some of the time was consumed listening to the radio. In those days, radio stations broadcast serial comedy and drama programs, much like television does today. For

Simpler Times; Better Times

boys in our age group the regular programs included The Lone Ranger, Sky King, The Shadow, The Green Hornet, Superman, Amos and Andy, Abbott and Costello, and Jack Benny. When one of these programs aired, we stretched out on the living-room floor and listened intently.

When not listening to the radio, I read—magazines, the newspaper, books, anything I could get my hands on. I visited the library a couple times a week and checked out several books each time—Hardy Boys, sports books, and biographies were all of interest. I found that books were much more interesting than a movie or a radio show. With a book, one imagined what the characters and locations looked like; with a movie, someone else did the imagining for you. A movie lasted for a little more than an hour—less if it was a serial episode; while a book took four or five hours to read and absorb, increasing one's pleasure time. With a movie, you had to go to the theater and sit in the same seat for the entire showing; while you could take a book anywhere and read it for as long as or as little as you wanted. By the time I was six-years-old, I much preferred reading a good book to almost any other form of entertainment. Moreover, every time I read something, I learned something new. Gramp often said: "If you don't learn something new each day, that day is a wasted day—one you will lose forever—but if you learn something new—something you can use in the future—you will recover a part of that day as soon as you use the knowledge gained." It made sense when he said it; it makes sense now. Few things equal reading for pleasure or learning.

CHAPTER TEN

From the first through the eighth grade, our prime activities during most of the week were school and play, but Sundays always started by attending church services.

Our family attended a Presbyterian church located five blocks from the house. Many of my friends, including Johnny and his family, attended the same church. In the earlier years, we were sent to "Sunday school" classes in the church basement, while our parents attended regular services upstairs.

Our first minister was an immense, obese guy whose personality was completely devoid of warmth and humor. His wife was as thin as a stick, acted prissy, had a constant frown on her bespectacled face, and was just as cold as her husband. I always thought they could have learned something from the old fairy tale that started out, "Jack Sprat could eat no fat; his wife could eat no lean." Somehow they'd managed to get the message in the verse exactly backwards.

The minister and his wife had a son, but neither of them seemed comfortable around children. We were expected to be prim, proper, and silent in their presence. If we weren't, we drew a scowl or scolding from one of them. Their son reflected his parents' rigid personalities and disciplinary practices. He didn't appear to own any informal clothes—jeans, shorts, or tee shirts—because he was always dressed in a shirt, tie, and suit. He was shy and aloof, didn't participate in any games or sports, didn't seem to have any friends, and was the image of a little sissy, making him the target of frequent teasing by other kids. I felt sorry for the guy. It seemed as if he'd gone straight from birth to adulthood, completely bypassing childhood.

The manner in which the minister and his family acted raised the first questions in my mind about the usefulness of church attendance and religious training. If following the minister's teaching was going to make us turn out like him and his family, I wasn't too sure I wanted any part of his message.

Simpler Times; Better Times

The minister's wife was in charge of Sunday school sessions; but most of the classes were actually conducted by members of the congregation. By the time we reached the age of eight or nine, the classes turned from a fun-and-games thing to more serious studies of various bible stories. I got off to a bad start in these classes.

One of our first lessons was devoted to the story of when Moses and his followers fled from Egypt. The part about the parting of the Red Sea got me thinking. I sat in the class and tried to visualize Manistee Lake and what it would look like if the lake opened up in the middle. It was an image that I had real trouble forming in my mind.

When I got home after church that Sunday, I pulled out the encyclopedia and looked up the Red Sea. The entry in the encyclopedia cited the length, width, and depth of the Red Sea and discussed its other attributes. It was a big sucker—a heck of a lot larger than Manistee Lake. If visualizing Manistee Lake separating in the middle was tough, forming an image of this huge body of water simply opening up in the center was impossible.

At the start of the next Sunday's class, I raised my hand and said to the teacher, one of the men from the congregation, that I had a few questions about the previous week's story. He seemed pleased that I'd paid enough attention to have questions, taking it as a sign that he was getting his message across. He said he welcomed any and all questions—a statement he'd later regret.

"First, where did the water go when the Red Sea parted?" I asked.

"What do you mean?"

"Well, did the water just kind of stack up or did the parting of the Sea cause the water to overflow the banks of the sea and flood the surrounding area?"

"I don't know," he said, scratching his head, "the Bible just says that the sea parted."

"The water that was in the portion that parted had to go someplace. If the sea flooded its banks, you'd think that would have been quite a story and the Bible would say something about it."

"The Bible doesn't say anything about a flood," the teacher answered.

"Okay, forget about the flood and assume the water just sort of stacked up, it must have been hundreds of feet high...would have been quite a sight. The story should mention something like that, don't you think?"

"The Bible doesn't say anything about that happening."

"Well, if neither of those things took place, what did happen with the water?"

"I don't know." Panic was starting to enter the teacher's eyes.

I scratched my chin. This wasn't getting me any place. I changed direction. "The encyclopedia says the Red Sea is really deep. If the water parted, how wide was the portion that parted?

"I don't know."

"With all those people following Moses, it must have been pretty wide. What kept the water in place? What stopped waves from filling the hole back up?"

"I don't know." Sweat was forming on the teacher's brow.

"Okay, forget about the water," I said, seeing that I wasn't going to get answers to those questions. "What about the fish and the seaweed?"

"What about them?" the teacher asked, seemingly perplexed by the question.

"Well, if the water was gone, wouldn't fish and seaweed have covered the path Moses and his followers walked down? In the lake that we go to in the summer, seaweed grows everywhere. If you took the water away, you'd have a giant mound of seaweed and a lot of dying fish. Why, just in Manistee Lake, I'll bet the seaweed would be way over my head. In the Red Sea, it would have to be much, much higher. How did Moses and his people get around it?"

"I don't know."

"You'd think that if the seaweed was still there—big piles of the stuff—the story would say something about it and the fish, too. It would have been pretty hard for those people to climb over all that wet, slimy stuff. People would remember that. So, why isn't it mentioned in the story?"

"There must not have been any fish or seaweed," the teacher said.

Simpler Times; Better Times

"Where did they go? Were the weeds ripped up by the roots? How did the fish disappear?"

"I don't know."

He was getting frustrated by the questions. I was getting frustrated by the lack of answers.

"How long did it take Moses to cross the sea?"

"I don't know."

"Well, in the encyclopedia, the Red Sea looks as big as Ohio. It must have taken days to walk across it. Did the sea remain parted the whole time?"

"It closed behind Moses, so the Egyptians couldn't follow," the teacher said.

"Was the part in front of them open the whole time? Or were they in something like a big moving hole?"

"The Bible says the sea parted. So, it must have been open in front of them," the teacher said, now completely frustrated. "Look, the parting of the Red Sea was a miracle. In miracles, anything can happen."

"Yeah, but you'd think the people who saw this miracle would have written more about it—about what happened to all the water, the fish, the seaweed, the size of the opening, and that kind of stuff. If I saw something like that, I'd sure say more than just `the sea parted.' Wouldn't you?"

"Well, that's all the Bible says." With that, he turned to another subject, leaving all the questions unanswered. I wasn't very satisfied with the discussion, and, by that point, neither were the rest of the kids in the class. They'd followed my questions and, like me, their curiosity wasn't sated.

The discussion must have been too much for the teacher—he never came back to the class. The next week, the minister's wife took over as our teacher.

A few weeks later, she told us the story of Noah and the Ark. When she got to the part about Noah loading two of every kind of animal on earth into the Ark, I interrupted the story to ask a few questions that were bothering me.

"You said Noah had two of each kind of animal. Does that mean he had two penguins?"

"Yes," the minister's wife replied.

"Did he have two polar bears?"

"Yes."
"Two lions?"
"Yes."
"Two elephants?"
"Yes."
"Two kangaroos?"

"Yes," the minister's wife said, her patience wearing thin. "I told you Noah had two of every kind of animal—a male and a female—aboard the ark."

"Well, tell me, how did he get the penguins from the South Pole to his ark and at the same time get two polar bears from the North Pole? They're at opposite ends of the earth."

She didn't say anything. She just looked at me like I was crazy or something.

"And how did he catch two wild lions? That must have been some trick."

"Are you trying to make trouble in here?"

"No...no...I'm just curious. I mean, how did Noah get two big elephants all the way from Africa to the Ark? Don't you wonder about that?"

"God had the animals come to Noah," she said, her mouth set in a tight, thin line.

"Really? How'd the kangaroos get across the ocean between Australia and where the ark was? Even if God sent them, they had to cross an ocean. I don't think kangaroos can swim, certainly not all the way across an ocean."

The minister's wife was starting to look like she was really ticked off. "God got the animals to Noah. Don't concern yourself about how they got there! They just did!"

I could see that was as far I was going to get with that line of questioning. "Okay. How big was this ark?"

"Big enough to hold all the animals."

"Geez—" She gave me a dirty look. "Sorry...that must have been the biggest boat ever built, because zoos don't have two of every animal in the world and they're huge."

"That is why it is called the `Great Ark,'" the minister's wife replied, a smug look on her face.

I shrugged my shoulders. What could I say to that? "How many days did you say they were on this ark?"

Simpler Times; Better Times

"Forty days and forty nights."

"How did the animals get fed during all of those days and nights?"

"Noah fed them."

"What?"

She glared at me. "What they usually eat."

"Well, lions, tigers, wolves, and other animals like that eat other animals. Did Noah take along extra animals in order to feed them to the ones that eat meat? You know, if Noah only took two of each animal, like the story says, he wouldn't have any extras, would he?"

"I don't know," the minister's wife said, by now completely exasperated by all the questions.

"And Noah must have needed oats for the horses; corn for the cows; carrots for rabbits; bananas for monkeys; and stuff like that for other animals. Where did he get all this food and where did he store it? It must have filled a big part of this 'Great Ark'."

"Yeah," one of the kids in the back of the room chipped in, "how did they get rid of the animal poop?"

"Who said that?" the minister's wife said, anger flashing in her bespectacled eyes. No one owned up to the question.

She ignored all other questions and changed subjects. From my perspective, it wasn't a very satisfactory class. The stories we were being asked to believe simply had too many missing details and unanswered questions to be plausible.

In the sessions that followed, we heard stories about Jonah, David and Goliath, and others. In each case, we asked what we thought were valid and logical questions and weren't given satisfactory answers.

It got to the point where we simply didn't believe anything the Sunday school teachers told us. The stories made no sense. We remarked to each other that if any of the excuses that we told our parents were as weak as the Bible stories we were being told, our back sides would be permanently tanned by all the whippings we'd receive.

The teachers were also tired of our questions and suggested—strongly suggested—that a few us spend all future Sundays in regular church. Apparently, they viewed us as disruptive forces in their classes. So, we stopped going to Sunday school and started attending regular services with our parents.

    Regular church service was the most boring hour of every week. After a few hymns and a Bible reading, the minister gave his sermon—fifteen minutes of lecture on a morality issue, delivered in an absolute monotone. I spent the time making paper airplanes out of the weekly church bulletin, drawing cartoon characters on the envelopes that were intended to be used for making the offering or tithe, and catching up on my sleep.
    I might have felt guilty about the lack of attention that I paid to the minister's sermons had it not been for the adults sitting around me. Dad usually fell into a deep sleep about halfway through each sermon. Most of the other men in the congregation could be seen nodding off, too, and a few even snored when their chins met their chests. You'd see wives jabbing elbows into their husbands' ribs in futile attempts to get them to open their eyes and sit up straight.
    The highlights of each Sunday's service were the hymns. Dad must have inherited his musical talents from Gram. Every note he sang was off key. To make matters worse, he made up for his tone-deafness with volume. Standing next to him as he blared out these hymns was an ear-splitting experience. In fact, I got a real kick out of most of the adults. Many of the women sounded like out-of-tune police sirens. The men made good imitations of bullfrogs with sore throats. And it seemed that the worst singers were always the loudest.
    The boredom of Sunday morning made a dramatic turn for the better when the church got a new minister. The old one accepted another position in the church hierarchy and was replaced by a young, energetic minister who had an equally young wife. The sermons shifted from lectures heavy on "shall not" to positive messages that told the members of the congregation about steps they could take to improve their daily lives. These sermons were delivered with great flair, as the minister's voice rose and fell, his primary points punctuated with dramatic hand gestures and active body language.
    Where the former minister and his wife seemed to dislike children, the new minister and his spouse were favorites with all of

Simpler Times; Better Times

us. The minister joked and played games with us, attended school functions, served as chaplain to area sports teams, and was visible everywhere in the local community. With his arrival, church activities were revitalized and membership soared. I even started looking forward to attending church services. And when I looked around at the adults in the congregation, no one was sleeping. Instead, their attention was riveted on the young minister and the message he was sending out to them.

In order to get more youths involved in church services, the new minister asked Johnny and me to serve as acolytes. It was the first time acolytes had been utilized by the church. We were each given white robes with gold trim to wear. At the start of each service we walked, side-by-side, down the center aisle and lit all of the candles on the altar. About halfway through the service, we assisted the ushers in passing the collection plates for the weekly offering. Then, at the end of the service, we extinguished the candles and followed behind the minister as he exited the church.

While the job was pretty simple, problems did arise from time to time. First, if we walked too fast, or there was a draft in the church, the torch-like device we carried to light the candles went out. When this happened, we had to bum a light from the other acolyte or reach in our pockets, get some matches, and relight the thing, which was easier said than done. It's a real trick to hold the torch and strike a match at the same time—you rapidly find that you're short one hand.

Second, when the candles were extinguished at the end of the previous service, the wicks may have been crushed into the molten wax. When this happened, it was hard to relight them, because the wicks weren't standing up high enough to accept the flame from the torch. Since neither Johnny or I was tall enough to reach up and free the wicks from the wax, the only option we had was to hold the torch against the candle long enough to melt the wax and free the wick. But, because the two of us had to coordinate our movements—arriving and leaving the altar at the same time—and because the time allotted to getting the candles lit was fairly short, sometimes there was nothing we could do but skip the candle, something the minister didn't approve of very much. When this happened, you found yourself staring at the stubborn

Jack D. Atchison

candle throughout the entire service, thinking that everyone else in the congregation must also be staring at the darn thing and wondering why the acolyte had failed to light it.

Johnny and I served as acolytes for a little over a year and then passed our torches and robes on to two younger kids. The minister then asked us to serve as ushers, greeting people as they entered the church, handing out the weekly bulletin, helping people find a seat, and passing the plates for the offering.

Johnny took to the usher's job like a duck to water. He was an extroverted, cocky kid, brimming with self-confidence and loved to stand at the church doors exchanging pleasantries with the arriving members of the congregation. I, on the other hand, was more introverted and less self-assured and found the usher's job a little intimidating at the onset. I tended to just mumble "Hi" to arriving churchgoers and thrust bulletins into their hands, hoping they wouldn't stop to chat. But as time passed, and I got to know most of the congregation, I became comfortable serving as an usher.

The usher's job gave me my first insights into the politics surrounding the church. Three groups—Trustees, Deacons, and Elders—were elected by the congregation to run the church's affairs. Over the years, Dad served in all three groups. The real political power lay with the Elders—the other two groups were more concerned with routine matters of running day-to-day church activities. The Elders watched over the finances, approved construction projects, and, effectively, hired and fired the minister.

Each Sunday, after the offering plates had been passed, the ushers took the money to the church office where it was counted and a deposit to the bank was prepared. When we got there, most of the Elders, having elected to skip the actual services, were usually sitting in the office smoking cigars and shooting the breeze. As I helped count the offering, I'd overhear the Elders' conversations. At first, they watched what they said in my presence, but as time passed, and they became accustomed to seeing me in the office every Sunday, they were less guarded and openly discussed church political matters.

Most of their discussions focused on various members of the congregation. In the fashion of gossip-mongers, they talked about specific families who were experiencing marital difficulties,

Simpler Times; Better Times

economic woes, problems with children, or behavioral problems, such as excessive drinking. It was obvious, even to a kid, that they were disclosing information that had been obtained by virtue of their positions in the church and had been told to them in strict confidence. Yet, every Sunday, they freely and openly breached these confidences, making me wonder why anyone in the congregation would ever trust these characters.

Now, one would think that the Elders would be the members with the most impeccable backgrounds, but I learned that wasn't the case. When one of the Elders was absent, the others talked about the missing person. Through these conversations, I learned one of the men was a reformed alcoholic who frequently fell off the wagon; another's daughter was sleeping around with a number of guys; and another had been involved in some questionable business deals.

About a year after I started serving as an usher, some church members began questioning whether they were being given credit for the amount they'd actually paid in their weekly tithes. Annually a member agreed to contribute a certain amount to the church. Each week, they wrote their name and the amount of that week's contribution on an envelope that they placed in the offering plate. When we counted the offering, we took the money out of the envelopes, compared it to the amount written on the envelope, and put it, along with the other offering money, in the bank deposit pouch. The individual envelopes were retained and given to the church's bookkeeper who posted the amount written on the envelopes to the member's tithing record. Every quarter, members were given a copy of their record.

Had only one member complained that they'd made contributions that weren't reflected on their tithing record, the church leaders would have assumed that the person's own records were in error. But it wasn't just one member. Over a dozen claimed they had contributed money and it had not been recorded by the church. It became apparent that money was somehow disappearing between the time it was placed in the offering plate and when the count was made in the office. At first, it was assumed that someone was taking money out of the plate as it passed by them. But that proved unlikely, because some of the affected members customarily sat on different sides of the aisle from other affected members. That meant that one of the ushers or one of the Elders in the office was responsible for taking the money.

The minister questioned each of the ushers about the missing money. We all walked together from the church to the office. If one usher dipped into the money, the other three would see it happen—and no one had seen any such thing. That left the Elders as the prime suspects.

On one Sunday, the minister put ten marked envelopes, each bearing a coded number, into the offering plates. After the offering was collected and counted, and before anyone left the office, the minister came in and looked for the marked envelopes. Two, each containing twenty dollars, were missing—proof-positive that someone in the office had lifted the envelopes from the plates.

The minister turned to the group in the office and said: "We have a problem. Two offering envelopes are missing from the collection plates. One of you is the person who took those envelopes and, over the course of the past several months, others like them. It'll be easier on everyone if that person steps forward and admits he is the guilty party."

Everyone in the room exchanged anxious and concerned glances, but no one said anything. One guy, a long-time Elder who passed out cigars each Sunday, looked ill, color drained from his face, sweat on his brow. After a few minutes of excruciating silence, during which eyes continued to dart around the room, this Elder tugged on the minister's sleeve and asked: "Can I talk with you in the hall for a minute?"

They left the room. The rest of us sat in silence, wondering what was going on in the hall outside the door. Ten minutes later, the minister reentered the room. "I'm sorry you all had to wait. The problem's been resolved."

"What happened?" one of the other Elder's asked.

"The problem is taken care of and that's all you need to know."

Later, I learned that the Elder had, indeed, pilfered money from the offering plates. He was fighting a losing battle against cancer and medical bills had exhausted his financial resources. One day, on the way home from school, I visited him at his home. It was a few weeks before he died. The cancer was in his stomach,

Simpler Times; Better Times

and, unable to keep any food down, he was wasting away as weight dropped from his once portly body. It was during this visit that he told me about the offering money. He was ashamed of what he'd done. At the time, he was worried about his medical bills and, desperate, wasn't thinking very straight. Once the minister saw his plight, he elicited help from friends, and the man's money problems were alleviated.

To the minister's credit, I don't think anyone, other than those who were in the church office on the Sunday morning when the marked envelopes were used, ever knew about the missing money. The records of complaining congregational members were corrected, and they were told it was a clerical error. In all, it was a practical lesson in how one's sins can be forgiven.

The new minister had several things he particularly enjoyed—cars, cigars, iced tea, and golf.

He found an old sports car, called a Playboy, in a farmer's field. The car had been built by a local Ohio company and was one of only a few hundred that were assembled before the company stopped production. The minister bought the old car from the farmer and partially restored it—only to the point where it could be driven.

One Saturday, the minister wanted to play golf and asked me to be his caddie. I showed up at the church manse where he lived and found him loading his clubs into the little sports car. He was a sight to behold. He had on a pair of wildly colored pants, a bright shirt that clashed violently with the pants, and one of those flat golfing hats.

Before we got into the car, he had to light up a cigar. He couldn't afford to buy high-quality stogies, so he bought seconds—ones that were flawed during the manufacturing process and therefore couldn't be sold except at a steep discount. He bought these cigars in bags of fifty, paying less than five cents a cigar. Because of the flaws, he found it difficult to draw smoke through the cigars. To cure the problem, he always carried a bunch of toothpicks. Before lighting a cigar, he rammed a toothpick into each end of it, twisting the toothpick around in an attempt to create a channel for the smoke to travel through. So, we stood there while he reamed out his cigar.

Jack D. Atchison

With the cigar lit and clamped between his teeth, we got into the sports car and headed for the golf course. We had not gone very far when he motioned for me to pour him a glass of iced-tea from a jug sitting on the floor. I poured the glass of tea and handed it to him. He was in seventh heaven—a cigar, sipping his tea, and driving his magnificent machine.

I'd never ridden in his car before and expected it to be a fast, nimble affair. I was wrong. The car had less power than today's riding lawn mower. Each time we approached a hill, the minister put the pedal to the metal and the car gradually built up to its top speed—about fifty miles per hour. As the car climbed the hill, it steadily lost speed. On bigger hills, we were lucky to make it over the top. Through all this, the minister sat there, cigar clamped in his teeth, a smile on his face, tea glass raised in a salute, acting like he was on the flag lap at the Indianapolis Speedway.

When we got to the golf course, he told me to get his clubs while he checked in with the starter. No two clubs were of the same brand or model. The strap on the bag was worn and frayed. The whole outfit looked like it had been salvaged from a local junkyard.

The minister came out of the club house and announced that he'd be playing alone, as a singleton. When we reached the first tee, he said, "Get the best ball out of the bag."

I opened the compartment where the balls were kept and sorted through them, looking for the best one. It was a tough search. Every ball had a cut in the cover.

"Where'd you get these balls?" I asked.

"I find them. Did you get a good one for me?"

I handed him the ball with the smallest cut. He teed it up and asked for his driver. I pulled a battered driver out of the bag and gave it to him. He addressed the ball, waggled the head of the club several times, wiggled his butt back and forth, and took a mighty swing, darn near jumping out of his shoes in the process. The ball shot down the fairway for about sixty yards and then abruptly duck-hooked into a copse of trees and weeds to the left of the fairway.

"Damn," the minister said. "Give me another ball. I'll take a mulligan."

Simpler Times; Better Times

Reaching for another ball, I asked, "What's a mulligan?"

"It's a second try on the first tee...it's customary in the game."

I gave him a ball that had a slightly larger cut than the first one. He placed it on the tee, addressed the ball, waggled the club, wiggled his butt, and took a mighty swing. The ball's flight path was almost identical to that of the first ball. "Damn," the minister said. "Let's go look for the balls."

We traipsed down the fairway to the copse of trees. For the next ten minutes, we foraged through weeds and found about a half-dozen balls. Apparently a lot of golfers had taken lessons from the minister, because the only way a ball could hit these weeds was if it was a vicious duck-hook.

"Throw one of the balls out onto the fairway," the minister said.

"I thought you had to hit it from here," I said, pointing to the weeds where we had found all the balls.

"No...no...I get to drop it in the fairway."

I tossed the best of the balls onto the fairway. He asked for a five iron. After his standard routine of waggling and wiggling, he hit the ball. Amazingly, it flew down the middle of the fairway. The minister, with a self-satisfied smile on his face, said, "Well, I've got the kinks worked out of my swing," and walked jauntily down the fairway.

When we got to the ball, he said, "I'll use this club again." The kinks must have reappeared, because this shot followed the duck-hook pattern of the first two, diving into a field to the left of the fairway. "Damn!" the minister shouted, as he buried the head of the club in the ground and angrily marched toward the weeds.

Using most of my strength, I extracted the buried club from the turf and followed him into the field. His temper abated when we found another half-dozen golf balls.

And so went the entire round. One or two good shots surrounded by a plethora of duck-hooks into weeds and trees. I rapidly learned that the outing was more a search for balls than it was a game of golf. The minister's anger over missed shots was always soothed by the retrieval of a few good balls. When the round ended, the bag was stuffed with balls, slightly fewer than the

Jack D. Atchison

number of strokes it had taken the minister to negotiate the course, however.

Later that summer, I was asked to caddie for Dad and the minister. They were to play at a local, semi-private course. The minister was attired in his traditional gaudy golfing clothes. Dad dressed as he normally did. He really didn't own any casual clothes per se. In the house and on weekends, he wore the pants from a worn-out suit—pants spattered with paint stains. On this occasion, he wore another pair of pants from an old suit, tennis shoes, a long-sleeved plaid shirt, and the brimmed hat he wore to work. He was not exactly a fashion plate, nor did he care one whit. Dad paid absolutely no attention to what he wore, nor did he care whether his clothes were in style or not. The only thing that mattered in his book was: Are they comfortable?

Dad's golf clubs were in even worse shape than the minister's. Not only were no two clubs made by the same manufacturer; no two were from the same decade. Half the clubs had wooden shafts. Most were held together by liberal doses of black friction tape. And, in total, his bag contained only six or seven clubs, far less than the norm.

It should be noted that the *woods* were, indeed, woods. The club heads were made of wood, rather than metal alloys like they are today; hence, the name woods. The irons, while maybe having club heads made of metal, or iron, often had wooden shafts, as did most putters in those days. Also, the golf balls had thin covers and cut easily. Any miss-hit shot resulted in a big gash in the ball. And the ball did not travel as far as modern golf balls do.

Dad believed that anything could be fixed with friction tape. If the cover of a baseball was ripped, he wrapped it with friction tape and declared it as good as new. A broken bat was nailed together and then wrapped in tape. The same with broken furniture or leaky pipes. I was convinced that if I ever broke an arm or leg, we'd save on doctor's bills by wrapping the injured limb with black friction tape.

When we got to the golf course, a kind of hoity-toity place, Dad and the minister stuck out like sore thumbs. The other people were dressed in the fashion of the day and sported matched clubs and big, bulky golf bags. Then, along came these two guys with their unique dress and ancient clubs. But if their appearance drew a

Simpler Times; Better Times

stare or two, Dad and the minister were completely oblivious to them. They firmly believed that "the man made the clothes," and not vice versa.

On the first tee, I saw I was in for a long day. The minister hit his normal duck-hook—the ball skidding into the left rough. Dad's drive was just the reverse, a sweeping slice that broke sharply to the right. All day long neither of them was ever on the same side of the course, and the short grass of the fairway was alien territory to both men.

The only thing that made my job easy was Dad's club selection. He used only three clubs: two iron, seven iron, and putter. He said that using more clubs made the game unnecessarily complex. And, for him, that was probably correct, because he demonstrated enough problems just hitting the ball with the ones he used.

But, all-in-all, it was great day. Even though the two guys weren't very skilled, they were intensely competitive. The round was punctuated with constant, good-humored badgering and baiting as they tried to best each other. More importantly, both men knew how to have a good time, nothing really bothered them. The anger over bad shots that the minister exhibited when he played alone was forgotten in this round. Each guy laughed off his bad shots—which were frequent—and moved on to the next.

And with two scavengers on the course, the ball-hunting expeditions into the roughs were a real experience. I don't think either guy gave a hoot about his golf score; the real competition was to see who could find the most balls. They'd forage deep into the trees and plow through fields in search of the little, white trophies. Until we reached the tenth hole, that is.

A small corn field bordered the left side of the tenth hole. A farmhouse sat on the edge of the field. It was owned by a little, old, white-haired lady who was fed up with golfers climbing over her fence in search of golf balls. The golfers trampled her garden and frightened her two dogs. To stop intrusions by golfers, she sat in a rocking chair on her back porch with a shotgun loaded with rock-salt in her hands. When a golfer was stupid enough to attempt to cross her fence, she'd blast away. More than one golfer beat a hasty retreat to the clubhouse with a butt full of rock salt. So, when the

Jack D. Atchison

minister's tee shot hooked into her field, we ignored the lost ball—the only one we didn't pursue the entire day.

CHAPTER ELEVEN

Along with church, scouting was intended to infuse young boys with strong moral principles. So, all the guys in the group that I ran around with were required to participate in scouting. First, Cub Scouts and, later, Boy Scouts.

Each year, one of our mothers got stuck with the job of acting as Den Mother for our Cub Scout den. Not only did she have to dream up things for us to do during our den meetings, but the den met in her home, meaning that, once a week, she had a real mess to clean up. Cub Scouts was largely devoted to completing a bunch of prescribed tests that were set forth in the Cub Scout handbook. After passing the first stage, you were designated a Fox, the next stage was Wolf and, finally, on to Bear.

Most of the projects in these various stages were fairly simple, and so attaining the various levels wasn't difficult. Thus, the meetings were not terribly exciting or very interesting.

The real reason most of us stayed in Cub Scouts was that we got to wear our uniforms once a week. The uniforms were blue with yellow trim, set off by a yellow scarf. As you passed each level, you got a badge to sew on your uniform pocket. Were it not for the fact that we didn't want to see our friends wearing a higher level badge than we were wearing, none of us would have bothered with the various tests we were required to pass.

I got my first introduction to Boy Scouts well before I was old enough to participate formally in a troop. Dad was one of the scoutmasters for a troop that met in the church basement. When the troop went on camping trips, he let me come along.

The Boy Scouts maintained a campground, complete with cabins, a few miles outside of Canton, and many, but not all, of the camping trips were to this camp. There were two kinds of cabins in the campgrounds: large, lodge-type structures suitable for housing a dozen or more people and small, three-sided affairs that were suitable for four to six people. Since most of our trips were in the fall or winter, when the temperature was cold, we usually stayed in one of the larger cabins.

My first trip with Dad's troop was in the late fall. Daytime temperatures were mild, but at night dropped well below freezing. In preparation for the weekend trip, Dad assembled his camping gear, some of which he'd brought home from the Army—mess kits, canteens, packs, and sleeping bags. To this he added cooking gear—coffee pot, fry pan, pots, spatula, and the like. We loaded one pack with our clothing, another with cooking gear, and a third with various foodstuffs.

Early Saturday morning, we met the other scoutmasters and the troop of scouts at the church. All told, there about twenty people going on this trip.

Most of the scouts were outdoor types and were experienced campers, having made several of these trips before, as well as having attended one or more summer camps where scouts spent a week in the campgrounds. With one exception, they were a rough-and-tumble group who liked physical activities and challenges.

The exception was a rotund kid, somewhat of a mama's boy, who tended to whine and complain about anything that required a little physical exertion. It was obvious that the others, including the scoutmasters, weren't too enthused that this kid was joining them on the camping trip. I saw the others roll their eyes and snicker when the kid's mother clucked around like a mother hen when the gear was being stowed in the cars. She checked to see if his clothing was warm enough; inquired about the food to be eaten on the trip; asked about the condition of the cabin; instructed the scoutmasters on how fast to drive on the way to and from the camp; and, in general, made a nuisance of herself.

Her son was no better. He sat like a bump on a log and sniffled and whined while the others did all the work, including loading his gear into the car. At the camp, the kid needed help carrying his sleeping bag and pack from the car to the cabin, saying it was too heavy. To make a point, Dad had me carry the kid's pack. I was the youngest in the group, by at least five years, and didn't weigh much more than the kid's pack, but I managed to get it from the car to the cabin without any difficulty.

Simpler Times; Better Times

In the cabin, the kid insisted on a lower-bunk bed located closest to the fireplace, claiming that if he got chilled during the night, he'd catch his death of pneumonia. It was clear the kid was going to be a royal pain in the butt throughout the whole weekend.

After we stowed our gear in the cabin, we loaded a few packs with the things we needed for lunch, filled our canteens with water, and set off on a hike. The area in which the campground was situated was marked with dense woods, streams and creeks, steep cliffs, and caves. Our hike followed paths that took us through the heart of the woods. The trail started out in a valley and led to higher ground, causing us to climb one hill after another. Along the way, we saw all kinds of birds, squirrels, rabbits, snakes, salamanders, and chipmunks.

By the time we stopped for lunch, we'd worked up a healthy sweat, our legs and feet were sore, and we were hungry. But, aside from the fat kid, who had complained incessantly throughout the morning, we had enjoyed ourselves. The weather had been ideal, neither too hot nor too cold for hiking. The scenery was outstanding. And the jocular bantering back and forth by the scouts was entertaining.

Lunch was to consist of hot dogs, hamburgers, fried potatoes, beans, and coffee. A few of the scouts rounded up some dry logs, branches, and twigs and built two fires. It took a half hour or so before the coals were right for cooking. Dad and another scoutmaster served as instructors and overseers while the scouts prepared the food. I rapidly learned that almost all food cooked over a campfire tastes the same—like charcoal. It doesn't matter whether it starts out as a hot dog or hamburger; in the end, it's converted into charcoal. The exceptions are those things, like beans, that remain in cans and, thus, escape direct contact with the flames.

I also learned that, after a long hike, it doesn't matter what the food tastes like. You're so darn hungry that if you can't get the fire started, you'll eat the stuff raw. By the same token, even if the cook burns the food to a crisp, you'll still eat it.

So it was that day. The hot dogs and hamburgers were indistinguishable from the logs in the fires. The fried potatoes looked like hockey pucks. The beans were great—hot and tasty.

And we ate every scrap of it—wolfed it down like it was our first meal in weeks.

The other thing I learned about cooking over a campfire is that cleaning up is a pain. Before the pots, pans, and mess kits can be put back into packs, they have to be cleaned. That means finding water. In this case, we found a creek about an eighth of a mile from where we had built the fires. A group of us had to drag all the cooking stuff and mess kits to the creek, scrub them in the ice-cold water, and haul them back. When we got back, our hands were cold and our clothes were covered with grease that had dripped from the pots and pans as we carried them to the creek.

After lunch, we took another route back to the cabin. Everything was fine until, three hours into the afternoon portion of the hike, we hit a stream that was about three-feet deep and fifteen-feet wide. People were sent upstream and downstream to see if they could find a place where we could cross the stream without getting unduly wet. They couldn't. Our options were limited to retracing our path to avoid the stream or wading across it.

No one was very enthused about walking back the way we had come; it would be well after dark, and hours past dinner time, before we reached the cabin. But wading also was a problem. The bottom of the creek was strewn with rocks. We'd have to keep our hiking boots on, meaning we'd have to walk the last three miles of the hike in wet shoes and socks.

After due deliberation, we opted to wade across the stream. It wasn't too bad for the scouts and scoutmasters; the water was about waist high at the deepest point in the stream. They took off their pants and underwear, held them above their heads, and walked across, donning their clothes on the other side. In my case, the water was chest high. I had to remove all my clothes, including my coat and shirts. By the time I redressed on the other side, I felt like I'd been encased in ice.

The next three miles were miserable. Wet shoes and socks produced quarter-size blisters on everyone's feet. As the temperature dropped in the late afternoon, our feet got cold. Yet, only one guy, the fat kid, complained. He whined and sniffled with each step, for three miles. The rest of us understood that being wet and cold, and having sore feet, was better than the other alternative we could have chosen to take, so we kept quiet.

Simpler Times; Better Times

As soon as we reached the cabin, we built a huge fire and dried our wet shoes and socks. The scoutmasters lanced blisters on our feet and drained them. Initially, this stung, but after a few minutes the pain subsided and our feet started to feel better.

By the time that dinner was ready—steaks, potatoes, biscuits, corn, and beans—we were in hog heaven. The cabin was warm. The food was good. And we were dead tired. While a few guys stayed up and shot the breeze over cups of hot coffee, the rest of us climbed into our sleeping bags and fell sound asleep.

In the morning, breakfast consisted of fried eggs, bacon, sausage, and pancakes. Dad made the pancakes. I knew in advance that they would be disasters. Even at home, on a hot griddle on the stove, he couldn't make decent pancakes. They were either too thick, leaving them uncooked in the middle, or they were too thin, making them as tough as shoe leather. These were the same, except now they tasted like charcoal. I confined my intake to bacon and eggs and, after a quick taste of Dad's handiwork with the griddle, so did everyone else, except Dad. He ate three mounds of his awful pancakes, grinning the whole time and professing that they were the best he'd ever eaten.

That day's activity was to hike to a cliff, climb down it, and return to camp. As we walked through the woods, the troop discussed the exercise of climbing down the cliff, and I started to get worried. They described it as a real test of courage, talking about people falling off the cliff and breaking arms and legs, or worse.

When we reached the edge of the cliff, I was more than apprehensive. The cliff was a sheer drop of over a hundred and fifty feet. Looking down, it appeared to be one big rock. Dad was watching me as I looked down and gulped. He walked over and said: "What's the matter? You look like you've seen a ghost."

"How...how are we going to get down this thing?"

"Don't worry. The side of the cliff is full of hand and toe holds. It's no different than climbing a tree." He clapped me on the back. "It's a piece of cake. You'll do fine."

"Yeah...but I heard guys talking about people falling off this thing and breaking their legs. That doesn't sound like a piece of cake to me."

Jack D. Atchison

Dad pointed to the fat kid. "They were just teasing him...getting him worked up. Forget about what you heard."

Well, their teasing worked. The fat kid absolutely refused to climb down the cliff. When a scoutmaster said he either had to climb the cliff or walk back to camp alone, the kid started blubbering and sniffling, tears rolling down his cheeks. The scoutmaster gave in to the kid's crying and agreed to accompany him back to the cabin.

I turned to Dad. "Maybe I'll walk back with those guys," I said, indicating the fat kid and the other scoutmaster.

Dad got a funny look on his face. "You don't want to be a sissy like that guy, do you?"

Yeah, I thought, I do, but I didn't think Dad wanted to hear that, so I said, "No."

"Okay, then let's get started."

Dad slid over the edge of the cliff and climbed down a few feet. "Okay," he said, "slide your legs over the side. I'll get a hold of you."

I lowered my legs over the side, and Dad directed my feet into some cracks in the cliff face. Then, as I lowered myself, he pointed out hand and toe holds. The cliff was not as sheer as I had imagined it to be. In addition to plenty of crags in the rock, small trees and bushes grew in the cliff face, providing climbers with added hand holds. I started climbing down, moving from one crag to another. When Dad saw the progress I was making, he picked up his pace and moved rapidly downward. Within minutes, a considerable distance separated the two of us.

Everything was going fine until, about halfway down, I hit a spot where the rock kind of bowed out. I didn't see a way to get around the bulge and panicked—simply froze in my tracks, unable to go either up or down. While I sat there clinging to my hand and toe holds, still sixty feet from the bottom, Dad was continuing his descent, unaware that I was frozen in place.

When he got to the bottom, he looked up and saw me. "What's the matter?" he yelled.

"I'm...I'm afraid! I can't move!"

"Move two feet to the left! There are plenty of places to put your hands and feet over there!"

Simpler Times; Better Times

I looked to the left and, in my panicked state of mind, saw nothing but sheer rock. "No...no, I'll fall!" I started to cry.

Dad tried again. "Just move a few feet to your left! If you reach over with your left hand, you'll find a big crack in the rock! Grab it!"

I wasn't about to move anywhere. "No!"

Seeing that he wasn't getting through to me, he started climbing back up the cliff. It took him about fifteen minutes to reach the point where I was clinging to the rock. He positioned himself on my left. "Look over here," he said.

I was looking straight ahead, right into the rock, afraid to look up, down, left, or right. Tears were streaming down my cheeks. I sobbed. "I can't."

"Well, son, you're going to have to move in some direction. You can't just stay in one place. Now, do you want to go up or down?"

"I don't want to go anywhere! I don't want to be on this rock at all! I told you I wanted to go back with those other guys!" I continued to cry, louder now.

Dad just kind of sighed. "Well, you are on the rock. You didn't go back to the cabin. And, now, you have to climb in some direction. Either up or down. It's up to you."

"You take me down," I cried.

"Nope," Dad said quietly. "I can't do that. You're going to have to do it yourself."

"Why won't you help me?"

"I will. I'll tell you where to put your hands and feet, but you have to do the climbing. Now, there are a bunch of guys watching us. You don't want them to see you afraid like this, do you?"

"I don't care what they see or think! I just want down!"

"Well, put your hand six inches to the left then," Dad said, his voice calm, like we were at home in the living room.

I looked over at him. He winked and said, "Ready to climb?"

I wasn't ready, but I couldn't see anything else to do. He said he wasn't going to take me down. No one else was coming up to help. I took a deep breath and slowly moved my left hand, making sure that my right hand and feet had a good grasp on the rock. I felt the crack that Dad was talking about.

"Good," he said. "Now move your left foot over." I did. "Now, put your right hand where your left one used to be." I did. "Now, move your right foot over." In this fashion, he slowly and patiently talked me down the rest of the cliff.

When we got to the bottom, he patted me on the back and said to the other guys, "Let's get back to camp." No one said anything about how I'd panicked. In fact, no one said much of anything at all. We just walked back to the cabin at a brisk pace.

When we got there, the other scoutmaster and the fat kid were waiting for us. We loaded up our gear, put it into the cars, and drove back to town. While the others in the car talked about sports, school, and other things, I remained silent.

We dropped the others off at the church and started for home. I looked over at Dad, who was dressed in his old army fatigues and battered hat. "I embarrassed you today, didn't I?"

He pulled the car over and stopped. "How do you think you embarrassed me?"

"Chickening out on the cliff...crying in front of the other guys." I shrugged my shoulders. "It must have been embarrassing for you. I know I feel ashamed about how I acted."

He smiled. One of his front teeth was chipped and the missing piece of tooth made his smile crooked and unique. He put his hand on my shoulder. "Anything is easy if you're not afraid of it. But it takes real courage to do things that frighten you. Even though you were frightened, you made it down that cliff. That took courage. I'm not embarrassed...never was...I'm proud you had the guts to finish what you started."

I thought about what he'd said. "How come you're never afraid of anything?"

He laughed. "What makes you think some things don't frighten me?"

"I've never seen you afraid of anything." I hadn't. Nothing ever seemed to bother Dad.

"You should have seen me when I was overseas in the Army."

"Were you afraid then?"

Very quietly, he said, "Everyday...everyday."

"What did you do to overcome the fear?"

He looked at me. "I didn't. Like everyone else over there, I just learned to live with it." He paused. "When you came down the rest of the cliff, you were still afraid weren't you?"

"Yes."

"You see, you don't have to eliminate fear; you just can't let it stop you. Next time we go to the camp, we'll climb the cliff again. You'll still be afraid. But, now, you know you can do it, so the fear won't stop you. That's learning to live with things that frighten you. Confront the fear. Challenge it. Don't let it stop you. Understand?"

"Yeah...I think so," not sure that I really did.

"Ready to go home?"

"Yeah."

"Okay." He whacked me on the shoulder.

The next spring, we returned to the camp with his scout troop. On the second day, we climbed down the cliff. I shook all the way down, but made it without stopping.

In the years that followed, every time I was confronted by something that frightened me, I thought about that cliff and Dad's words in the car. So far, I've been able to live with fears, and none has stopped me from doing what I needed to do.

When I finally moved from Cub Scouts to the Boy Scout troop, I had to undergo the initiation that all new members were required to go through. The initiation rites were held in the church's basement, where the troop held its weekly meetings, and were conducted by the existing members of the troop.

The initiates were asked to assemble in the hallway outside the meeting room. One by one, we were blindfolded and led into the meeting area. I was the first to go.

Inside, I was greeted by one of the scouts, who said: "The purpose of this initiation is to test your courage and your willingness to follow the commands of your scout leaders. You will be asked to pass a series of tests. Are you willing to submit yourself to these tests?"

"Yes," I said, with some apprehension in my voice.

Still blindfolded, I was led by the elbow to a table in the middle of the room. The lead scout said: "There is a large bowl in front of you. The bowl is filled with the warm, bloody guts of a bunch of rabbits we just killed. Buried in the guts is a key. Reach into the bowl and get the key for me."

I shuddered a little and reached out with my hand. As my hand entered the bowl, I felt warm, squishy, slimy stuff that, indeed, felt like the guts of the fish we cleaned at the cottage. I sifted through the stuff until I felt a metal key. I grasped the key and pulled it from the bowl. "Here's your key."

"Good job," the scout said, "but your hand is covered with blood and guts. Before you pass on to the next test, you'll have to clean your hand."

"Give me a towel."

"We don't have a towel."

"How am I supposed to get this stuff off my hand then?"

"Lick it clean."

"What!"

"You heard me," the scout said; his voice calm and serious. "Lick it clean."

"You've got to be kidding."

"Not at all. If you have any courage, you won't let the thought of a little blood stop you. None of the others in the troop did."

I thought, these guys are nuts. But Dad was the scoutmaster, and he'd be real disappointed if I didn't pass the initiation. I didn't see much choice in the matter. If others had done the same thing, it couldn't be too bad.

Forcing myself not to gag, I lifted my hand and licked my thumb. As my tongue hit the goop on my thumb, I thought that I'd heave. The stuff was warm, thick, and tasted terrible. Nonetheless, I licked my thumb clean and moved on to the next finger and did the same. When I started licking my middle finger, my tongue touched something that was stringy and slimy. Quickly, I pulled my hand away from my mouth. Geez, I thought, I must have a piece of a rabbit's guts on my hand. As I started shaking my hand to get the piece of guts off, someone grabbed my wrist.

"What are you doing?" a voice asked.

"I've got some of those guts on my hand. I'm trying to get it off."

"You'll mess up the floor," the voice said. "Eat it."

Simpler Times; Better Times

"No way!"
"Do you want in this troop?"
"Yes."
"Then eat it."

I took a deep breath, raised my hand, and sucked the slimy thing into my mouth. When it hit the back of my throat, I gagged. Choking back the urge to heave, the darn thing slid down my throat. Not wanting to prolong this any longer, I quickly sucked the other fingers clean, and then licked the rest of the stuff off my hand, having to swallow one more piece of warm guts. When I was done, I felt woozy and sweat broke out on my forehead. I was sure I was going to upchuck all over the floor.

A couple of deep breaths calmed my stomach. The worst is over, I thought.

"Now," the lead scout said, "you know that we do a lot of camping, right?"

"Yes."

"Well, sometimes a scout gets separated from the troop and becomes lost in the woods. It can take days to find him. When that happens, he has to live off the land...eat what he can find. If he doesn't have any matches, and can't start a fire, he has to eat the animals he catches raw. That is what this initiation is all about—to see if you can survive in the woods. We're using rabbits for this test, because they are the easiest animals to catch. You've already gotten over the hurdle of being able to eat guts and a little blood. Now, let's go to the next test."

He grabbed my elbow and walked me to the end of the table. "The most nutritious parts of the rabbit are the eyeballs," he said. "There's a bowl in front of you. Eyeballs from rabbits we killed are in the bowl. Reach in and get one."

With great reluctance, I reached into the bowl. I felt a bunch of slippery, little balls and took one in my hand. "Okay, I've got one."

"Good," the lead scout said. "Now put it in your mouth and eat it. Be sure to chew it well or it will be hard to digest."

I really didn't want to do this. The eyeball in my hand was cold, wet, and slippery. I pictured an eye in my mind, and thought, Geez, how can anyone eat an eyeball?

"What are you waiting for?"

I couldn't put it off. I took another deep breath and popped the eyeball into my mouth. When I started to chew, the darn thing collapsed and fluid filled my mouth. I didn't chew a second time; I just swallowed. As the eyeball slid down my throat, I choked and gagged.

One of the scouts said, "Here, drink this," and handed me a glass.

I took a big gulp. Immediately, I thought I was on fire. My mouth and throat felt like they were overcome by flames. Without thinking, I spit the stuff out.

"Geez! What's that?"

"It's just something to clear your mouth," a scout said.

"Clear it! It almost burnt the inside of my mouth away!"

"Do you want more?" the scout asked; the voice of innocence and sincerity.

"No...no. Let's get this over with," I said; my mouth still on fire.

"There's just one more test," the scout leader said. "Come over here." He led me across the room. "In front of you is a tub that's filled with the blood of the rabbits. The tub is six feet deep and five feet around. We're going to have you stand on a plank. We'll raise the plank up to a point where it's level with the tub. Your job is to jump far enough to get over the tub. The depth of the blood is over your head and blood is thicker than water. If you don't jump far enough, you'll land in the blood and have to swim out of it or you'll drown. Understand?"

"Yeah...I think so. I just have to jump as far as I can."

"Right," the scout leader said. "Remember, you'll be six feet off the ground. So, after you leap over the tub, you still have to land. Be prepared to hit the floor pretty hard."

"Okay."

He led me to the plank. With my hands on the shoulders of two scouts, I stepped onto it. The plank started to rise and I had to bend at the waist in order to keep my hands on the scouts' shoulders. "You'll have to take your hands off their shoulders and balance yourself," the scout leader said, as the plank rose higher. I removed my hands, straightened up, and, teetering back and forth, fought to maintain my balance.

Simpler Times; Better Times

When the movement of the plank stopped, the scout leader shouted, "Jump!"

I gathered myself and leaped as hard as I could. Suddenly, my feet hit the floor. I thought my knees, which were unbent when I hit the floor in a straight-legged posture, were going through my chest. I fell over and crashed into a heap on the floor as the troop broke out in laughter.

A hand removed the blindfold from my eyes. I saw fifteen Boy Scouts, bent over, clutching their sides, laughing so hard that tears were streaming down their faces. Dad was in the middle of the group, laughing harder than anyone.

I was still somewhat befuddled when the lead scout shook my hand and said, "Congratulations. You passed the tests. You can now watch the other initiates go through theirs. But whatever happens, you can't laugh or make a sound. Got it?"

"Yeah...I think so," not sure that I understood what had happened or what was about to happen to the others.

When I watched the next initiate go through the tests, I learned a great deal about the power of suggestion and its ability to trick the mind.

The bowl of rabbits' guts and blood was nothing more than spaghetti covered with tomato sauce laced with a little mustard, horseradish, and a few other ingredients. The eyeballs were grapes resting in raw egg yolks. The drink I was handed was a concoction of Tabasco Sauce, horseradish, vinegar, and water. But the plank was the real work of art.

First, there was no tub. Two scouts, the biggest guys in the troop, lifted the plank a few inches off the floor and then slowly squatted down. As they squatted, they lowered their shoulders, giving the person on the plank the feeling that he was rising. When the command of "Jump!" was given, the person was a mere four inches from the floor. Expecting a six-foot drop, the person was completely unprepared for the quick landing.

Every initiate was sucked in by the power of suggestion. Everyone gagged and choked. One kid actually tossed his cookies over the eyeball gag. And everyone darn near broke their legs on their determined, four-inch leap. It was a real education.

Jack D. Atchison

Each summer, the Boy Scout troop attended a week-long summer camp. Camp activities were fairly typical of most summer camps: hiking, swimming, arts and crafts, and competitive games. With all these activities, the summer camp should have been fun.

It wasn't.

Scouts stayed in three-sided cabins. There were six scouts per cabin, with each being assigned a bunk. The cabins were supervised by a group of former scouts, primarily high-school and college students who were hired for the summer to supervise one group of campers after another.

Some of the supervisors viewed their role to be that of a strong disciplinarian, acting like a drill sergeant in the military. It didn't take long for most of the campers to run up against one of these characters. I did the first night in camp.

Everyone in the cabin was from my own troop. On the first night, we were still excited about the schedule of events that lay before us. When the supervisor for our group of cabins ordered us to turn out the lights and go to sleep, we continued to lie on our bunks, shooting the breeze about the next day's planned activities.

We'd been yakking for about fifteen minutes when, suddenly, the lights came on. Our supervisor, a college kid, stood in the middle of the cabin, hands on his hips, and said: "I guess you are hard of hearing. You were told to turn out your lights and go to bed. You must not be tired, so I have a way to make you sleep better. You two," he pointed to another kid and me, "get over here."

We jumped off our bunks and walked to where he was standing. "Get down and give me twenty push-ups." We did. It was no big deal. We were used to doing push-ups from gym class and our YMCA activities. Twenty push-ups were a cinch.

The supervisor saw, primarily because of the satisfied smirks on our faces, that the push-ups didn't faze either of us. It teed him off. "Come outside," he said.

We followed him out of the open side of the cabin. He pointed to two fire buckets—gallon-sized buckets filled with sand—hanging on the side of the cabin. "Each of you get a bucket," he ordered.

We grabbed the buckets from the hooks on which they were hanging.

Simpler Times; Better Times

"Take the bucket handle in both hands, extend your arms, and hold the bucket straight out in front of you."

We did as he said and held the buckets in front of us. Within a few minutes, our shoulders and arms ached. Then, our arms began trembling. I lowered the bucket.

"Get that bucket back at eye level," the supervisor shouted.

I raised the bucket. It didn't take long for it to lower again. The strength in my arms and shoulders was gone. The other scout was having the same problem. Each time we let the buckets lower, the supervisor yelled, "Get those buckets up."

Finally, it got to the point where we simply couldn't hold the buckets anymore. Our arms were shaking uncontrollably and our shoulders were knotted in pain. Seeing that we were defeated, the supervisor told us to put the fire buckets back on their hooks. Then he said: "If I hear another peep from this cabin tonight, you guys will get to hold those buckets until you drop. Now, get back to bed."

I had trouble sleeping that night. My arms and shoulders were really sore. Every time I tried to find a comfortable position to lie in, I felt another stab of pain. In the morning, I was tired and ached all over. As a consequence, I enjoyed very little of that day's activities.

As the week continued, others got a dose of the fire-bucket treatment. One guy had to hold both buckets, his arms spread out at his sides, shoulder high. It took only a few minutes for him to break down in pain. Another guy, who had been talking after lights went out, was told to empty the sand out of a bucket and to hold the empty bucket in his teeth. As he did so, the supervisor slowly put sand back into the bucket. The kid almost broke his jaws before giving up.

The rest of the camp's activities were also conducted like a military boot camp. Hikes were longer than they had to be and rest stops were too infrequent. Hikers weren't given enough water to drink. We all hated the daily hikes, viewing them more as a kind of torture than as enjoyable activities.

If a kid goofed off or didn't respond fast enough to a supervisor's orders, the punishment was a set of push-ups or sit-ups. With supervisors constantly hovering around and barking out

Jack D. Atchison

inane orders, no one had any free time. By the end of the third day, we were ready to go home. It was not a good experience.

During my second year in Boy Scouts, Dad's job forced him to step down as the head scoutmaster. His work involved a great deal of out-of-state travel, and he simply couldn't commit the necessary time to the scouting program.

Dad's replacement was a guy of Irish extraction named Mike. He was a big guy with rosy cheeks and a cheerful manner who had a repertoire of thousands of jokes and limericks.

During World War II, Mike had been stationed with an infantry group near the Black Forest in Germany. Mike's unit, expecting a morning attack by German foot soldiers, was dug-in in a series of defensive trenches along the edge of the forest. On the day of the expected attack, hours before sunrise, Mike and the others in his unit heard the noise of approaching German troops. But instead of attacking with foot soldiers, the Germans hit Mike's position with a Panzer unit. The huge tanks rolled over the trenches containing Mike and the other Americans, burying them beneath the dark, wet dirt. To insure they'd done maximum damage, the German tanks ran back and forth over the collapsed trenches, tamping down the earth with their heavy treads.

Mike was one of the few who survived the attack. He was rescued when a soldier from another American unit that had been assigned to look for survivors saw Mike's hand move. The hand and one side of his head were the only parts of Mike's body that were not buried. A tank had crushed the right side of Mike's chest when it rolled over the trench. It took months in the hospital and a series of reconstructive surgeries before Mike was able to use the upper part of his right side. Even then, because some ribs had to be removed, that side of his chest felt like a big marshmallow.

Mike was an outdoors type and felt that cabins were for sissies; real campers stayed in tents. So, as soon as he took over the troop, we stopped using the Boy Scout campgrounds and started taking trips to state and federal parks where we pitched tents.

Our first trip was in the late fall. We were going to a small state park that contained a good-sized lake reputed to contain a plentiful stock of pan fish and bass. We were all instructed to bring

Simpler Times; Better Times

our fishing gear. Mike hoped we'd catch enough fish on Saturday to have a fish fry before we broke camp Sunday afternoon.

When we assembled at the church Saturday morning, the sky was overcast, the wind blustery, the temperature was dropping, and rain appeared to be on the way. Mike had managed to round up two field tents, each of which could accommodate six to eight people, and three two-man pup tents.

The first task we had to accomplish at the lake was pitching the tents. We'd selected a campsite on a small hill that ran down to the lake. The tents were to be pitched in a row, starting near the crest of the hill. Mike decided that one of the big tents should be first in line, followed by the pup tents, and then the remaining big tent. We drew lots to see who would be in each tent. I ended up in one of the pup tents with another scout as my bunk mate.

To pitch a big tent, the scouts laid it out on the ground, put the two main tent poles in place, lifted the canvass tent onto the poles, stretched out the tent ropes, and secured the ropes to pegs that they'd pounded into the ground. Because of the number of hands required to perform this sequence of steps, it took a half-dozen guys to pitch these tents.

Pup tents were easy to set up. The tent resembled a large canvass bag, or tube, and had door-like flaps on both ends. To pitch the tent, you laid it on the ground, stuck small tent poles at each end of the tent to raise the canvass, strung two ropes from each tent pole to pegs in the ground, and pounded in a series of additional pegs to secure the sides of the tent. The whole operation took about five minutes.

After my partner and I pitched our tent and put our sleeping bags and packs inside, we grabbed our fishing gear and headed for the lake, hoping to get a head start on the other guys. We'd only taken a few steps, when Mike shouted: "Hey, you guys aren't done! Get back here!"

We walked back to our tent, where Mike was standing, hands on hips.

"What's the problem?" I asked. "Our tent's up."

"You have to dig a four-inch-deep trench all around your tent. When you're done, dig another trench extending out from that one and head it down the hill."

"Why?"

"If it rains, and it looks like it will, the rain will run off the sides of the tent and into the trenches. The trenches will carry the water away from your tent and send it downhill to the lake. Without the trenches, the rain will run under your tent and you'll get soaked. So, start digging." He handed us a small collapsible shovel like the one soldiers used to dig foxholes.

As Mike walked over to the other tents, my partner asked: "Have you looked inside the big tents?"

"No."

"Well, they don't have floors. The sleeping bags are sitting on dirt. The trenches that Mike talked about make sense for those tents. But look at ours. It has a canvass bottom. The bottom is attached to the sides. How can water get in?"

He had a good point. "Maybe it can come in at the ends where the flaps are," I suggested.

"Okay. Let's dig trenches at the ends. But I don't see any reason to dig them on the sides."

"Sounds good to me," I said, not wanting to do any more digging than necessary.

It took us less than ten minutes to dig a trench at each end of the tent. We gave our shovel to the guys who were trenching around one of the big tents, grabbed our rods and reels, and headed for the lake again.

Mike stopped us. "You guys get the trenches dug?"

"Yep," we answered.

"Okay. Good fishing."

We rapidly learned there were only two species of fish we could catch from the shore: carp and catfish. Both are scavengers that live off the lake bottom. They'll eat anything. And wherever you find them, it's a cinch you won't find any decent fish.

Carp are ugly-looking creatures, with big gulping mouths. They're filled with bones, making it darn near impossible to eat them. Even if you think you can handle the bones, they are filthy things. They have a strong fish smell and taste worse than any fresh-water fish in America. The only real use for a carp is fertilizer. Bury them in the soil and maybe your garden will grow. Of course, it'll smell like dead fish, but the plants will be bigger and more bountiful. But, from my perspective, a ton of cow manure is better fertilizer and smells a lot more pleasant than a ton of dead carp.

Catfish are a little better—but not by much. I've found that it's impossible to kill them, except if you chop their heads off. If you throw them on the bank, and keep them out of water, when you toss them back into the water at the end of the day, they'll gulp once or twice and swim away. Any other fish dies after being out of water for a few minutes. If you stomp on catfish, smack them with a hammer, or stab them with a knife, they'll spit in your eye and swim away.

After having grown accustomed to eating perch, walleye, and trout, I'd boil a pair of old tennis shoes and eat them before I'd touch either carp or catfish. As luck would have it, all we caught during the entire day were carp and catfish. The other guys shared my opinion of the carp, so we threw all of them back into the lake. But Mike said he knew a way to fry catfish to make them edible, so we kept them. By the end of the day, there were three or four dozen of the vile creatures flopping around on the hill overlooking the lake. Killing and cooking them was Mike's problem.

We built a big fire in a pit close to the lake's shore. When the sun went down, it was really needed. The sky was full of thunderclouds. The wind was brisk. And the temperature, which had continued to drop throughout the day, was hovering just over the freezing mark. Without the warmth of the fire, we'd have been miserable.

We were sitting around the fire listening to Mike tell one joke after another when the first drops of rain started to fall. Mike said: "We better get into the tents before we all get wet. One thing about the tents that you should know is: If you touch the canvass, the water will come through. It's waterproof only if you don't touch it, so make sure your sleeping bags aren't touching the tent walls." As soon as my partner and I got into our little pup tent, we followed Mike's advice and made sure that our bags weren't touching the sides of the tent.

Rain fell gently for the next two hours. The sound of it pitter-pattering on the tent lulled us to sleep.

About three o'clock in the morning, the gentle rain turned into a downpour. It came down in buckets. A half-hour after the heavy rain started, I awoke. It felt like my sleeping bag was moving. I reached my hand out. Water was streaming through our tent. The tent bottom was covered with an inch of water and my sleeping bag was wet. It was just a matter of time before the outside of the bag became saturated and the inside filled with water.

I punched my bunk mate. "Hey, wake up!"

He lurched awake. "What's wrong?"

"The tent's full of water."

He turned on his flashlight. The light showed that the bottom of the tent was flooded. Our sleeping bags were sitting in a pool that was rapidly getting deeper.

"Where's it coming from?" he asked.

"I don't know. Check the front and back of the tent."

He flashed his light on the rear of the tent. The trench outside was full of water, but it seemed to be doing its job, carrying the water away from us. The same was true in front. "If it's not coming in at the ends, where is it coming from?" he asked.

"It's got to be coming through the sides or bottom of the tent." Then, it hit me. "Geez, we're lying on the canvass bottom. Mike said that if we touched the canvass, it would leak. That's what it's doing."

We both crawled out of our bags and stuck our heads out the front of the tent. We were the next to last tent in the row. Only the big tent at the end of the line was further down the hill than we were. The light from my partner's flashlight showed that the water was running out of the trenches around the tents further up the hill and was coming directly toward us like a small river. With no trenches on the sides of our tent to divert the water, it was running right under us.

"Geez," I said. "If this keeps up, we're going to wash away."

"Everything in here is already soaked."

"Yeah, we better get our packs off the ground or we won't have any dry clothes," I said—too late. Our packs were already full of water and the clothes inside were soaked.

We'd each brought a poncho with us. We put them on and decided to abandon the tent. We were better off outside. If we stayed in the tent, we'd be sitting on the ground and the water would eventually soak the clothes we were wearing. Outside we

Simpler Times; Better Times

could at least keep some parts of our clothing dry—those covered by our ponchos.

As soon as we got out of the tent, cold wind instantly chilled us to the bone. "We can't stay out in this wind," I said.

"Where are we going to go?"

"Maybe we can squeeze into one of the big tents."

As we were discussing this option, Mike poked his head out of the big tent next to ours. "What are you doing out in the rain?"

"Our tent is leaking. The floor's an inch deep with water," I said.

"Give me a minute." We waited until he came out in his poncho. "Let's see what the problem is." He walked toward our tent. "Hell, there aren't any trenches on the side of the tent. Didn't I tell you to dig a four-inch-deep trench on each side?" he asked, hands on hips, eyes glaring at us.

"Yes...yes," my partner stammered. "But the tent has a canvass bottom. I figured we'd be alright if we just took care of the ends."

"You figured wrong. You should have done what I told you to do."

"Well, we screwed up," I said.

"Sure looks that way. You guys tried to get out of a little work...so you could goof off...now you've got a real problem."

I shrugged. He was right. There was nothing we could say. "Uh...can we squeeze into one of the big tents?"

Mike smiled—kind of a wicked little grin. "Nope."

"Why not?" My partner asked. "It looks like there's room for another guy in each of them."

"There probably is," Mike agreed. "But if you'd done what you were told, you wouldn't need to get into those tents...yours would be nice and dry, just like all the others. While you two were goofing off, everyone else was working. Now they're warm and dry, and you have to pay the price for goofing off."

"You mean we have to stay out here in the rain?" my partner asked, hoping Mike wasn't serious.

"That's exactly what I mean. It'll teach you to listen better." He opened the flap of his tent and started in. Then, he turned and smiled. "Have a good night, guys."

Jack D. Atchison

"What do we do now?" my partner asked.

"Just hope the night passes fast, I guess." I walked down to the pit where our fire had been and sat on one on the logs bordering the pit. With my back to the wind, I hunkered down in my poncho. A few minutes later, my partner joined me. We sat there the rest of the night, cursing our stupidity and wishing we had followed Mike's directions.

As the sun rose over the lake, the clouds lifted and the rain turned into a slight drizzle. We'd been sitting on the log for well over three hours and were almost frozen stiff. I got up and went to our tent to assess the damage. The tent still had a couple inches of water in it. Our packs, including our extra clothing, were soaked. It was clear that we'd have to wear what we had on until we got home later in the day.

The other scouts were emerging from their tents as I headed back to the log. Mike came out and said to us, "See if you can find any wood for a fire. Look for dead trees—ones where you can chop off branches. Don't take anything from the ground, because it'll be too wet to burn."

I went with a few other guys to look for wood. We were lucky and found two dead trees in a small copse at the top of the hill. Before long, we had enough wood to last the rest of the day.

It was still pretty cold out and everyone was anxious to get warm. Even with the dead wood from the trees, it took a while to get the fire going. When we did, Mike put his coffee pot, containing the last of the coffee that he'd brought with him, in the middle of the fire, saying: "I have to have a cup of coffee in the morning. Without it, I'm miserable."

While the coffee was brewing, Mike suggested we put a few fishing lines out in the water. He thought the rain might have brought the bass in closer to the shoreline. Maybe we could catch some of them, rather than the carp and catfish we'd caught the day before.

I got my rod and reel and cast a line out into the lake. My hands were cold from sitting all night on the log. Instead of holding onto my rod, I laid it down, put a rock on it to hold it in place, and returned to my seat by the fire.

I'd only been sitting for a few minutes when one of the guys yelled, "Jack, something's on your line!"

Simpler Times; Better Times

I looked down and saw my rod was being pulled out from under the rock. Whatever was on the other end of the line was dragging the rod toward the water. Not wanting to lose the rod and reel, I jumped up and leaped across the fire. As I did so, my foot hit Mike's coffee pot, knocking it over and spilling the contents into the fire.

Mike let out a roar. "Damn it, you spilled my coffee!"

As I grabbed my rod, I looked back to see Mike coming after me, fire in his eyes, cheeks aflame with anger. I tossed my rod to the guy next to me. "Here, hold this!" I started to run, Mike hot on my heels.

Mike chased me down the shoreline, up the hill, and down the road, shouting curses and threatening me with bodily harm. After a couple hundred yards, he ran out of gas and had to stop. I stood a few feet away and watched him, bent over, hands resting on his knees, trying to catch his breath. He looked so tired and ragged that I couldn't help laughing. As I laughed, he did, too.

"You gave me a good run," he said.

"I wasn't about to let you catch me. Your threats sounded pretty real."

"They were. I have to go all morning without any coffee. I hate that."

"You don't have to go without coffee."

"How's that?"

"Well, I don't know about you, but I'm cold, wet, and sick of this place. I sure don't intend to eat any of those catfish. I think we should ditch the fish, pack up our stuff, and get to the nearest restaurant. You can get some coffee. I can get warm. We can both have a decent breakfast. And we all get out of this crappy weather."

"For such a clumsy kid, that ain't half bad. I agree, let's get out of here."

The others in the troop didn't require any convincing. It took less than thirty minutes to tear down the tents, stow our gear, and hit the road.

We found a truck stop about fifteen minutes later. I was sitting in a booth with Mike, my tent mate, and two other guys. Mike was on his second cup of hot coffee and looked like a new

man. He looked over at me. "Next time we go camping...if there's a next time...you remember to put a trench around your tent."
"I will."
"One other thing."
"Yeah."
"Stay away from the damn fire and my coffee pot."

When Mike's year as our scoutmaster was over, an ex-military guy who had the demeanor of a drill instructor from a Marine boot camp replaced him. Gone were Mike's jokes and casual scout meetings dominated by fun and games. In their place was an emphasis on discipline. At each meeting, scouts stood inspection while the scoutmaster checked our uniforms to see if they were neat, all badges were in order, and scarves were tied properly. We were even taught to march in a military style. With his spit-and-polish attitude, the new scoutmaster removed most of the enjoyment from our scouting activities.

On one of the first camping trips under the new scoutmaster's leadership, Gary had his first real encounter with the scoutmaster's disciplinary tactics. The troop had gone to the Boy Scout campgrounds and would be staying in some of the bigger cabins. The scoutmaster assigned everyone to bunks. He told us to stow our packs under our bunks and to put our sleeping bags neatly on top of the bunks. He then laid down a series of rules we were expected to follow while in the campgrounds.

Gary was suffering from a cold or allergies and his nose and chest were congested. After Gary stowed his gear in the cabin, carefully following the scoutmaster's instructions, he went outside to join the other scouts. As Gary walked out the door, he coughed a couple times to clear his throat, hacking up phlegm in the process. Doing what any young kid would do, he spit the phlegm out onto the ground. He'd only taken a few steps away from the cabin when a voice shouted out harshly: "You! The redhead! Stop right there!"

Gary turned to see the scoutmaster angrily approaching him. Gary pointed to his chest. "Me?"

"Yes, you, mister! Get over here!" Pointing to the ground, the scoutmaster said, "What's that?"

Gary looked where the scoutmaster was pointing. "What? I don't see anything."

Simpler Times; Better Times

"Look again. I see an offending gob of spit in front of me, mister."

Gary nodded. He, too, saw the gob of yellowish phlegm that he'd just expectorated onto the ground. "So?"

"I've warned you people about spitting." Indeed, he had. He found spitting offensive and told many of us to stop spitting at scout functions.

This was hard to do. Part of being a boy is acquiring the ability to launch a respectable gob of spit from your mouth. Everyone knows if you want to hit a baseball, you have to spit two or three times before entering the batter's box. You have to spit again just before the pitcher releases the ball. It's an art form—one not fully perfected until a guy gets to that stage in life when he can chew tobacco, at which point he can really work up the stream of saliva necessary to spit at will. Major league baseball players are testimony to this common wisdom.

Spitting isn't restricted to the baseball diamond. It plays a bigger role. It separates "real" guys—tough, macho ones—from girls and sissies. Girls and sissies don't spit; "real" guys do. Real guys spit anytime, anywhere. They learn to spit through their teeth, so the stream of saliva shoots out of their mouth with power and accuracy, and none of it dribbles down their chin.

In furtherance of this concept and image, we practiced spitting all the time, developing our own individual styles. We spit spitballs, pumpkin seeds, and watermelon seeds. To simulate the effect of using chewing tobacco, we bought black licorice whips and chewed it as a tobacco substitute, launching streams of blackened saliva all over the ball field. We even had contests to see who could spit the farthest.

With all this tradition, and to preserve our own images, we paid little attention to the scoutmaster's concerns about the evils of spitting. When he wasn't looking, we spit. It is the American way.

But, in Gary's case, it wasn't image; it was a necessity. Again, everyone knows, when you have a cold, you have to get rid of "hockers," the gobs of phlegm that inevitably find their way into the back of your throat when you sniffle, snarf or cough. If you don't carry a handkerchief—and no real man does, because who needs a handkerchief when he has shirtsleeves, a forearm, or the backs of his hands—the only way to get rid of a hocker is to spit.

Now, the scoutmaster was making a big deal out of one of life's necessities.

"I know you don't like us to spit, but I've got a cold. I had to spit some stuff out of my throat," Gary said—an explanation that should satisfy any sane person.

The scoutmaster was unmoved by Gary's solid logic and reasonable explanation. "You're going to get rid of that offensive mess on the ground," pointing once again to the gob in front of them. "Go into the cabin and get the field shovel."

The field shovel was the collapsible shovel we used to throw dirt on fires. Gary did as he was told. He got the shovel and returned to the scoutmaster.

"Dig under that offensive spit and put it in on the shovel," the scoutmaster ordered.

Gary slid the shovel under the spit, lifting the piece of dirt on which it rested onto the shovel blade.

"Now, come with me." The scoutmaster led Gary along a path that entered the woods near the cabin. They walked several hundred yards into the woods, stopping at a small clearing in the trees. Pointing to the shovel Gary was carrying, the scoutmaster said: "Place that dirt carefully on the ground. Be sure that you don't disturb the spit when you do."

Gary placed the small mound of dirt on the ground.

"Now," the scoutmaster said, "you're going to dig a grave for that offensive matter and you're going to bury it."

"A grave?"

"Yes, a standard grave. Three-feet wide. Six-feet long. Six-feet deep."

Gary laughed.

"What's so funny?"

"This is a joke. Right?"

"It's no joke, mister. You need to be taught a lesson." The scoutmaster used his foot to draw the dimensions of the grave in the dirt. "Now, start digging."

Still not sure whether the guy was serious, Gary started digging. The soil was reasonably loose and, within a few minutes, he was piling up the dirt from the hole the scoutmaster had outlined.

Simpler Times; Better Times

The scoutmaster, hands on hips, watched Gary dig. When the hole was about six-inches deep, the scoutmaster said, "I'm going back to the rest of the troop. When you've got the grave dug, come and get me before you bury the spit. I want to see it go into the grave." With that, he walked away, leaving Gary to finish digging the hole.

As the hole deepened, the digging became more difficult. The dirt was laced with roots from nearby trees and the field shovel, with its small blade and short handle, wasn't suitable for cutting through the roots. At about the three-foot level, Gary could dig no deeper. Besides, by then, his arm and back muscles were sore, the cold worse, and his hands were blistered. He stuck the shovel in the mound of dirt next to the hole and went to get the scoutmaster.

When Gary entered the cabin, where the scoutmaster was resting on his bunk, the scoutmaster said: "Are you done already?"

"I've gone as far as I can. There are too many tree roots to go any deeper."

"We'll see about that," the scoutmaster said, as he rose from the bunk.

They walked from the cabin to the clearing in the woods. Apparently satisfied that the roots were, indeed, too thick and too big to cut through, the scoutmaster said, "Okay, go get the piece of dirt with the spit on it."

Gary picked up the shovel and retrieved the piece of dirt.

"Place it carefully at the bottom of the grave," the scoutmaster said.

Gary climbed into the hole and put the chunk of dirt on the floor of the hole. "Now what?"

"Now, you cover the grave."

With his sore hands and muscles, Gary shoveled the mound of dirt back into the hole. It took almost as long to fill the hole as it had taken to dig it. When he was done, he was beat.

The scoutmaster stayed to watch the covering of the grave. "Now," he said to Gary, "if I ever see you spit again, you'll be digging another grave. Got that, mister?"

"Yeah."

"You mean, yes, sir, don't you?"

"Yes, sir."

Jack D. Atchison

"Alright, go join the rest of the troop."
By the time Gary got to the rest of the troop, the day was shot. He'd missed most of the activities. The camping trip was ruined and he simply wanted it to end, so he could get home.

Not long after the burial experience, we, along with most of our friends, quit scouting. The fun was gone. Leave it to a few misguided adults to screw up a good thing.

Simpler Times; Better Times

CHAPTER TWELVE

Like most parents, Mom and Dad gave Gary and me a weekly allowance—starting at a dime it increased each year, reaching twenty-five cents a week by the time I hit the fourth grade. It was enough to buy a couple of cokes and a candy bar, but it wasn't sufficient to fund all the things we wanted to do. To make up the difference, we needed to earn money, and that meant we had to find odd jobs that people were willing to pay us to perform.

The first job for most of us was to shovel snow. When the snowfall resulted in an accumulation of an inch or more on the ground, we got out our snow shovels and started going door-to-door throughout the neighborhood.

If the snow wasn't too deep—less than three inches—we offered to shovel a sidewalk for a quarter and a driveway for another quarter. Since most of the houses in the neighborhood didn't have paved drives, most jobs involved sidewalks only. On a good day, we shoveled the sidewalks in front of a half-dozen to a dozen houses. If we did a good job, the residents of those houses became regular customers—people who hired us every time it snowed. So, there was an incentive to do the work well and keep the customers happy. If we did, we earned between three and six bucks a week, every week of the winter.

One problem with living in Ohio was the inconsistency in the types of snowstorms that we experienced. Some consisted of light, fluffy snow—easy stuff to shovel because it wasn't heavy and it didn't stick to the sidewalk. Light snow only fell when the temperature was really frigid. So, while the snow was easy to shovel, the cold air made the job very unpleasant. Within a few minutes, your hands and toes were cold, your nose started to run, and your cheeks and ears stung. In order to avoid getting frostbitten, you bundled up and went inside to warm up every hour or so, which tended to limit how many sidewalks you could shovel on a given day.

But more often than not, the snowstorms featured a combination of snow and freezing rain. When this occurred, shoveling snow was hard, hard work. The wet snow was heavy and taxed the strength of an eight-year-old. And the freezing rain formed ice beneath and on top of the snow, meaning you had to chip the ice off the sidewalk with the shovel—a time-consuming, back-breaking undertaking, even for adults.

Despite the unpleasant aspects of shoveling snow, we all looked forward to lining up a list of steady customers each winter. Virtually every guy in our group had at least a dozen regulars, allowing all of us to have money in our pockets.

When spring arrived and the snow melted, the more industrious of us kept our regular customers. Instead of shoveling their walks, we mowed their lawns. The going rate was about a dollar to mow the front, back, and side yards and another quarter to trim the grass along all sidewalks, drives, and flower beds—a job that took about two hours. The average kid could do one yard each night after school and three on Saturday and, again, on Sunday, giving the kid an income potential of more than twelve dollars a week, excluding tips. The tips increased the weekly take by a few dollars.

We didn't have power mowers in those days. Instead, ours were reel-type mowers that one had to push before the reel of blades rotated to cut the grass. In order to push these mowers, one had to be tall enough and have sufficient strength. Some smaller guys in our group lacked both the height and strength required to push the mowers. Barred by their physical attributes, the smaller guys teamed up with bigger guys. While the bigger kid mowed, the smaller one did the trim work. Then, they split the money.

The old reel mowers didn't work well when the grass was higher than two inches. The taller the grass, the more difficult it was to push the mower. And with tall grass, the blades cut unevenly, leaving occasional clumps of uncut grass. This meant that you had to mow the lawn a second time to get the clumps left behind on the first mowing. In order to avoid these problems, we tried to get our customers to allow us to mow their yards before the grass grew too high. Most customers went along with this request, but the more frugal ones didn't, so we had a few problem jobs each week.

Simpler Times; Better Times

Trimming wasn't a particularly easy job either. The trimmer was a device that you squeezed in order to draw the blades together, much like a pair of scissors. In order to use the trimmer, you had to get down on hands and knees. By the time you finished a good-sized yard, or one with a lot of trees and flower beds, your hands, knees, and back ached.

In the fall, we raked leaves. And at odd times during the year, we spread fertilizer, pulled weeds, raked thatch, and did other small jobs for our customers. All of this was hard work for kids that were not yet ten years old. It was fatiguing and required the commitment of a great deal of time if the job was to be done correctly and to the customer's satisfaction. But, again, the money was good and we competed with each other to get a stable of regular customers.

By the fifth grade, some of the guys got paper routes. There were two papers in the area that offered home delivery—<u>The Cleveland Plain Dealer</u>, a morning paper, and <u>The Canton Repository</u>, with afternoon delivery. A route for delivering the <u>Repository</u> was, by far, the most desirable, as it was the paper most favored by Canton's residents.

The typical route had between sixty and one hundred customers. The papers were dropped off, in bulk, at the paperboy's house. The paperboy folded the papers and put them into a delivery bag, which he either carried over one shoulder or strapped onto the handlebars of his bicycle. He then delivered the papers to the individual customers on his route. This entire process took about an hour and a half each night.

The primary factor that determined how long it took to service a route was the paperboy's skill in folding and tossing the papers. No one used rubber bands or plastic bags to wrap the papers, as is customary today. Instead, the paper was folded three times and one edge was inserted into the open side of another edge. If the fold was done properly, it was every bit as effective as putting a rubber band around the rolled paper.

Most customers allowed the paper to be tossed on their front porch, although some had a box on the porch where they wanted the paper placed. Others wanted it put in a garage or inside the storm door. A skilled paperboy could speed by a house on his

Jack D. Atchison

bike, grab a paper from the bag, and toss it on the fly, hitting his target every time. Beginners or unskilled paperboys were a different story.

My first experience in delivering papers was as a substitute for a guy who was on vacation. The first problem was folding the papers. I did exactly what the guy told me to do. Carefully, I folded the paper into equal thirds, inserted one edge into the other, and rolled it to tighten the bond. As soon as I put it into the bag, it unfurled. It took three attempts before it stayed together. As I went through the eighty papers I had to deliver, it took two or more attempts to get each of them to stay tightly folded. By the time I had the bag loaded, I was a half an hour behind schedule.

I rode my bike to the first house on the route, reached into the bag, grabbed a paper, and tossed it toward the porch. What a disaster. In tossing the paper, I lost control of the bike and fell in the customer's driveway. Papers flew out of the bag hanging on the handlebar and scattered all over the drive, half of them popped open as the fold gave way. As for the paper that I'd tossed, it popped open and fell about ten feet short of the porch. Rubbing the knee I'd scraped when I fell off the bike, I limped over, retrieved the paper from the middle of the yard, and put it inside the customer's storm door. Then, I picked up the papers which were strewn all over the drive, refolded them and returned them to the bag, wasting another fifteen minutes.

The next half-dozen delivery attempts were no better. I fell two more times. Some of the papers landed in shrubbery; some popped open; and one even sailed onto a porch roof. It was getting dark and I'd barely started the route. In order to finish without any further disasters, I rode up to each remaining porch, got off the bike, and placed the paper on the porch. It took me twice as long to deliver the papers as it would have taken the regular delivery boy, and it was pitch dark when I finished, but at least I got done.

When I finally got home, I spent hours folding and refolding our own newspaper, intent on mastering the skill. Not that I had any real choice in the matter. I'd committed to taking the route for two weeks. If I didn't eliminate the problems I had experienced, the nightmare of the first day would replay itself thirteen more times.

Simpler Times; Better Times

After the third day, I was able to get through the route without falling off the bike and without having more than a half-dozen papers fly terribly wide of their intended targets. I was beginning to feel pretty good about the whole experience. It was a premature feeling of well-being—the awful job of collecting cash from the customers on the route lay ahead.

The first trick was in trying to get someone to answer the knock on the door. At some homes, there was no car in the garage or drive, and no sounds could be heard from within the house—reasonable evidence that the occupants of the house were not at home. But at other houses, there was a car in the drive, and I heard sounds coming from inside the house—evidence that the occupants were home. Yet, knocks on the door went unanswered. In fact, in a few cases, people actually peered out from a crack in the drapes, saw me standing on the porch with my collection book in hand, and still refused to acknowledge the knock on their door. I finally realized they were hiding, so they wouldn't have to pay their bill.

When people did answer the door, I heard every lame excuse imaginable as to why they couldn't pay.

"My husband (wife) pays the bills and he's (she's) not home. Come back later."

"Gee, I forget to cash a check and don't have any cash. Come back later."

"We pay every other week. Come back next Saturday."

"We're just visiting. The owners will be home later. Come back then."

At every house, there was another excuse. In the end, I collected from about half the houses on the route, which, from my standpoint, was a real problem. As a substitute, I received half the pay that the guy who controlled the route received—he kept the other half because he "owned" the route. But I got to keep all the tips I collected. It was the lure of the tips that caused me to agree to act as a substitute. With half of the people not paying, the tips were nowhere near what I had been led to believe they would be.

Moreover, I found that many customers didn't tip a substitute carrier, presumably because they didn't figure a tip to a substitute would improve or maintain the level of service they received. They looked to the regular paperboy for that and, therefore, reserved their tips for him.

Jack D. Atchison

Unfortunately, the only way a guy could get a paper route was to serve first as a substitute for another guy. The other guy knew he had a good deal. If he got some poor schmuck to deliver the papers, while he retained half the income, he'd never give up the route—he'd just run through one substitute after another and benefit from their labor. About the only ways a route changed hands was when the existing holder of the route went away to college or got tired of dealing with the problems of collecting from dead-beat customers. Then he turned the route over to someone else. I served as a substitute for one guy for over six months. When he showed no sign of relinquishing the route, I quit and moved on to better things.

Some guys were lucky. After working as a substitute for less than three months, Johnny got a good route. He kept the route for several years, then handed it down to his brother. For him it was a good deal, because a decent route allowed a kid to earn a steady stream of income, and delivering papers was an easy job compared to mowing lawns or shoveling snow.

One day in the fall of the year, at the age of about nine or ten, I was leafing through a magazine when an advertisement hit my eyes. It promoted a company that made greeting cards and, in bold type, it solicited people to sell cards door-to-door, offering the promise of generous rewards to those who took up the offer. The idea of selling cards appealed to me. Christmas was not far off, and everybody in the neighborhood sent cards to friends and relatives. They had to buy the cards from someone: Why not from me?

I responded to the ad and, in a few weeks, received a huge sample book, displaying several dozen different cards, and an order book, along with instructions on how to process an order. After reading the accompanying materials, the whole deal looked pretty straightforward. The cards appeared to be of high quality and, after comparing them with what a couple of stores in the shopping center offered in the way of Christmas cards, I thought the prices seemed fair.

Armed with my sample book and order pad, I started knocking on doors in the neighborhood. Because I'd never tried anything like this before, I concentrated on friends first—later learning that this approach is standard fare for sellers of life

Simpler Times; Better Times

insurance, cosmetics, and other products. To my surprise, and delight, people responded well to my pitch and to the cards that I was offering. On the first day, I received well over fifty dollars worth of orders, earning a commission of about five dollars.

As I moved away from friends and simply made cold calls on houses in the neighborhood, the ratio of orders received to calls made dropped dramatically. But still, I got enough orders to more than justify the effort. In the end, the cards I sold that year allowed me to earn around seventy-five dollars, not an insignificant sum to a kid in the early fifties.

I continued to sell the cards for several years, expanding my offerings to include Valentine's Day, Easter, Mother's Day and general greeting cards, making it a year-round business. It was a valuable experience, and I learned a great deal about salesmanship—how to identify a customer's needs, make a pitch, overcome buyer resistance, counteract excuses not to buy, and close a deal. And when I moved on to other ventures, I sold my route of over two hundred regular buyers to another kid for a nice profit.

The card deal worked out so well that I scanned magazines for other opportunities. I noticed that a number of magazines carried ads placed by companies who were selling collectible postage stamps. One of the ads that appeared in several of the magazines offered a stamp book and bag of stamps for ten cents, stating that other stamps would be sent "on approval" to anyone responding to the ad. I didn't know what "on approval" meant, but what the heck, it's only a dime, so I might as well see what the deal is all about. I clipped the ad and responded to it.

Within a week or so, I got a big package from the company. Inside was a colorful stamp book; a bag containing several hundred canceled stamps issued by countries all over the world; a packet of glued "hinges," used for affixing the stamps in the book; and a couple dozen sheets of stamps that were offered "on approval."

I rapidly discovered the meaning of "on approval." Each of these stamps had a price included for it. If you wanted to keep the stamp, you sent the company the price it was asking. If you didn't want to keep the on-approval stamps, you returned them to the company.

Jack D. Atchison

Well, the prices for these stamps were more than I wanted to pay. Besides I didn't know anything about stamps or their values—I'd responded to the ad out of simple curiosity and for no other reason. So, I sent them all back to the company. Then, I discovered something else about these stamp companies—they won't take "no" for an answer. Two weeks later, I received another batch of on-approval stamps. I sent them back—and promptly got another batch in the mail. I'd entered the world of the on-approval monster.

As I leafed through the free stamps I had received, I found quite a few of them fit in the stamp book. Using the hinges, I started to fill up the book. As more and more of the pages had colorful stamps glued to them, the book started to look pretty impressive and my interest in stamps grew. I responded to dozens of other "free offers" that I found in magazine ads.

Within weeks, I was awash in free stamps—thousands of them, most of which were duplicates, sometimes scores of the same stamp. And I had an impressive stack of stamp books; because every company felt compelled to send one to you "free." I was also buried in on-approval stamps.

I had to do something about these on-approval stamps. The postage cost of returning them was getting out of hand. So, with each return, I enclosed a note that said: "Please don't send me any more stamps. I'm not interested in buying them."

The note didn't do the trick, the stamps continued to come—a packet almost every day, the on-approval monster was on a rampage. I enclosed a stronger note that said: "I'm ten years old. I don't want to buy any stamps. Don't send me anymore. If you do, I won't return them and I won't pay for them. I'll just keep them. So, no more, please."

They continued to come and, true to the words in my last note to the various stamp companies, I kept everything they sent, without tendering any payment.

Well, that didn't sit well with the stamp companies. I started to receive a series of letters from each of them. Each letter was a little more threatening than the one which preceded it. The general gist of the letters was: "Return the stamps or make payment. If you don't, we'll take legal action." At first, this sounded fairly ominous.

Simpler Times; Better Times

But a curious thing was happening. On the same day or a day or so after I received a threatening missive, I also got another batch of on-approval stamps from the same company. This got me thinking. First, if they were really concerned about me holding their stamps without payment, why were they sending more of them? Didn't the people who sent the nasty letters talk to the ones who sent the stamps? Second, what were they really going to do to me? I was a kid. I couldn't see some lawyer coming after a ten-year-old. I concluded that their threats were hollow. Nonetheless, one last time, I sent back all their stamps with another note saying I'd keep any future ones. I continued to get them and, this time, I had no intention of sending them back. If the stamp companies wanted them, they could come get them—I'd had it.

During the months that followed, I squirreled away hundreds and hundreds of these on-approval stamps—just stashed them in a drawer. Soon, they stopped arriving, and so did the threatening letters. After a couple months of calm—no stamps and no letters—I figured the issue was dead. The companies had seen the error of their ways and taken their lumps, accepting the loss of the unwanted stamps they had sent to me.

The next summer—months after the last word from the stamp companies—I got out the stamp books and the thousands of stamps I now possessed. I figured there must be a way to get something out of these stamps. I returned to the task of mounting stamps in the book I'd started earlier. It wasn't long until every page was full of colorful stamps picturing flags, birds, flowers, animals, historical figures, and all kinds of images. It really was impressive.

Now, a number of my friends were pretty gullible—they were also somewhat greedy, always looking for a way to make a quick buck without having to do any hard work to earn it. They seemed like good prospects for an idea that was forming in the back of my head.

I invited several guys over to the house under the pretense that we'd go to the playground and pitch horseshoes. Before they arrived, I spread out the stamp book and a sampling of stamps on my bed. The stamps that I put on the bed were the most exotic ones—stamps issued by island nations and countries in Africa, like Tanganyika, French Equatorial Africa, French Guinea,

Mozambique, and others. I was busy putting stamps in my book when three guys clomped up the steps to my bedroom.

"Hey, are you ready to go to the playground?" one of them yelled as they climbed the steps.

"Yeah, give me a minute to finish this," I said, feigning more interest in the stamps than I really had.

"What's this?" Chuck said, pointing to the stamps.

"Huh...." I pretended to be totally absorbed in finding a place for a stamp I held in my hand, acting as if I didn't hear his question.

"What are you doing?" Chuck asked, louder this time.

"Oh..." I looked up. "I'm working on my stamp collection. I'll just be a minute...then we can go."

"You collect stamps?" Lee asked; derision in his voice. "I thought only sissies collected stamps."

I shrugged my shoulders. "Maybe...but there's a lot of money to be made in collecting stamps." I paused, letting that thought pique their interest. "You can get rich off these things."

"Oh, yeah? How?" Lee asked in a challenging tone of voice.

I pushed my book aside, making sure it was right under Chuck's and Pete's noses. "Look, some of these stamps are over fifty years old. They don't issue them anymore. As time goes by, more and more of them get lost or destroyed. The ones remaining get rarer and rarer, causing the price to go up. So, I buy now and sell later, making money when the price rises."

"Sure," Lee said, still skeptical, "who's going to buy them?"

I looked at him and shook my head. "Don't you know anything? There are thousands...maybe millions...of stamp collectors in the world. Go look in the phone book. There are four stores right here in Canton that do nothing but buy and sell stamps to collectors." I got the phone book off the floor where I'd put it earlier, opened it up to "stamp dealers," and shoved it to Lee. "Look for yourself. Do you think there'd be four stores if there wasn't big money in this stuff?"

The deal with the phone book firmly planted the hooks in their mouths. The fish were on the line. Pete and Chuck were staring at the mound of stamps on the bed—dollar signs visible in their eyes—and Lee's skepticism was gone, greed starting to take

Simpler Times; Better Times

its place. I pushed them a little farther. "See these," I shoved a few pages of paper with on-approval stamps attached to them toward my three fish. "Look at the prices the dealers want for these stamps." The prices ranged from a quarter to several dollars for a single stamp.

"Where'd you get these?" Chuck asked.

"From dealers," I said nonchalantly. "As an active collector, I get stuff from them all the time."

"And you're making money selling them?" Lee asked.

"I haven't chosen to sell any yet, but the value of these stamps is hundreds of dollars higher than what I paid." Which was true. I hadn't paid anything for the on-approval stamps I hadn't sent back.

"You bought all these?" Chuck asked, as he tried to imagine the price of the hundreds of stamps on the bed.

"Yeah, I paid for most of them...the dealers haven't been paid for some of the others yet." I didn't add that the ones I paid for were a dime a bag for hundreds of stamps and that I had no intention of paying for any of the others. "I've got more than these on the bed." I opened a dresser drawer and showed them thousands of stamps, mostly ones hinged to on-approval sheets from various dealers.

"How long have you been doing this?" Pete asked.

"Months and months."

"Was it hard to get started?" Chuck asked.

"No, but it costs a little money." Very little—only about two dollars to get all the bulk stamps and books on the bed. But no sense telling them that piece of information. "And the dealers are a real pain." Especially when you don't return their stamps; but I didn't add that fact either.

I could see wheels turning in their heads. With each turn, a dollar signed flashed across their eyeballs. "I'll tell you what, if this stuff interests any of you, I have some extra books and those stamps," I pointed to a pile on the end of my bed, "are duplicates. I'll give you a book and you can have any of the duplicates you want. That'll get you started. Of course, as Lee said, you might think this is sissy stuff--"

"I didn't mean that," Lee said quickly. "I just didn't know anything about stamps. Forget what I said."

Jack D. Atchison

I gave each of them a book—even then I had dozens more in stock. Within seconds, all three were pawing through stamps that I'd gotten in dime bags. Every few minutes, one of them shouted "I found one" and put it in his book, using the packet of hinges that I gave each of them.

After they'd been at it for a good half-hour, I said, "Hey, if we're going to get in some horseshoes, we better get going."

Lee, the former skeptic, said, "If you don't mind, I'd like to stay here and look in this pile for more stamps."

"Me, too," the others echoed in unison.

"Well, okay," I said, forcing disappointment into my voice. "If that's what you guys want to do, it's alright with me." I thought "alright" isn't the word, "fantastic" is the right word. The fish were thoroughly hooked and all three were flopping there on the end of my bed, ready for the kill.

Two hours later, Chuck finally asked the sixty-four-dollar question. "How do we get some of these other stamps?" He pointed to some of the more colorful commemorative stamps in my book.

"All those come from dealers," I said. I pulled some of the on-approval sheets from my dresser drawer. "These are what you want. Right?"

The three of them looked at the array of stamps on the sheets. "Yeah," Lee said, "how do we buy those?"

"Well, you can write to dealers and they'll mail you stamps they're offering for sale. But, I've got to tell you, it's a real pain in the neck. They send you all kinds of stuff that you don't want and can't afford. Then, you get stuck with the cost of mailing it back to them." I could see the disappointment in their faces. "But there might be another way."

"What's that?" Pete asked.

"I got most of these for a real good price." Nothing actually, since I'd never paid for them. "I'll sell you anything you want for one-half the price shown on these sheets. And if you see any stamps in these boxes," I pointed to two boxes of the better stamps that I'd separated out of the dime bags, "let me know and I'll give you a price."

"Hey, that's sounds like a good deal," Chuck said.

"Well, I'm always writing to dealers," usually to tell them to get off my back and stop sending anymore on-approvals to me, "and probably will in the future. So, I'm used to the headaches. By buying from me, your price is lower and you avoid the problems. But it's up to you."

With an easy path to follow, and thoughts of bargains in their heads, they bit like starved barracudas. During the next half-hour, each committed to buy about ten bucks worth of stamps, often bidding against each other for the same stamp.

"Since some of you want to buy the same stamp, I'll hold your order until tomorrow afternoon. If you pay me before then, the stamps are yours. If you don't, the deal is off and anyone can buy them." All three paid by the next afternoon, and, in fact, all bought more stamps.

Over the next several months, I gave stamp books to six or seven other guys, and all of them bought stamps. Before their interest in collecting stamps waned, I made a couple hundred bucks selling stamps. What started as curiosity turned out to be a neat economic windfall.

Now, I wasn't the only one who pulled a scam on his buddies; they all had their turn as well. I got suckered into buying, at inflated prices, baseball cards, yo-yos, marbles, and a collection of other junk from these characters. So, it wasn't a one-way street. We each thought of ways to hustle the other guys and to separate them from their cash. In the end, all of these deals probably canceled each other out. But it was a lot of fun to carry off a really good scam.

In the eighth grade, I was ready for a real job. I got one working in a store in which paint and related products were sold, on both a retail and wholesale basis. The owner was a friend of Mom's and Dad's. They met when Mom had shared a hospital room with his wife during Jann's birth. The owner's wife was delivering one of their eleven children—ten boys and then, finally, the girl they both wanted.

The paint store, a two-story affair, was located in the shopping center at the end of our street. The basement level served as a large warehouse area where inventory was stored. The second floor, at the upper-street level, was the retail showroom and also housed a small office area. The retail area was stocked with paint, wallpaper, unfinished furniture, brushes, buckets, drop cloths, and other painting supplies.

My initial job was that of stock boy. My duties included stocking the shelves; carrying inventory from delivery trucks to the warehouse space; maintaining the inventory records; notifying the owner when items needed to be reordered; sweeping all the floors; and running errands. For this, I received seventy-five cents an hour.

It was not easy work. The store didn't have an elevator. I had to carry the stock from the basement to the first floor where I put it on shelves. The most common inventory item was a gallon of paint. A case of paint—four gallons—weighed over thirty pounds. Since, at the time, I weighed less than one hundred and ten pounds, it was no mean trick to carry several dozen cases of paint up the story-and-a-half flight of stairs each night.

On delivery days, it was even worse. Our typical delivery was for over two-hundred-and-fifty cases of paint. I helped the driver unload the truck, stacking the goods just inside the delivery door. Then, I checked the bill of lading to be sure we had gotten everything we had ordered and for which we would be charged by the paint company. Once I determined that the order was complete, I carried the goods to the warehouse area.

The paint was stored in stacks, usually ones that were six cases high and four to six cases deep. The policy was to store all new deliveries in the back, on the bottom. To do so, I tore down the stacks, rotated the oldest goods to the front and top of the stacks, and then restacked everything. In practical terms, it meant moving darn near every item in the inventory. After every delivery day, I was dead tired.

I also assisted the salespeople. I mixed paint, assembled orders, and carried orders from the store to customers' cars. I didn't mind this part of the job, because it was usually a good way to earn a few extra dollars in tips.

When I had a few minutes of downtime, I read brochures and asked the salespeople questions about the differences between various brands of paint, about painting and wallpapering techniques, and about the merits of the other products in the store. After working in the store for six months, I had a fairly thorough knowledge of most of the products and their use.

Simpler Times; Better Times

I also watched how the salespeople dealt with customers. I wasn't terribly impressed. They seemed to be order takers, getting the customer only what the customer asked for and not trying to sell the customer other goods. I thought I could do better.

One Saturday morning, I asked the owner, "Can I work here on the floor awhile? I'd like to try my hand at selling to customers."

He hesitated. Technically, he wasn't supposed to hire anyone under the age of sixteen. I was almost thirteen. As long as I was in the basement, no one saw me. On the floor, people would.

I saw his hesitation. "Come on. Just give me a chance. If I screw up, I'll go back down and sweep the basement."

The store was starting to get busy, as it always did on Saturday mornings. "Okay," the owner said reluctantly, "wait on the woman over there." He pointed to a woman who was studying some brochures containing sample paint chips.

I walked over to her. "Can I help you?"

She looked at me with a funny expression on her face. "Are you a salesman?"

"Yes. How can I help you?"

"I need some paint for my children's rooms," she said, still not convinced I was the person to help her.

"How old are the children?"

"My son is four and my daughter is six."

"Then, they're still at the age where they get fingerprints and marks on the walls."

"Oh, yes," she said, laughing. "That's why I need to paint them."

I pointed to the brochure that she was holding. "Well, the paint you're looking at is an oil-based, flat paint. I don't believe it's what you want."

"Why not?"

"It's hard to work with, and will show every fingerprint. It's also difficult to clean. You want a latex-base, semi-gloss paint. It's easy to use, durable, and can be washed with soap and water. Come over here." We walked to where the latex, semi-gloss paint was displayed. I handed her a card of color chips.

She studied it for a minute. "I like the mint green for the boy's room and peach for the girl's."

Jack D. Atchison

I looked at her selections. "I think you'll be pleased with the green, but the peach has a pink cast to it. When it goes on the wall, it'll be more pink than peach." I pointed to another chip. "This is more of a light peach color...more orange and less pink than the other one."

"Thanks," she said; a sign of respect now in her voice.

"How big are the rooms?" I asked. She told me the dimensions. "Okay. It'll take a little less than a gallon for each room. What colors are the walls now?"

"The boy's room is blue. The girl's is a dark pink."

"You may need two coats to cover those colors. They're darker than the ones you want to use. Why don't you take two gallons of each color? If one coat works, you can return the other gallon."

"Okay."

I got the four gallons of paint and put them on the counter. "Are you going to use a roller or a brush?"

"I have an old brush that I was going to use."

"Are the bristles stiff?"

"A little. The brush was used before. Is that bad?"

"Well, it could leave streaks or bristle marks," I said.

"Should I get a new brush?"

"You could. Some people prefer to use a brush. But, frankly, a roller is faster and easier to use and, unless you're a skilled painter, it also does a better job."

"Okay. I'll get a roller."

We walked over to where the rollers were stored. "You'll also need a pan." I got a pan and roller and showed her how to use them. "Now, when you change colors you can wash out the roller cover with water and reuse it. But, if it was me, I'd just change roller covers. It's easier and not as messy." She bought an extra roller cover.

Back at the counter, I asked her, "Do you have a drop cloth?"

"I was going to use newspapers."

"They'll work," I said. "But be sure that you don't tear them. If you do, paint will seep through the torn area."

"The same thing will happen with a drop cloth, won't it?"

Simpler Times; Better Times

"Not if you use one of these heavier ones," I said, pointing to a stack of drop cloths.

"You better give me one."

"Do you have masking tape for the windows?"

"No. I forgot about tape. You better get me a roll." I did.

As I started writing up the order, I handed her a tool used to paint trim and borders. "You might want to consider this. It'll make your job easier."

"Okay."

I finished writing up the order. The woman had entered the store expecting to buy two cans of paint. She left with four gallons of paint, a roller, roller covers, roller pan, drop cloth, masking tape, and trim tool. And she was a satisfied customer. She needed all the items she had purchased. Each item would make her job easier and more professional looking. A few months later, she returned to the store to get supplies to paint her living room. She asked specifically for me to help her. She knew I would assist her in getting the things she needed to do the task properly.

As I finished with my first customer, I noticed that the store owner had been watching me, evaluating my performance. When I returned from carrying the order to the customer's car, he came up to me. "Well, I've finally got a salesman in here," he said. "The others would have let her walk out of here with two cans of paint. You didn't. Good job."

"Does that mean I can stay here on the floor?"

"When you're done with your other tasks, you can wait on customers."

During the next few weeks, I busted my tail to stock the shelves and get the warehouse area done as quickly as possible, allowing me to spend more time dealing directly with customers.

I found that by asking simple, direct questions, I could identify all the customers' needs. Then, I could match our inventory against those needs. The end result was that the orders I wrote averaged twice the dollar value of the orders taken by the other salespeople. It didn't take long for the owner to recognize I was more valuable to him on the sales floor than I was in the storeroom. He hired one of my friends to stock the shelves, and, from that point on, I worked as a salesman, getting a nice raise in pay in the process.

Jack D. Atchison

At one point, the owner asked me where I had learned how to sell. I told him that, even though I was only thirteen, I'd been selling things for years—lawn services, greeting cards, and stamps to my friends. In the process, I learned that all selling was the same: listen to a customer's needs, wants, and desires and, then, match your product or service to those same needs, wants, and desires. If you do, the customer will "buy"; you don't need to "sell." He asked me to explain that subtly to his adult salespeople. It was a lesson they hadn't learned.

Our early jobs, and even the scams we pulled on each other, were learning experiences. We learned how to sell our time and skills to others; promote a product or idea; close a deal; collect the money; manage money; and keep customers happy with our services.

We also learned to appreciate the value of money and to understand the nature of work. A dollar earned from spending two hours in the hot sun mowing a lawn meant more than a dollar received as an allowance or gift. You made sure that the dollar you earned was spent judiciously, because you knew the effort that would be required to replace it.

We understood that work was hard. It requires effort, is fatiguing, and takes away time that can otherwise be used for play and personal entertainment. We learned that when you accepted a job, you had to do it right and finish it as promised. If you didn't, you'd never work for that customer again—the customer would find someone more reliable. We also learned that if you failed to satisfy too many customers, you wouldn't get any future work—period. And if that happened, you wouldn't be able to earn the money you needed to buy the things you wanted. So, we all did our best to perform satisfactorily on every job we committed to undertake—no matter how difficult it turned out to be or how long it took to complete.

CHAPTER THIRTEEN

While we learned many positive lessons from church, scouting and the discipline our parents meted out, we, nonetheless, were far from being angels and sometimes failed to live up to the citizenship standards that we had been taught to uphold.

Our walk to and from elementary school caused us to pass by one of the strangest families in the neighborhood. There was a boy in the family, a year younger than Gary, who was hyper and emotionally imbalanced. As kids walked by his house, he'd spit, throw things, attempt to punch or kick or bite them—the human equivalent of a rabid dog.

The father was an attorney with the City of Canton. He had a real temper and cursed any kid that walked across his yard or tried to fend off his nutty son. In effect, he was a taller, older, and heavier version of the little monster he'd helped to spawn.

The mother was also a few bricks short of a full load. Because her kid was such a problem, she often had to drive him to and from school. When she did, she was a menace to anyone on the streets and sidewalks. She drove fast and erratically, often swerving up and over the curb as she negotiated corners. If she was at home, she'd stand at her screen door and scream invectives at us as we passed by the house.

One day, in late spring, the mother had already picked up her rabid son and driven him home from school. She was in her front yard, trimming shrubs with a big pair of garden shears. The kid was playing in the driveway. The drive was made of gravel, but the family was about to pave it with concrete. Cement bags were stacked inside their garage, a sign the paving project was about to begin.

Three or four of us were on our way home. As we approached this demented family's property line, the kid started pegging pieces of gravel at us. The stones—marble size—weren't big enough to cause injury, unless they struck an eye, but they stung when they hit. The closer we got to the kid, the more the stones stung.

Jack D. Atchison

By the time we'd reached the midpoint of their lot, he'd already hit me two or three times. When the little monster ran out of stones, he charged at us, kicking out with his feet, trying to nail our shins. He missed one of the other guys and turned on me. In an attempt to ward him off, I threw a stiff-arm that knocked him down. As soon as he hit the ground, he started crying and screaming for his mother.

His mother had obviously seen the kid pegging stones and saw him trying to kick us, but had done nothing to stop him. But, when he was the victim rather than the victimizer, it was a different story. She let out a war whoop and, with garden shears in hand, started running toward us, cursing a blue streak.

It only took one quick look at this she-devil to set our feet in motion. But before we could pick up speed, she closed in on us and began swinging the garden shears. The sharp shears literally missed our heads by inches. Fortunately, we were faster than she was and we quickly gained ground, getting safely out of her range. She soon gave up chasing us.

When we stopped running, we talked about our frustration with the members of this strange family. And we hatched a plan to get our revenge for the mother's shears-swinging behavior.

Late that night, four of us sneaked out of our respective homes and met at the corner of the street leading to the demented family's house. It was pitch dark; the moon and stars covered by clouds. When we got to their house, all the lights were out.

We went to the garage. The door was open, which was customary in our neighborhood, because no one was concerned about theft. Working in pairs, we carried cement bags from the garage to the backyard. Using the garden shears we were threatened with earlier in the day, we opened one end of each bag and spread its contents, as evenly as we could, over the grass in the yard. We emptied the entire stack of bags, about forty in all, covering most of the yard with an inch-high blanket of dry cement.

Next, we got the garden hose out of the garage and attached it to the tap extending from the rear wall of the house. We turned the water on and placed the end of the hose in a position where the water ran down the sloping backyard. Then, we took off, sneaked back into our own homes, and went to bed.

Simpler Times; Better Times

Our efforts were aided by Mother Nature. Early in the morning, the cloudy sky released a light drizzle of rain—a gentle downfall that lasted for about an hour—just long enough to thoroughly wet the cement in our adversaries' backyard. When the rain stopped, the clouds lifted and the sun came out.

As we walked to school the next morning, we were greeted by a sight that made our day. Cars, including two cop cars, were parked in front of the demented family's house. A group of adults was standing in front of the house trying to calm down the nutty kid's thoroughly agitated father, who was red in the face, gesturing wildly with his hands, and cursing at everyone in sight.

All the neighbors were outside watching the proceedings. I asked one of the neighbor ladies: "What's going on?"

"Someone emptied a bunch of cement bags in their yard and the whole backyard in now a solid slab of concrete." She laughed. "It couldn't have happened to a better family."

Gary, who wasn't in on the attack, and didn't know that I had been, asked: "Gee, what are they going to do?"

The neighbor lady laughed again. "That's what they're trying to figure out. One of those men," she pointed to a guy in workman's clothing, "says they need to break up the cement with sledgehammers or jackhammers in order to haul it away. But they're having a hard time reasoning with him," indicating the kid's red-faced father.

Unfortunately, we had to get to school and couldn't watch the rest of the scene. The guy in the workman's clothes must have prevailed, however, because when we walked by the place that afternoon on our way home from school, workmen were using wheelbarrows to carry big chunks of concrete from the backyard and loading it into trucks parked out front. While we suffered some pangs of guilt over the financial cost of the prank to this family, the sight did wonders for our hearts. It served them right for tormenting the neighborhood.

Starting just above Johnny's house, Whipple Road ran down hill, reached its low point at the end of the block, and then rose again, following the hill leading to West Tusc. A single storm sewer was located at the nadir of the depression between the two hills. When it rained, water flowed off both hills and collected in the depression. If the rain was heavy, the storm sewer wasn't large enough to handle the runoff and the roadway flooded, the water often rising to depths of three feet or more.

We kept some cement blocks stacked against the playground fence next to the storm sewer just for those occasions when the road flooded. As the water rose, we put on bathing suits or took off our shoes and rolled up our Levis. Then, we got our cement blocks, stacked them on the shoulder of the road, and stood on them. As we stood on the blocks, it created the illusion that the water was only a foot deep, rather than three feet.

Now, as soon as it started raining, city maintenance crews placed barricades on both hills, warning motorists about the flooding and directing them to detour around the area. But we understood the adult mentality. If an adult thought the water wasn't very deep, and was looking to save a few minutes, he or she would ignore the warning signs and try to drive through the floodwaters, making them perfect targets for the illusion we had created.

With every storm, we counted on a few foolhardy motorists to see us standing in the water. We knew they would assume that the water was only a foot deep and they'd disregard the signs, go around the barricade, and attempt to drive through the floodwaters. When they did, they found themselves in two feet of water, and the car's motor began stalling out. The smart ones stopped right there. The dumber ones gunned the car and tried to bull their way through the water, thinking the worst was behind them, only to get into deeper trouble as the water rose almost level with the windows.

Either way, whether stalled in two feet or three feet of water, the motorist had a problem. The motor was dead and wouldn't start. If the motorist opened the car door, the water would rush in and flood the interior. This is the point where we came to the rescue.

When a car stalled in the floodwaters, we gave the motorist a few moments to contemplate the dilemma facing them. Then, we got off our cement blocks and waded over to the car. We told the driver that, in exchange for ten bucks, we'd push them onto dry ground. If they agreed to our proposal, and paid our asking price—they always did—a gang of us pushed them back up the hill.

Simpler Times; Better Times

On a good day, we took in forty to fifty bucks. What would we have done without adults?

Twice a day—once in the morning and again in the afternoon—we were given a twenty-minute "recess" period. Weather permitting, all students were released from their classrooms and allowed to go to the playground.

The playground at Harter Elementary School had three distinct areas: a blacktop portion, where kids could play games like hopscotch, jacks, and jump rope; a grass and dirt section, where kids played tag, ran races, or played marbles; and a basketball court, an area generally taken over and used exclusively by boys in the seventh and eighth grades.

Recess, while intended to be a time for kids to burn off excess energy and relax from the rigors of their schoolwork, was also an integral part of the educational process. It was here, on the playground, where social skills were learned and provided an opportunity for kids to get to know one another and for friendships to form.

Occasionally, fights occurred on the playground and they were the most humorous part of the relationship-building process. They generally started over some small, insignificant disagreement or imagined wrong and escalated from there. The first stage of battle consisted of trading insults.

"You're stupid!"
"Oh yeah, you're ugly!"
"Where'd you get those clothes, a junkyard?"
"Where'd you get yours? From your sister?"
"Least my ears aren't as big as an elephant's!"
"But your teeth stick out like a rabbit's."
"Screw you, four eyes!"
"Oh, yeah! Want to make something of it?"
"Yeah!"
"You're chicken!"
"Am not!"
"Are too!"
"Am not!"
"Are too!"

By this time a circle would have gathered around the two guys who were trading insults, each getting redder in the face as tempers grew. The guys who formed the circle egged them on, suggesting new barbs, better insults, hoping a fight would break out. The circle didn't care who won or lost, nor did they necessarily support either one of the prospective combatants, their interest was purely in the entertainment to be derived from watching a good fight.

The taunts would continue until the ultimate insult was delivered—the one that no self-respecting guy could ignore.

"Oh yeah! Your mother wears combat boots!"

Those were fighting words. It was all right if you were insulted, or your brother or sister, even your Dad, but never your mother. If anyone said anything disparaging about your mother, no matter how trivial or ridiculous the comment, you were honor bound to defend her good name. You were absolutely required to pop the other guy in the mouth. Failure to do so labeled you a chicken of the worst kind—a guy no one wanted to be seen with. So, when a guy's mother entered the contest, fists flew.

The fights were always short-lived. A few punches followed by some wrestling on the ground. Then, a teacher usually interceded and broke up the fight or, if no teacher was around, it ended when blood was drawn—a bloody nose or cut lip. Within minutes of its end, the two combatants would grudgingly shake hands. By the time recess ended, they'd be buddies again, best of friends, the fight completely forgotten.

Through these contests, respect was earned and friendships were tested and solidified. Dirty tactics, such as kicking, using rocks or other objects, or ganging up on a person, were not tolerated. No one ever intended to render real harm to the other and, so these confrontations could hardly be considered violent.

And, make no mistake about it, even with the disciplinary rules in the school we were not always angels in the classroom—far from it. We spent a good deal of time trying to figure out ways to torment those who were seated around us, including, on occasions, our teachers.

For example, we would take a wooden matchstick, push a sewing needle into one end of it, and attach pieces of paper, in the shape of wings, to the other end of the stick. When we were done, we had a miniature dart. Most of us always had two or three of these little missiles in our desk. When the teacher turned her back to the class, it was not uncommon to see one of the darts fly through the air and land in the back of an unsuspecting classmate, producing a loud "Yeow" from its victim.

We would also string a rubber band between our thumb and forefinger to form a slingshot. These little slingshots were used to launch bobby pins at the backs of our classmates. Again, whenever the bobby pin found its mark, a loud "Yeow" was the reward.

During the fourth grade, my desk was near the front of the classroom. Before the year was half over, my back resembled a pin cushion from receiving more than its fair share of darts and bobby pins. After that year, I never sat in the front of a classroom again.

Johnny was the master of the "fart machine." He bent a piece of clothes hanger into the shape of a "U," attached rubber bands to each arm of the "U," and tied the other ends of the rubber bands to a metal washer. Before class started, he twisted the washer in the middle of his contraption, which wound the rubber bands into a taut, spring-like condition, and placed the device inside one of his books. When the teacher turned her back, Johnny lifted the cover of his book, allowing the rubber bands to unwind, thereby spinning the washer which produced the hideous sound of flatulence; hence, the name "fart machine."

Each time we engaged in these types of activity, we knew there could be adverse consequences. If the teacher spotted us, it was a certain trip to the principal's office for a taste of the paddle. But that did not deter us. Every day, one of us took the chance and pushed the rules.

Every neighborhood has a few grumpy characters. Ours was no exception. In almost every block, there was at least one guy who didn't care for kids. These guys wouldn't let us play in their yards, or even cut through them. They yelled at us if they thought we were making too much noise when we played in someone else's yard. They were the same guys who didn't tip paperboys; paid the lowest price for their yard work and snow shoveling; and stiffed us at Halloween by pretending they weren't home. They became the prime targets of many of our pranks.

Jack D. Atchison

Because of their overly protective attitude toward their property, they could be expected to react swiftly, and with emotion, anytime their space was invaded. It was this aspect of their personality that we exploited.

A lot of our pranks involved doors. One started with a length of clothesline rope. We tied one end of the rope to the handle of a screen or storm door and the other end to the mailbox, which in our neighborhood was mounted near the door, making sure there was very little play in the rope. Then, we rang the doorbell, pounded on the door, hooted, hollered, and yelled. When we heard someone come to the door, or as the porch light went on, we ran for cover, usually hiding behind a neighbor's shrubs.

If our strategy worked, and more often than not it did, the incensed grump tried to storm out of his house to chase us. When he did, he got a surprise. When he hit the door and started to rush through it, the rope stopped him. Then, one of several things usually happened. He might ram his hand through the screen door, ripping the screening from the frame. He might push the door hard enough to rip the mailbox from the wall. Or he might simply bang his nose on the door. In any event, his own anger, along with a little rope, did him in, and we got a good laugh at his expense.

We also used variations of this same theme. In the most popular, we got a large paper bag and went around the neighborhood to those houses where dogs were kept as pets. Using a makeshift pooper-scooper, we filled the bag with doggie droppings—the fresher, the better. The filled bag was placed on the target's doorstep, a safe distance away from any shrubs or other flammable materials. As the rest of the group rang the doorbell, knocked on the door, and otherwise made a lot of noise, one guy held a match close to the bag. When we heard someone approach the door, the guy with the match set the paper bag on fire and we all took off.

The target usually opened the door, saw the fire, and did what anyone would do under those circumstances. He stomped out the fire, splattering his porch and shoes with doggie-do in the process.

This trick even worked on guys who had previously fallen for the rope deal. They checked their door to see that it wasn't tied shut, and, seeing it wasn't, they opened the door and stomped on

Simpler Times; Better Times

the paper bag. Again, it was their own rage that got them in trouble.

Once, and only once, we tried another variation. There was guy who lived near our school who absolutely hated kids. If a kid crossed his yard, even the corner of it, he'd call the school and complain, getting the offending kid in trouble. As we walked to and from school, the crotchety guy sat on his porch and, without any provocation, shouted curses at us. He was so mean most of us were truly frightened—too frightened to pull any pranks on him. Until we were in the eighth grade, that is.

It was Halloween. One of the guys got his hands on a starter's pistol—the kind used in track meets—one that shot blanks. The pistol was completely harmless, unless it was pointed too near a person's ear, in which case damage to the eardrum could occur, or too close to a person's body, in which case the muzzle flash or wadding from the blank cartridge could cause injury.

As we visited various houses to beg for Halloween candy, we came to this old guy's house. The rest of the kids were bypassing it, partly out of fear of the old duffer, and partly because they knew from experience that he wouldn't open the door or, if by chance he did, he'd refuse to give them any candy.

The standard treatment for a house where the occupants refused to give out candy was for kids to soap the windows. In the past, a few kids had tried to soap the windows of this guy's house, only to have him call the police, asserting vandalism. Then, either the police or the old guy chased the kids or called their parents. Based on these experiences, and the stories surrounding this particular character, kids didn't even attempt to soap his windows.

The kid with the starter's pistol had a different idea. He thought he could teach the old grump a lesson. As the rest of us stood on the walk leading to the house, our friend walked up to the door and rang the doorbell, yelling "trick or treat" as loud as he could. Even though there were lights on in the house, and we saw people walking past the windows, no one answered the door. The kid rang the doorbell again. And again. And again. Finally, the door swung open. Our friend stepped back.

"Get off my porch!" the man yelled.

"Trick or treat," we all shouted.

Jack D. Atchison

"Beat it or I'll call the police!" the man shouted, coming toward our friend, menace in his eyes.

Our friend jumped off the porch and reached into his pocket to withdraw the starter's pistol. From a distance of about eight feet, he pointed the gun at the old guy. "Take this you old fart!" our friend shouted as he pulled the trigger. The gun blasted twice, the muzzle flashes brilliant in the darkness of the night.

The old man screamed, "Oh, my God, I've been shot...I've been shot!" and started holding his chest and stomach.

We took off running in all directions, knowing the guy hadn't been shot, but somewhat concerned that he may have had a heart attack or been scared to death. Immediately, we realized this trick had not been a good idea—not good at all.

Later, we learned that the guy's wife called the police, believing her husband, who was lying on the porch, holding his chest and searching for signs of bleeding, had been shot. Of course, when the police arrived—several squad cars full of them—they found no evidence that a shooting had occurred. The guy wasn't bleeding. There were no bullet holes in the walls of the porch. There were no spent shells—the starter's gun didn't eject shells. The cops wrote the whole thing off as a figment of an overactive imagination. Case closed.

But we knew there had been a "shooting." It just wasn't with real bullets. We also knew the guy believed someone had shot at him. All this ultimately worked to our advantage. First, the guy no longer terrorized kids. When he saw kids coming in his direction, he turned tail and ran, fearing that every kid in the neighborhood was armed and out to do him harm. Second, when he showed any sign of reverting to his old self and cursed at or harassed kids who walked past his house, a few well-placed firecrackers drove him back into his shell. Anything that remotely sounded like a gunshot appeared to scare him out of his wits. So, while the idea of using the starter's pistol had not been a good one, and one most of us regretted, it did serve to neutralize an enemy of all the kids in the area.

The desire of many adults to catch and punish any kid whom they believe is acting inappropriately, and an adult male's love affair with his car, were the underpinnings of our favorite wintertime prank—bombing cars with snowballs.

There was a house on a corner lot near the home of one of our friends that was the ideal venue for tossing snowballs at passing cars. The backyard of this house was enclosed by a white picket fence—one of the few fences in the entire neighborhood. There were gates on each side of the fence. One gate led to the street. The other gate led to the driveway between this house and our friend's home.

The occupants of the house didn't care if we played in their yard. The fence had not been built to keep kids out of the yard but, rather, to keep a little dog in. The dog had died several years earlier and hadn't been replaced by another pet. Thus, the fence was decorative as opposed to functional, except when it came to our snowball-throwing episodes, and then it was very functional.

We started these episodes by tying a piece of white clothesline rope between the posts of the gate leading from the yard to the street. The rope was intentionally placed about two feet off the ground and was tied as taut as we could make it. During most portions of a typical winter, this put the rope about a foot above the snow.

As darkness started to fall, we packed a supply of snowballs and stacked them near the fence. Then, we positioned ourselves in the yard, close to the fence, and lay in wait for passing cars. While the street wasn't a major thoroughfare, it was, nonetheless, a busy one, and we could count on a car passing by every few minutes.

As a car approached the intersection on our side of the street, or went through the intersection on the other side of the street, it was in our target zone. At this point, several of us launched snowballs, aiming for the car's doors. If our aim was true, the snowballs banged into the car, producing one hell of a racket.

It should be noted that cars in those days were built with heavier gauges of steel than they are today. A snowball didn't dent or otherwise damage a car, unless it contained a rock, and we were careful to see to it that there were no rocks in any of our snowballs. Our intent was not to cause damage but rather to get a rise out of the driver of the car.

After they got hit with a barrage of snowballs, many of the cars, if not most, kept on going. Drivers might have been irritated by the noise of the snowballs colliding with their car, but not enough so to stop and confront us. But there were a few drivers, always males, who decided to chase and catch us in order to teach us a lesson. These were the guys whom we looked forward to encountering.

The behavior of these guys was always the same, and thus quite predictable. They slammed on their brakes and jumped out of the car to start their pursuit, at which point we pelted them with a liberal barrage of snowballs, further feeding their anger and causing them to storm after us. When we saw them start to run, we took off through the gate on the other side of the yard and split up, running in different directions, agreeing to meet later at another friend's house a block away. But before we bolted in all-out flight, we always waited to see our pursuer enter the yard.

Most pursuers stopped at the gate. They stopped there because the rope tied across the gate hit them shin high, sending them into a less-than-graceful swan dive into the foot-deep snow. After they rose from their pratfall, and wiped their face to clear away the snow that was invariably packed into their eyes, ears, nose, and mouth, the fight was gone and nineteen out of twenty beat a hasty retreat to their car and continued on their way.

About one in twenty continued the chase. They had no chance of catching us because we knew the neighborhood like the backs of our hands. We knew which yards to cut through; where hedges needed to be jumped; which streets dead-ended; and every hiding place within three blocks of the attack site. So, whether we were pursued by someone on foot or by a guy in a car, we literally disappeared before the pursuer laid a hand on us—unless, of course, one of us was careless.

One night, when the snow was about two-feet deep, six of us were bombing cars with snowballs from this preferred site. We nailed a couple dozen cars. Two guys had already stopped their cars and chased after us, only to be tripped by the rope across the gate. Once they dusted themselves off, they gave up and continued on their way.

We were positioned behind the fence when another car entered the intersection. As it slowed for the stop sign, each of us

Simpler Times; Better Times

launched a snowball. All six snowballs found their mark, banging off the door panels of the car. Suddenly, the car swerved to the curb and braked to a stop. The driver leaped out of the car and started running in our direction. We each picked up a couple snowballs and threw them at him before running across the yard and out the other gate. We hesitated in our friend's drive to watch our pursuer come through the gate on the other side of the snow-filled yard. When he reached the gate, he hit the rope and did an amazing cartwheel into the snow, arms and legs flying in all directions. As soon as he landed in the snow, we threw more snowballs. They nailed him just as he was sitting up. He let out a howl of rage, rose to his feet, and, slipping and sliding in the snow, tried to run after us.

As soon as we saw him start to get up, we ran, scattering in six different directions. He ran for about fifty yards, with Gary as his primary target, and then appeared to give up, returning to his car. We continued to duck and dodge through various back yards until we reached the house where we had earlier agreed to meet. Within a few minutes, everyone, except Gary, arrived at the meeting spot. We waited for fifteen minutes, but Gary never showed. We assumed he'd gotten tired of throwing snowballs and had gone home. So, we returned to the attack site without him and nailed a few more cars before calling it a night.

As it turned out, Gary had run through a few back yards like the rest of us had, but the deep snow started to tire him. Believing our pursuer had given up; he stopped and hid behind a garage while he tried to catch his breath. The guy from the car had not given up. He followed Gary's tracks and, while Gary was leaning against the garage, walked up and nabbed him.

The guy shook Gary by the shoulders. "Are you one of the kids who hit my car with snowballs?"

Gary was too scared to deny it.

"Who are the other kids?"

Gary named us all.

"Where do you live?"

Gary told him.

"Well," the guy said, "you're coming with me. We're going to have a talk with your parents." With that, he loaded Gary into his car, where the guy's wife and kids had been waiting, and they drove to our house. There, the guy told Dad that we'd thrown snowballs at his car and at him. He demanded that Dad punish us. Then, he told Dad that Gary told him the names of everyone else and he intended to call their parents as well.

When I got home, Dad was waiting for me. "Where have you been?"

"Out playing in the snow?"

"Were you throwing snowballs at cars?"

"Yes," I said with great reluctance. "But we didn't do any damage."

"Was Gary with you?"

"Yes, but he left early."

"Why did he leave?"

"Some guy chased us. We got away, but Gary didn't show up at the place where we were supposed to meet." I shrugged my shoulders. "I guess he got tired and came home. He's here, isn't he?"

"Yes, he's in his room." Dad hesitated a minute, forming his next question. "What if your brother didn't get tired? What if someone chased him and caught him...tried to hurt him?"

"How could he get caught? We had escape routes. He had to get away...and, anyway, you said he's in his room."

"He's home because the driver of a car you kids hit with snowballs brought him here."

I was stunned. "How did he get caught? We saw him get away. He was running through some yards, and no one was behind him."

"Well, he did get caught. He was lucky. The guy who caught him could have really hurt him. You shouldn't have left him--"

"I didn't leave him. I didn't know he was in trouble. We thought he just came home."

"But you didn't know that, did you? You just thought that he came home."

"Yeah...I guess so."

"And you didn't check to see if he was in trouble, did you?"

"No."

With that, Dad yelled upstairs to Gary. "Come down to the basement." Then, he said to me, "You go down there, too."

Simpler Times; Better Times

I knew we were in trouble. We got sent to the basement for only one reason: a whipping. I reluctantly trudged down the basement steps and took off my snow clothes, expecting the worst.

Gary came down the steps as I was removing my snow pants. "You jerk! How'd you get caught?"

"I—"

Before he could answer, Dad came down the stairs, folded belt in hand. He motioned to me. "You first."

"But Dad, we didn't do any damage," I protested.

"I'm not whipping you because you were throwing snowballs."

I was confused. "Then, why are you whipping me?"

"Because you didn't check to see if your brother was alright. When you two go out together, you're supposed to watch out for each other. You didn't. Your brother could have been hurt and you did nothing to prevent that from happening. Now, bend over."

I got three sharp, hard smacks on the fanny. They stung like heck.

Dad then turned his attention to Gary. "As for you, you're getting whipped because you squealed on your brother and the others—"

"But—"

"No buts. You are responsible for your own behavior. If you do something wrong, you take responsibility for it. Don't tattle on others. They have to account for their actions, and it's not up to you to do it for them. Now, bend over." He also got three smacks.

"Now, about the snowballs," Dad said. "While you may not do any direct damage to the cars you hit, throwing snowballs at cars is very dangerous. The sound of the snowball hitting the car can cause the driver to lose control of the vehicle, especially on snow-covered, slippery streets. You could easily be responsible for causing a serious accident. When you learn to drive, you'll understand more about what I'm saying. So, no more snowballs. Got it?"

We did. That was the end of our snowball-throwing careers.

Jack D. Atchison

There was one other incident where throwing objects got us in real trouble.

A kid, who was one year older than me, lived at the end of our block. For a time, we played together, and then a rift developed between us. Because he was older, the kid was bigger than we were and tended to bully the rest of us around. Our solution to his bully tactics was to ostracize him from our activities.

As a form of retaliation, he lay on his garage roof with a BB-gun and plinked us with BBs as we walked through our backyard. The BBs didn't hurt that bad, but they did sting. We complained about his use of the gun, in voices loud enough for his parents to hear, but they never did anything to stop him from shooting at us. The combination of his actions and his parents' failure to stop him ticked us off. We decided to get even.

The neighbors who lived behind them had a small vegetable garden that wasn't well attended. Rotten tomatoes hung from numerous vines.

One summer's evening, after it was dark, we went to the vegetable garden and tossed dozens of rotten tomatoes at the back of our offending neighbor's house. We simply expected to cause a mess in the kid's yard, hoping he'd be forced to clean it up.

The next day, Dad was working in the backyard when the kid's father approached him.

"Last night, while we were gone, someone threw tomatoes at our house. We'd left our windows open and some of the tomatoes came into the house, splattering our furniture and carpets. I want to know if your boys were involved in this vandalism. If they were, I expect you to pay for the cost of cleaning up the damage."

Dad said, "I don't think the boys had anything to do with it, but let me ask them."

We were playing in the front yard. Dad called for us to come to the backyard. When we got there, he asked, pointing to the kid's father, "Did you two throw tomatoes at their house?"

Not knowing about the open windows, and believing we'd just made a mess in the yard, I quickly answered, "No."

"I think you're lying," the kid's father said.

Before I could say anything, Dad, who suddenly was very angry, told the kid's father: "If my boys say they didn't do it, they didn't. Don't you call them liars, or you and I are going to have problems with each other."

Seeing how angry Dad was, the kid's father backed off and apologized.

After he left, I asked Dad, "What was he so upset about?"

"They weren't home last night. They left their windows open, and the tomatoes dirtied up their furniture and carpets. They want the people who are responsible for throwing the tomatoes to pay for the clean-up costs." Dad paused. "I don't blame him for being upset. I would be, too, if it happened to our house. I hope he finds out who did it."

He returned to his work. Gary and I looked at each other; both of us were feeling very guilty. Gary whispered to me, "You better tell him."

Reluctantly, I approached Dad and interrupted his work. "There's something we need to tell you."

He leaned on his rake. "What?"

"We did throw those tomatoes."

Dad's face turned crimson red. "Do you mean you lied to me? Right in front of him?"

"Yes," I said, with my eyes turned to the ground, not wanting to face Dad's intense and very angry glare. He was seething.

"First things first," he said, appearing to calm down a little. "Both of you march down to the neighbor's house. Tell them you lied about throwing the tomatoes. Tell them you are fully responsible for any damages. And tell them you'll pay any and all clean-up costs...and, believe me, you will pay. Now, go!"

Two very concerned and very frightened little boys slowly walked through three yards to the neighbor's house. At the door, we told the kid's father we had lied, we were responsible for the damages to his house, and we would pay the costs of making things right.

He was satisfied with our confession, but asked, "Why did you do it?"

I told him we were angry over being popped by the BB-gun all the time, but added that that was no excuse for what we did. I said: "Our beef is with your son. We should have handled it with him. Instead, we harmed you. For that, we are sorry."

Jack D. Atchison

We did pay for what we did. The easy part was paying the monetary costs. It took everything both of us had saved, plus some. We worked for several months paying off the extra costs.

The hard part was facing Dad. We'd let him down; and we knew it. When we got home from confessing to the neighbors, he tanned our hides for lying and embarrassing him in front of the kid's father. It was a tanning we truly deserved, and, while it hurt for a while, it was nowhere near as painful as seeing the disappointment in Dad's eyes. That was the worst price we had to pay—by far.

Simpler Times; Better Times

CHAPTER FOURTEEN

While play, scouting and work occupied some of our time, school is still where we spent the better part of each year. A grade-school education in the late 1940s and 1950s was different from what it is today. The principal teaching method was memorization, or learning by rote.

In learning arithmetic, students memorized addition, subtraction, multiplication, and division tables. Using flash cards, teachers repeatedly drilled students on these tables, requiring students to repeat from memory the answers to problem after problem. As the problems became more complex, and therefore didn't lend themselves to the memorization technique, students were required to solve the problem using pencil and paper, showing the teacher each step in the solution of the problem. In these instances, the student was expected to apply a standard approach to problem solving and any deviation from the teacher's preferred approach was as serious a transgression as arriving at the wrong answer to the problem.

The most perplexing problems to me were what we called "story problems." These nasty things started to show up in about the sixth grade and continued on in seventh and eighth grade math classes. A typical story problem went something like this:

A farmer in Toledo wants to trade 10 cows to a farmer in Canton for 50 chickens. The distance between Toledo and Canton is 200 miles. They agree to meet between the two cities to make the trade. The Toledo farmer drives at an average speed of 35 miles per hour and the Canton farmer's average speed is 45 miles per hour. If both leave their farms at the same time how far will each farmer travel before they meet?

While everyone else in the class diligently tried to solve the problem posed by the last question in the paragraph, I would get hung up by the very first sentence. I mean why would any farmer in his right mind trade 10 cows for a measly 50 chickens? Even a city kid knew this was a dumb trade, because 10 cows had to be way more valuable than 50 chickens. A cow must cost hundreds of dollars, while a chicken couldn't cost more than a few bucks. The Toledo farmer was getting ripped off.

By the time I got done pondering the fairness of the trade, time would be up and, the papers collected, and my answer space would be blank. Consequently, I got a double dose of homework to make up for missing the problem. This penalty came after explaining to the teacher the absurdity of the trade—an explanation that, for some reason, the teacher was not eager to hear. So much for the logic of math.

Students learned to expand their working vocabularies by memorizing the proper spelling and dictionary definition of thousands of words. Almost daily, students had to commit the spelling and meaning of more than two dozen words to memory. To test the student's ability to retain these words in his or her memory, the teacher conducted weekly spelldowns using words drawn from a year-to-date list. Students lined up along one wall of the classroom, and the teacher went down the line asking each successive student to define and spell a given word. If the student erred, he or she was asked to take a seat. In the end, only one student remained standing, the champion of that week's spelldown. Winning was an honor, while having to make an early return to one's seat was a disgrace.

Augmenting the spelldowns were weekly tests. The teacher read a list of words, and each student had to write the word and a brief definition on his or her test paper. By the end of a school year, the list of words that a student had to retain in memory numbered in the hundreds, if not well over a thousand.

In learning grammar, students were required to memorize parts of speech and punctuation rules. Each day, students were given several sentences, or paragraphs, to diagram. A student had to identify the subject, predicate, adjectives, adverbs, prepositional phrases, and so on. In order to challenge the students, teachers introduced usage errors into the sentences and then required the students to identify and correct all the errors.

Students were also required to write brief compositions, usually reporting on a book they had been assigned to read. These compositions were graded for spelling, use of grammar, and content. The teacher's evaluation focused on both the student's understanding of the subject matter of the assigned reading material, as well as his or her ability to communicate that understanding in written form.

As students moved from the first grade, to the second, the third, and up the line, each year's lessons built upon the knowledge acquired in the preceding grades. The entire process was based on repetition, constant testing, and drill, which pounded facts and data into the students' heads, imbedding it in their memory, requiring them to retrieve it on demand. The process required hard work and mental discipline on the part of students and teachers alike.

Discipline in the classroom was demanded from students on more than just a mental level; they were also required to behave in accordance with stringent rules laid down by the teachers. Disobedience, classroom antics, disruptions of the class, and failure to do one's homework were not tolerated. An offending student was dealt with immediately and, often, harshly. Talking back to a teacher or unruly behavior resulted in corporal punishment and reports to a student's parents.

The corporal punishment usually consisted of spanking. The offending student was forced to bend over, either in front of the class or privately in a hallway or the principal's office, and received one or more swats on the behind with a wooden paddle. The paddles were made out of pine; were a half-inch thick, three inches wide, and two feet long; and most had several dozen holes drilled into them, reducing air resistance and allowing them to be swung faster and with more authority. The holes also increased the sting when the paddle connected with a student's backside. When an offense was particularly egregious the paddle was wielded by one of the male teachers—an early version of baseball's designated hitter—assuring that the paddle was swung with speed, maximizing the sting.

Our parents did not disapprove of the school's use of spanking—it was an accepted disciplinary tactic within most families. In fact, parents were an integral part of the school's disciplinary framework. If a student violated any of the school's rules, his or her parents were notified of the transgression. More often than not, the notification resulted in the student receiving additional punishment upon arriving home.

Parents also supervised homework assignments, making sure their son or daughter did the required work. In my case, Mom helped me with assignments in reading, spelling, grammar, and history. Dad worked with me on solving math problems. In effect, Mom and Dad served as teacher's aides, explaining materials and concepts, drilling us on spelling words and math tables, and setting work hours and performance standards. Their objective was to see that I got the most out of my education.

Mom and Dad were not unique. The parents of all my classmates came from working-class backgrounds. One of their dreams was to see that their children were better educated than they had been. Many, but certainly not all, of the parents wanted their children to receive a college education and, therefore, saw grade school and high school simply as means to an end. They understood that education is essential to coping in an increasingly complex society and they were determined to see that their kids had the necessary tools to succeed.

Through the PTA, parents participated directly in the affairs of the school. The parents of virtually every member of my class attended the monthly PTA meetings. During these sessions, they reviewed the curriculum, approved school policies, got to know the teachers, and planned events to raise money for extracurricular activities. Most parents served on one or more of the various committees of the PTA, and so it was not unusual to see them in the school during class hours.

The partnership between parents and the school provided benefits to both parties. The parents got to know the people who were teaching and disciplining their children; they had an effective forum for lodging complaints or making suggestions; and, through PTA activities, they became friends with the parents of their child's classmates. The school benefited financially from the PTA's activities; received parental support for its programs and teachers; and gained a cadre of concerned partners to help maintain a disciplined school environment.

While the methods and practices of the 1940s and 1950s may have been unimaginative and harsh, they were effective and I and my peers received a sound education. Moreover, the school environment was safe and secure. There's not much more that a kid can ask of his school.

Simpler Times; Better Times

Again, in our day, parents viewed the neighborhood school as being "ours." It didn't belong to some bureaucratic school system; it belonged to the people in the neighborhood. Backing up their claim of ownership, the neighborhood played a significant role in funding many of the school's activities. If the school needed athletic uniforms, band instruments, playground equipment, audio/visual equipment, or money for field trips and special events, it didn't turn to a school board for the funds or wait for a bureaucrat to put the request into a budget appropriation, the school turned to its PTA members and asked them to raise the money—and they did.

Long before "environmental issues" were a cause celebre for American politicians and activists, recycling was a key element in funding school activities. Rather than throw used newspapers and magazines into the trash, area residents stored them in stacks in their garages or basements. Twice a year, the school held "paper drives" to collect the stored newspapers and magazines. The drives were held on weekdays and usually ran for two consecutive days.

On the first day, kids went door-to-door collecting newspapers and magazines from houses in the neighborhood. They loaded newspapers and magazines onto wagons or into family cars. The kids, or their parents, then delivered the paper to the school playground, where it was accumulated in huge stacks, with separate stacks for each classroom in the school. This effort required each student to make scores of trips back and forth to the playground, as the collection part of the drive started early in the morning and continued until darkness arrived, and there were hundreds of homes to canvass.

On the second day of the drive, older students stayed on the school grounds, where they bundled the newspapers and magazines into bales, tying each bale with hemp rope. The bales were weighed on a scale and then loaded into trailers for transport to the recycling facility. It was back-breaking work because the typical paper drive resulted in collecting hundreds of tons of paper. While the older kids bundled paper and loaded trucks, the younger ones continued canvassing the rest of the neighborhood, visiting homes that were not covered the first day.

While the work associated with a paper drive was hard, the events were always festive occasions. There was a competition among all of the classrooms. The classroom that collected the highest tonnage of paper won a trophy plus a treat, usually soft drinks and candy bars. On the first day, the older students held the advantage because they were stronger and able to carry heavier loads. But on the second day, they had to stay on the school grounds to bale paper and load the trucks, giving the advantage to younger kids who were still roaming the streets collecting more paper. In the end, the competition was always close, with the winning classroom beating the others by less than a ton.

Parents joined in the effort. Fathers drove cars to ferry paper from intermediate staging areas to the school grounds. Mothers helped bale paper and supplied the workers with lemonade and cookies. By the end of each day, everyone was gathered on the school grounds, fathers and mothers baling or loading paper and kids climbing over the stacks like an army of ants.

In addition to paper drives, classrooms also collected soft-drink bottles. In those days, all soft drinks were sold in bottles, as cans were not yet used by bottlers. A twelve-ounce bottle of Coke or Pepsi cost a dime, with two cents being the bottle deposit. A six-ounce bottle cost a nickel, with one cent being the deposit. Because the deposit represented twenty-percent of the purchase price, it was significant, and few people tossed soft-drink bottles into the trash. Periodic drives were conducted to collect bottles, which were returned to the bottlers for the deposit.

These paper and bottle drives drew the entire neighborhood together as everyone worked toward a common goal. The school received payment based on the number of tons of paper delivered to the recycler or the number of bottles delivered to bottlers. A typical drive raised several thousand dollars—big money in those times—so reaching the goal was important to everyone. Success meant the school could pay for its extracurricular activities without dipping into taxpayer monies. So, parents saw the drives as a way to keep taxes down without sacrificing school events. This was sufficient motivation to mobilize the entire community and was what kept parents involved and committed. As for the students, it was two days without school—no other motivation was required.

Simpler Times; Better Times

When I entered the sixth grade, at the age of eleven, one kid in the class was almost eighteen years old. He was over six feet tall and was barely able to fit into the desk assigned to him. And he was certainly the only guy in the class who had to worry about shaving before coming to school. I was told that he had repeated the third, fourth, and fifth grades and was now taking his third shot at the sixth grade. I didn't know whether any of this was true or not, but he sure was older than the rest of us, so something had to be wrong with the guy.

When I talked to this kid, which wasn't very often because he tended to stay pretty much to himself, he seemed reasonably bright. So, I didn't know what his problem was.

A few weeks after school started, I was in the car with Dad when we passed by this older kid. I pointed to him. "See that guy, Dad."

"Yes."

"Well, he's in my class. The guy's eighteen and he's still in the sixth grade. He must be retarded or something."

"Maybe he has some personal problems."

"Yeah. His personal problem is that he's not too smart."

Dad gave me a dirty look—as if he were angry. "Listen, until you know what a person's circumstances are, don't jump to conclusions." Dad paused. "Do you know where he lives?"

"Nope."

"Well, why don't you get to know him better? See what his circumstances are. You might be surprised."

"Yeah, okay," I said, dropping the subject of this kid.

A couple days later, I was talking to the older kid—he sat next to me in class. He hadn't done his homework and the teacher had chewed him out.

"Why didn't you do the assignments?" I asked. "They weren't very hard."

The kid shrugged. "I had some work to do and just didn't have time to get to the homework."

"What kind of work?"

"I live on a farm and had to do some things in the fields."

"Really. What kind of farm is it?"

"It's my uncle's place. We grow vegetables—tomatoes, bell peppers, beans, and corn. I take care of the fields and pick most of the crops."

"Sounds like hard work."

The kid shrugged again. "It's not bad."

"It must be fun living on a farm."

The kid gave me a funny look. "It's okay." After a pause, his face brightened. "I have some traps on the place. I catch muskrats...skin them for their pelts. It's kind of fun and I make extra money when I sell the pelts."

That sounded fun. "Hey, can I come see your traps?"

He hesitated. "I guess so."

"Great! How about tonight...after school?"

He seemed uncomfortable but said, "Okay."

When school was over, I walked home with him. As we walked along together, his height and my relative shortness made us look like Mutt and Jeff.

The farm was on the outskirts of Canton—about a mile and a half from the school. When we reached it, we walked down rows of corn until we reached a series of irrigation ditches.

"I put my traps in these ditches," the kid said. "The muskrats swim in the water in search of food. Here, I'll show you." He reached down into the water and withdrew a steel trap that was attached to a wooden stake by a length of chain.

I peered at the lethal-looking trap. "How many traps do you have?"

"About two dozen."

"Do you catch many muskrats?"

He shrugged. "If I'm lucky, I get two or three a week. There aren't that many here, and they're hard to catch."

We walked around the field and checked the rest of his traps—no muskrats. When we finished with the last trap, we were standing near a run-down shack that stood in the middle of the farm field. I pointed to it. "What's that?"

The kid was looking down at the ground, shuffling his feet, as if embarrassed. "That's where I live."

"Oh," I said. I was now embarrassed.

"Yeah, it's not much," he said with a sigh. "Come on, I'll put these traps away," indicating the two traps in his hands, "then

Simpler Times; Better Times

I'll walk you back to the edge of the farm." He started walking toward the shack.

When we reached the shack, he dropped the traps into a box near the door. "Come on in while I get some gloves."

The shack consisted of one room—I'd seen an outhouse out back when we got closer to the place. A pot-belly stove stood in the center of the room and three beds were aligned along the walls. A couple of lanterns provided the light. Other than the beds, the only furniture was a wooden table, three rickety chairs, and a battered dresser. A white-haired woman was lying in one of the beds, apparently asleep, because she gave no indication that she had heard us enter the shack.

The kid got a pair of work gloves off one of the beds and returned to the door. When we got outside, he said, "Not much, is it?"

I didn't know what to say. "Huh...was that your mom?"

"Yeah," he sighed. "She's been sick for several years and has to stay in bed."

"What about your dad?"

"He died about six years ago. Since then, I've had to provide for the family—my mom and younger sister. That's why I miss so much school. Every year, something comes up and I have to drop out. Don't know if I'll ever finish."

Just then, another kid from our class yelled across the field, "Hey, you've got work to do! You better get to it or Dad will be pissed!"

The older kid let out a deep sigh. "That's my cousin. He lives up there." The kid pointed to a huge, white house on the edge of the field. "I've got to get going or my uncle will dock my pay. Can you find your way home?"

"Sure," I said as the kid started to walk toward his cousin. "See you later." I turned and headed home.

Later that night, I told Dad about the kid's living conditions. As I talked, Dad just nodded his head, as if he knew all about it. When I finished, I asked: "Did you know where he lives and how hard he has to work?"

"No. But there are a number of kids in your class who have to cope with hard times. Some lost their fathers in the war. With others, their fathers were wounded and are unable to work. All these families suffer hardships, and it affects how the kids perform in school and how they act. So, before you judge anyone, take the time to learn about their situation. When you do, you won't jump to premature conclusions."

Dad was right. A number of the kids had to deal with some real problems. Over the years, it was these kids—the ones who had to struggle with adversity—whom, among all my friends, Dad liked the most. He was always a champion of the underdog.

And whenever Gary or I complained about not being able to afford something, Dad would always tell us not to lament the things we didn't have but rather to be thankful for what we did have. As he put it: "There are always people who are worse off than you are."

It was Dad's compassion for and understanding of those who struggled that made him such a special person. He never passed judgment and always focused on a person's good points—and he found something good in everyone. Nor did he ever make a person who was down on his luck feel bad about his plight; instead, Dad gave him a helping hand—a hand of friendship, never charity or pity.

As for the kid in my class, he dropped out of school a few months later so he could work full time. I never saw him again.

The school held an annual bake sale and fair to raise money. Mothers baked cakes, pies, cookies, bread, and pastries. These items were displayed and offered for sale in the school's combination auditorium/gymnasium. The bake sale was held the Friday and Saturday of the fair and went from noon until eleven o'clock at night, the closing time for the fair. All proceeds from the bake sale went to the PTA.

The fair consisted of a number of carnival type games—balloons and darts, milk bottles and baseballs, coin tosses, basketball free throws, ring tosses, and the like—as well as the sale of snow cones, cotton candy, and candied apples. All the games and booths were manned by students and their fathers.

When I was in the seventh grade and Gary in the sixth, Dad was in charge of the dart and balloon game. The booth was about ten feet long by eight feet wide, with a waist-high counter in the front and a large board, constructed out of bulletin-board material, in the back. Gary and I blew up balloons and, using thumbtacks, attached them to the board in the back of the booth.

    A customer bought three darts for a quarter. The object of the game was to throw the darts at the balloons. One popped balloon yielded the customer a small prize; two balloons a slightly larger prize; and, if the customer popped a balloon with each of the three darts, the prize was a stuffed animal. It was always one of the most popular games in the fair.

    Midway through the second night of the fair, a young child—maybe six-years old—approached the booth and held out a quarter, asking for three darts. The kid was so short that the top of his head didn't clear the countertop in front of the booth, making it impossible for him to throw the darts at the balloons.

    Seeing the problem, Dad told the kid, "Duck under the counter and come inside," allowing the kid to stand inside the booth about eight feet from the balloons.

    The little guy wound up and hurled the first dart with all his might. The dart left his hand at an odd angle and flew out of the booth, striking Gary, who was blowing up balloons, in the forehead, right between the eyes, boring in a good half of an inch. Gary must not have felt anything because he didn't react; he just stood there, balloons in hand, with the wooden barrel and red feathers of the dart protruding from his forehead.

    Dad hadn't realized where the dart had flown until he looked in Gary's direction. When he saw the dart sticking out of Gary's head, his jaw dropped in shock. He ran over to Gary, who still didn't completely realize that he'd been struck by the dart, and tugged at the barrel of the dart, trying to ease it out of Gary's forehead. The dart didn't budge. It was lodged tightly in bone.

    Dad turned to me. "Take Gary to your mother and see if there's a doctor around to remove this thing," pointing to the dart. "I can't leave the booth."

    I'm not sure whether his request was based more on not being able to leave the booth or on not wanting to face Mom. In any event, I took Gary by the arm—he was now fully aware of the dart and was starting to panic—and walked him to the auditorium where Mom was running one of the bake-sale booths. As we walked across the schoolyard, we were greeted with stares of amazement as people noticed the red dart sticking out from between Gary's eyes.

When we reached Mom's booth, she was busy arranging some baked goods on a table and her back was turned toward us.

"Mom, we've got a little problem," I said; a slight understatement.

"I'm busy," she said, not turning around.

"You better look at this."

"Oh, okay." She turned. Immediately, she honed in on the dart, her mouth dropped open, and her eyes widened. "Oh, my God!" she said, raising her hands to her mouth.

"Dad couldn't pull this out," I said, calmly pointing to the red dart. "He wants to know if there's a doctor around."

Mom didn't answer. She just stood staring at the dart, frozen in place, unable to move.

"Let me look at it," someone behind me said.

I turned to face the local undertaker, a tall, thin guy whose complexion was as gray and demeanor as cold and stiff as the cadavers in his funeral parlor. He pulled on the dart and got the same result that Dad experienced—it didn't give at all. "I have some tools in my shop that'll take care of the problem," he said, motioning for Mom and me to follow him as he took Gary by the hand.

Mom followed in a daze as we walked to the undertaker's car. His funeral home was located about three blocks away, so it only took a few minutes to drive there. When we arrived, he escorted us into one of the rooms he used to embalm bodies. He went to a cabinet and pulled out a couple of instruments that looked like pliers. Using one of them, he grasped the barrel of the dart and, with a turning motion, pulled. His hand snapped back as the dart yielded. When he looked at the pliers-like instrument, he was holding the wooden barrel of the dart, but not the tip, which was still imbedded in Gary's forehead.

If anything, Gary looked more grotesque. The steel tip of the dart made it look like someone had pounded a nail into his head—somewhat reminiscent of the time when I nailed him into the doghouse.

Unfazed, the undertaker selected another instrument, again one that looked like pliers. This time, the prongs had small grooves

Simpler Times; Better Times

in them, increasing their ability to grip objects. He grasped the tip of the dart with the instrument and tugged. We heard a sickening, sucking sound as the tip was pulled out of the bone in Gary's forehead. Surprisingly, very little blood oozed from the wound. The undertaker stuck a small piece of tape over the wound and pronounced Gary as fit as a fiddle. Within a few minutes we were back at the fair, acting as if nothing unusual had happened.

    The seventh grade marked one's entry into the leadership of the elementary school, as seventh and eighth graders were regarded as the school's upperclassmen. One of the most important roles assumed by seventh-grade boys was serving on the junior police squad.

    The junior police manned all of the street crossings located within four blocks of the school. Armed with flags, badges, and bright yellow shoulder harnesses, junior police officers were empowered to stop traffic at these intersections, allowing students to cross the street safely. In the morning and at lunchtime, the junior police arrived at their assigned intersections a half-hour before school started and remained there until the bell rang, marking the start of classes. At the end of the school day, the junior police officers left ten minutes early and stayed at their posts for a half-hour after the bell that marked the end of classes.

    If any driver failed to stop on the junior police officer's signal or breached the officer's "stop" flag, the junior policeman recorded the driver's license plate number and turned it into the police department, who issued arrest warrants and traffic citations to all offenders. Likewise, any student who disobeyed a junior policeman's orders at an intersection, or who was seen by a junior policeman violating other school rules, such as fighting with another student, damaging property, or crossing streets in improper places, was subject to punishment by school authorities. Thus, the position of junior police officer carried with it strong responsibilities and authority. Students were therefore carefully screened for these roles—only those with strong academic and citizenship records qualified.

    The junior police corps, like many functions in the school, was organized and administered by students, with faculty members acting as advisors or overseers. The three most important people in the junior police corps were the captain and his two lieutenants. They were responsible for assigning all the members to their posts; seeing that everyone showed up when they were supposed to; and supervising the officers at the three major intersections leading to the school. These officers were, subject to the approval of the faculty advisor, elected to their positions by the membership.

During our seventh-grade year, Johnny and I were the only students who held the positions of both captain and lieutenant. Our service in these capacities provided us with an interesting and rewarding experience. We were in the position of having to ask our peers to comply with the school's rules—and, if they didn't, we had the responsibility and authority to enforce the rules, as well as to mete out punishment for any noncompliance. In effect, we became a part of the school's administration, and we didn't take our roles lightly.

It was interesting to see the effect that wearing a badge had on our peers' attitudes toward us. Our buddies complied with our instructions and didn't make jokes or try to hassle us when we were at our posts—in fact, they treated us the same as they did adult authority figures in the school. And I learned how it feels to be "in charge" of things—somewhat awesome feelings of responsibility and accountability.

Finally, the junior police corps effectively gave parents the confidence that their child could walk safely to and from the school. In those days, there were no school buses serving Harter Elementary School, and many students, even those in kindergarten and the earlier grades, walked a mile or more to school, crossing several busy intersections en route. In the eight years that I attended the school, there were no serious accidents or any cases of a child being badly injured by another student or outside party. And ours was a neighborhood that few would have considered to be affluent or privileged.

During our grade school years, the dropping of the atom bombs on Japan, which had occurred less than ten years earlier, gave rise to the fear that the United States might someday be the target of a similar bomb attack. So every week, classes were interrupted by "air raid warnings." When these occurred, sirens blared, bells rang, and all students dropped to the floor and took

Simpler Times; Better Times

positions under their desks or filed into the "air-raid shelter" in the school basement. I never figured out how an old, wooden desk was supposed to ward off the effects of an atomic bomb. But someone in the school administration must have believed that the desks were impervious to atomic fallout, because these exercises took place week after week, year after year.

Graduation from the eighth grade marked our passage from childhood to teenage years, bringing to an end the first stage of our maturation from children into adults. We would be leaving the comfort of our local school and our neighborhood to join kids from four other grade schools when we entered high school.

For me, the eighth-grade graduation ceremonies held special significance. I had entered Harter Elementary School under less than ideal circumstances and was rapidly labeled a slow learner, a kid who was not expected to get very far in life. But with the help of my peers, other teachers, ministers, scoutmasters, neighbors and grandparents and parents, I survived that rocky start. I received the American Legion Award as the most outstanding student in my class. As awards go, it was no big deal; unless, of course, you were the recipient. To me, it was a tangible affirmation that my future held promise and I could go forward without the fear of failure.

I and my classmates left Harter School excited about what awaited us. We looked forward to new playing fields, new friends and new adventures, comforted by the fact that we had healthy support systems—friends and families—to protect and guide us as we got on with the rest of our lives.

Years later we, my childhood friends, look back on the period from 1942 to 1956 as the very best of times. We were, if not the greatest, certainly the luckiest generation. Our childhood years were easier and more comfortable than those experienced by our parents and freer and more exhilarating than those experienced by our children and grandchildren.

Today, many children's daily lives are completely planned and controlled by parents or other adults, such as daycare or pre-school teachers and supervisors. Many games—football, baseball and soccer, for example—are conducted in leagues with adult coaches and organizers. Kids are driven to school in school buses or by parents. After-school play has been replaced, for many, by organized activities—dance lessons, musical instrument lessons, after-school care programs—or by sitting in front of some electronic device—a computer, game controller, DVD player, or television set.

Without controlling their own play, choosing their own teams, making and enforcing their own rules, today's kids do not have the opportunity to learn many of the valuable lessons that we learned. Play is supposed to be "fun," but it can also be very instructive; but not if adults make all the important decisions and the kids make few or none of them.

If today's dieticians looked at the meals that we ate—meals loaded with red meat, starches, carbohydrates, and lots of fat—they would shake their heads in disgust. But despite the high fat content, our meals were healthier than the junk kids eat today. Mom made our meals from scratch using mostly natural ingredients—no preservatives, additives, artificial flavors and coloring; it was real food, not a bunch of chemicals. Our food came right from the butcher, the dairy, the baker and the produce stand; it did not come out of a can, a frozen food package or, worse, from some fast-food or carryout place.

Moreover, because we walked to and from school and played actively outdoors—every day—and worked at jobs that required physical labor, we burned tons of calories. If you had looked in our classrooms, you would have been hard pressed to find a single overweight kid and, if you looked at the kids' parents, you would have been hard pressed to find many overweight adults. Large numbers of today's inactive, sedentary kids, and their equally inactive parents, are not only overweight; they are obese, many morbidly so. If you doubt this conclusion, visit your local Wal-Mart or McDonald's and you can observe scores of overweight patrons. Today's kids will end up paying for the rotten food that they consume and for their lack of physical activity with a host of adult-onset diseases and shortened life spans—call it the cost of progress.

The greatest freedom that we had as kids was the freedom to fail. We were encouraged to try new things, to strive for new goals, and, if we did not succeed, we were not shamed or embarrassed; instead, we were encouraged to forget about the minor injuries or bruised egos that we might have suffered and to try again. In the end, we all learned more from our mistakes and failures than we did from our successes. We all remember the games we lost, but can hardly recall the games we won.

Our parents, our school, and our friends all made sure that we understood the rules that we were expected to follow and the standards that we were expected to meet and we understood that if we did not follow the rules or achieve the expected standards that there would be consequences. We were then given considerable freedom to act or behave as we, on our own accord, chose to act or behave. If we ignored or failed to follow the rules, standards or admonishments, we got no sympathy for the failing grade, fat lip, bloody nose, black eye, stitches, broken bone, or spanking that we may have received as a consequence.

Our parents understood that if they coddled us as children—protected us against minor failures and disappointments—or made decisions for us, when we became adults we would not have developed the judgment, confidence, resiliency, perseverance, and courage that we would need to cope with life's challenges. Each of us learned that freedom, responsibility and accountability all were bundled together, with none being more important than the others.

Progress has given our children and grandchildren television, computers, DVDs, shopping centers, big box stores, fast-food restaurants, fancier homes and cars, modern appliances and conveniences and greater affluence than we had. But progress also has eliminated, among so many other things, the fields, swamps, soda fountains, five-and-dime stores, Saturday matinees, 45rpm records, clamp-on roller skates, nights around the radio, ice-cold glass soft drink bottles, unfenced yards, and personal freedom that we enjoyed. For my part, I would never trade places with the kids of today. Ours were simpler times and better times to be a kid.

Before we go, you might wonder what happened to the little core group of ten guys who hung together through our grade-school years. We all attended and graduated from college; some with advanced degrees. Our occupations include: school superintendent, chemical engineer, aerospace engineer, college professor, certified public accountant, Air Force Colonel and

Jack D. Atchison

fighter pilot, FBI agent, mechanical engineer, and business executive. We all have children and grandchildren. One of our friends died at a relatively early age, but the rest of us are still alive and kicking. All in all, not bad for a group of mischievous kids who started out on the very lowest rung of the middle-class ladder.

Printed in Great Britain
by Amazon